Hymns as Homilies

For Chris—

HYMNS
AS HOMILIES

A small appreciation
by
of your wonderfully

PETER NEWMAN BROOKS

*Kind way you take
care of us — and our organ—
at Barnsley
THANKYOU
Rosemary.*

Gracewing.
*This should have been
with you at Easter.* R

First published in 1997

Gracewing
Fowler Wright Books
2 Southern Avenue
Leominster
Herefordshire HR6 0QF

ISBN 0 85244 281 5

Typesetting by
Action Typesetting Ltd, Gloucester, GL1 1SP

Printed by Cromwell Press
Broughton Gifford, Wiltshire SN12 8PH

TABLE OF CONTENTS

Dedication, ii

Acknowledgements, vii

A Note on the Illustrations x

Preface xii

1   Martin Luther
and *'Ein feste Burg'*, 3

2   Thomas Ken
and *'Awake, my soul, and with the sun'*, pp. 21

3   Philip Doddridge
and *'Hark the glad sound'*, pp. 37

4   Isaac Watts
and *'When I survey the wondrous Cross'*, pp. 49

5   Charles Wesley
and *'Love divine, all loves excelling'*, pp. 65

6   Augustus Montague Toplady
and *'Rock of Ages'*, pp. 81

7   John Newton
and *'How sweet the name of Jesus sounds'*, pp. 99

8   John Keble *'Blest are the pure in heart'*
and *The Christian Year*, pp. 125

9   John Henry Newman
and *'Firmly I believe and truly'*, pp. 157

10   Charlotte Elliott
     and *'Just as I am, without one plea'*, pp. 179
11   Fanny Alexander
     and *'There is a green hill far away'*, pp. 199
12   John Ellerton
     and *'The day Thou gavest, Lord, is ended'*, pp. 221

Appendices
1   A Note on Text and Tune, pp. 243
2   A Chronological Chart: Hymns in Context, 1600–
     1900, pp. 247
3   Select Bibliography, pp. 261

Index, pp. 267

In the text, necessary references appear in [brackets].

ACKNOWLEDGEMENTS

Good hymns, well sung, have always proved inspirational. Carefully chosen, they make the milestones of life meaningful, often adding another dimension. Hymns can deepen intimacy in the personal commitment of communion; and on family occasions like baptisms and weddings, funerals and memorial services, they can widen a fellowship of praise and thanksgiving. The increasing demands of contemporary society have made human existence a veritable marathon. Runners need regular sustenance to cope with all its peaks and troughs. Yet through long centuries dedicated hymnwriters have faithfully catered for congregations and individuals with both sensitivity and panache – even with what some would term 'gusto'! For strangely, the best hymns make demands that, if essentially religious, are also decidedly physical.

In an essay of acknowledgements, the reader must pardon some measure of autobiographical comment. An ordinand's high point in the good old days of an unapologetic English Church has to be the hymn that by tradition the 'gospeller' can choose; and with the choir and organ of Canterbury Cathedral involved, Dr Martin's 'A mighty Fortress' (*Ein feste Burg ist unser Gott*) echoed forth to confirm the confidence of all Lutherans who prize it as heaven's national anthem! If sceptics scorn such emotional peaks as merely 'soulful' and far from the true terrain of the Spirit, let them do so. But let them also listen to a fine recording of George Guest – who directed Music at Downing when the writer was Fellow and Director of Studies in History. For, superbly trained and conducted, the Choir of St John's College, Cambridge, singing *Psalms of Consolation and Hope* is altogether memorable.

The experience of an erstwhile Precentor – untrained but once acclaimed by Downing's Organ Scholar, Carl Jackson, FRCO, as 'of perfect pitch' – is more appropriate to a lecture tour than to written record. The fame of that Choir as a marriage bureau has become legendary; and no book of mine on hymns can fail to make honourable mention of Mr Gareth Hayward, bass. Selected by Dr Sydney Watson of blessed memory, he was the triumphant treble who not only rose to be Head Chorister of Christ Church Cathedral, Oxford, but whose vocal endurance saved the Walker organ of All Saints', Landbeach. For his 'Sponsored Hymn Sing' – Gareth gave voice to the first and last verses of every entry in *Ancient & Modern Revised* – raised over £1,500 in 1986. A far cry from the timid ten year-old who, in 1969, chose 'There is a green hill' for his Oxford audition, and set a challenge to his church historian father-in-law to explore the high mystery and magic of the many hymns that, with a tribe of tenacious trebles like Thomas, William and Richard Peter as irrefutable evidence, testify to the tryst with Jenny through the Downing College Choir.

Other debts, less complex, demand gratulatory reference: the joy of American experiences with great Choirs as varied as those of Bethesda-by-the-Sea, Palm Beach, Florida; the United Church of Indian Hill, Cincinnati; All Saints', Chevy Chase; St Peter's, Saint Louis, Missouri; and St John's, Logan, Utah; the 'New-Every-Morning' faithfulness of the BBC Religious Broadcasting, and of late, when a Summer heat wave in enervating Cambridge climes almost stifled endeavour, an evening 'second wind' gained from the 'Songs of Praise' *Hymnformation with Henry Sandon.* Then too, for fascinating debates about the Wesley brothers with a pupil, the Methodist ordinand Mr 'Uel' McBratney of Wesley House; lively conversations and London weekend hospitality from Cambridge *alumni* Sheridan and Lynne Swinson; immensely helpful conversations and correspondence with Miss J.P. Nash; and every consideration and support from my Secretary at Robinson College, Mrs Helen Wright, without which a busy Cambridge Tutor for Admissions, with heavy Faculty commitments, could not possibly have found time for research and writing.

Professional tributes also go to Dr Richard Marlow, revered for his transformation of the Chapel Choir since my halcyon days as a Trinity undergraduate; to Dr John Chadwick, FBA, an admired colleague from my time as Fellow and Dean of Downing; to generous support from the Principal of Westminster College and his secretary Mrs Marilyn Russell for every access to the fine Edward Alfred Elias Library of Hymnology, and permission to photograph a rare portrait of Charlotte Elliott; and of course to the Publishing House of Gracewing, for the careful oversight of Jo Ashworth, Publications Manager; and to the Managing Director, Tom Longford, for the critical encouragement only the best in the business can provide.

Robinson College,   P.N.B.
Cambridge   August, 1996

A NOTE ON THE ILLUSTRATIONS

To enlarge the reader's understanding of the various individuals whose life and ministry is reviewed in these pages, a portrait likeness of the hymnwriter appears at the start of every chapter. Chosen for clear characterization, the illustrations provide the best contemporary focus of artists whose powers of observation highlight the simple piety of their subjects. They will enhance awareness of remarkable men and women who endured troubled times with the full assurance of those whose vocation enabled them to face challenge with commmitment and, above all, to inspire future generations in their pilgrimage.

Martin Luther by Lucas Cranach the Elder (1522–24) - a last portrait of the Wittenberg Reformer wearing the habit of an Augustinian Friar, this likeness was painted at roughly the time Luther was composing and writing most of his hymns.

Thomas Ken - from an engraving made by G. Vertue in the bishop's seventy-third year (reproduced from an edition of Ken's *Works* in the Edward Alfred Elias Library of Hymnology, by kind permission of the Principal of Westminster College, Cambridge).

Philip Doddridge - from an engraving by N. Branwhite (repro-duced from an edition of the writings of Doddridge by kind permission of the Syndics of the Cambridge University Library).

Isaac Watts - from a frontispiece engraving of the works of Isaac Watts (based on the portrait by Godfrey Kneller, and reproduced by kind permission of the Syndics of the Cambridge University Library).

Charles Wesley - from a frontispiece in an edition of Wesley's poetry in the Library of Wesley House, Cambridge, the engraving is reproduced by kind permission of the Principal.

Augustus Montague Toplady - from a contemporary study, posthumously published as a frontispiece to Toplady's *Works* in

1828, this engraving is reproduced by kind permission of the Syndics of the Cambridge University Library.

John Newton – from the complete edition of Newton's *Works* this engraving of J. Collyer, ARA, is reproduced by kind permission of the Principal of Westminster College, Cambridge.

John Keble – by George Richmond, RA. Reproduced by permission of the Warden and Fellows of Keble College, Oxford.

John Henry Newman – by Sir William Ross. Reproduced by permission of the Warden and Fellows of Keble College, Oxford.

Charlotte Elliott – from the frontispiece of the Religious Tract Society's edition of her sister E.B.'s *Memoir,* this rare illustration of Miss Elliott is reproduced by kind permission of the Principal of Westminster College, Cambridge, and the Edward Alfred Elias wLibrary of Hymnology.

Cecil Frances Alexander – from a photo portrait of Elliott and Fry, this likeness of Mrs Alexander is reproduced by kind permission of the Principal of Westminster College, Cambridge.

The Reverend John Ellerton – from a rare photo portrait.

PREFACE

Through long centuries, psalms and hymns have proved inspirational in traditional worship. They have sustained the people of God, and continue to minister to every aspect of the human predicament. When first composed, most verse excites at least a passing fancy; but some goes on to gain real appeal and oblige successive generations to prize its enduring worth. Like revered passages of sacred Scripture – the Holy Writ that is customarily their source and fountain head – such stanzas stimulate a stronger heartbeat and add new strength to Christian spirituality. Although familiar and often taken for granted too, hymns can prove the most effective of teaching aids. For at the hands of very different, but always dedicated, writers, they have made the crucial transposition from complexity – in psalms or catechisms – to attain simplicity and a compelling appeal.

Enshrining the sacred liturgy, the early music of monks in choir spread far beyond the calm of the cloister to extend a sublime influence of devotion. Nor has the Gregorian chant lost its fascination for our contemporary society, sound recordings from Ampleforth and Santo Domingo de Silos rising high in the musical charts to indicate the timeless attraction of a serene and calming tradition. Centuries earlier, others questioned medieval certainties. They determined to secure a response from remote hierarchies and councils committed to the use of Latin in worship. Liturgical chant, psalms and responses guaranteed religious solemnity whenever and wherever the priesthood chose to observe rites sanctioned by authority. But were they effective in teaching the faith to the vast majority of ordinary unlettered folk? However fashionable its deconstruction to dons in university research at the close of the present century, the Reformation of the sixteenth century sought to solve this dilemma and offer answers to such questions. Luther's own stand was itself a protest from the world of learning, and it cannot be doubted that he sought to communicate his 're-discovery' of Christ's gospel by every possible means in his work as a pastor. Isolated at first, the Reformer of Wittenberg was soon joined by others, and a convinced and growing clamour for revival arose in the groves of academe. Initially this must have seemed as remote to simple parishioners as the notorious debates of medieval schoolmen. But once pastoral considerations were given priority, even those opposed to new doctrines recognized that worship with a common touch had a teaching potential to rival the miracle of the Mass. Albeit an age of sound, heat and furious issues contemporaries dismiss as *odium theologicum*, there was sufficient light to ensure a new focus on the Christian gospel. Forceful hymns, like those Luther adapted from familiar psalms, popularized 'the new religion' and took Europe not so much by force as by song.

This little book attempts to trace the progress of that great endeavour. It does so in a series of self-contained chapters as the work of key hymnwriters in the English religious tradition parades something of a people's pageant before the reader. That progress properly starts with the work of Martin Luther who anticipated so much in the development and use of the hymn. He was, for example, not merely convinced that 'only the simplest and most common words should be used for singing', but also supremely capable of composing rousing melodies of musical genius to convey the gospel to his Saxon people. But in a work primarily concerned with worship in English, the concentrated focus of this book falls elsewhere. It selects an arbitrary sample of renowned hymns, carefully sets them in context, and in spiritual treasuries selected from lesser-known compositions of the writers involved, provides devotional material intended to stimulate thought, deepen understanding, and prompt meditation. Such focus may cause the orthodox to stray from St Augustine's celebrated definition of a hymn★, yet the By-Path Meadow experience by no means leads to Doubting Castle. Rather will its very breadth offer the widest scope for strength in the continuing pilgrimage of Christian life. For the traditional 'office' worship of

★*see* below, p. 211.

Thomas Ken; the simple devotion of Philip Doddridge; the renewal of a worship 'in the Name of Jesus' Isaac Watts was clear could save 'the ruin'd and degenerate World'; the gospel faith of Charles Wesley's universal love 'born in song'; 'the ever-memorable' and controversial Augustus Montague Toplady; the flawed but fervent discipleship of John Newton, Evangelical apologist; the 'practical religion' of John Keble, paragon country parson; the adoration of John Henry Newman's Catholic orthodoxy; the 'plaintive lyre' of Charlotte Elliott's fellowship of suffering; the respectability and commitment of Fanny Alexander; and the principled priorities of John Ellerton: all afford a genuine mosaic to refract and reflect 'kindly light' as the daily light of no mean spiritual inspiration. Or to change the metaphor, like the best in quality antiques, they are at once period pieces and timeless treasures. So when faith is challenged and under threat, hymns used as homilies can convey both profundity of doctrine and a spiritual wisdom beyond compare.

For in days when sermons are invariably short, sharp and evasive, all too many Christian people find themselves frustrated in their faith. Preachers could once be relied on to expound gospel truth, but now prefer to convey varied assortments of helpful hints on harmful habits, and those who mount the pulpit often lack the conviction of men and women with a real message for those committed to their charge. Young people seem almost to expect such a state of affairs, and new philosophies influence the religious education they receive in school and college. As a result, many mature believers have been side-lined. Increasingly bewildered by the trials they experience, faithful folk are made to face long periods of spiritual loneliness, even daily despair. After all, in barely half a lifetime, many of the certainties of their childhood religion have either been lost or wilfully abandoned by the official church. Holy Writ appointed for reading in public worship has surrendered much dignity of language to racy contemporary translations, or worse to what a leading article in *The Times* recently described as 'the prose of the management manual rather than the Authorised Version' [The King James' Bible] (*see* 'The Empty Pew', 11 April 1996). Ancient liturgies that, like Cranmer's *Book of Common Prayer*, have in splendour sustained the prayers of a people through long centuries, have largely been replaced. And even the friendly face of society's most traditional figure, the resident clergyman, is now rarely seen and increasingly exchanged for fleeting glimpses of unfamiliar 'group' or circuit ministers on irregular, migratory visits.

Yet a constant can be found, for these are also times when, on sound and vision, the media have popularized what Gordon Rupp once termed 'the divine cheerfulness' of traditional hymns. In the knowledge that such programmes have stirred many a soul, this is an attempt to focus the attention of both the faithful, and not so faithful, on the poetry of well-loved hymns as a source of both inspiration and meditation. It by no means chooses to challenge or undermine belief in the manner of some recent scholarship. (Much of the work of Lionel Adey, in, for example, *Hymns and the Christian 'Myth'* (1986), could go into the dock here.) Quite the reverse, for, no exercise in hindsight, this essay has tried to weigh and convey the spiritual worth of great hymns both in their own context and as an incomparable heritage of no mere phase or fashion but of timeless truth. For when used in the praise of church worship, or simply read in a pensive mood of silent prayer, such hymns afford key and durable threads in the rich tapestry of the altar cloth of Christendom. No less than the music on which they ascend as incense, their very words in dignity of language hallow the treasure house of a Great Tradition to inspire, enlighten and reassure pilgrims along the Way.

St Augustine of Hippo,   PETER NEWMAN BROOKS
28 August, 1996

Chapter 1

MARTIN LUTHER

and

'A mighty fortress'
(Ein feste Burg ist unser Gott)

1 A safe stronghold our God is still,
   A trusty shield and weapon;
He'll help us clear from all the ill
   That hath us now o'ertaken.
         The ancient prince of hell
         Hath risen with purpose fell;
         Strong mail of craft and power
         He weareth in this hour;
On earth is not his fellow.

2 With force of arms we nothing can,
   Full soon were we down-ridden;
But for us fights the proper Man,
   Whom God himself hath bidden.
         Ask ye, Who is this same?
         Christ Jesus is his name,
         The Lord Sabaoth's Son;
         He, and no other one,
Shall conquer in the battle.

3 And were this world all devils o'er,
   And watching to devour us,
We lay it not to heart so sore;
   Not they can overpower us.
         And let the prince of ill
         Look grim as e'er he will,
         He harms us not a whit;
         For why? – his doom is writ;
A word shall quickly slay him.

4 God's word, for all their craft and force,
   One moment will not linger,
But spite of hell, shall have its course;
   'Tis written by his finger.
         And though they take our life,
         Goods, honour, children, wife,
         Yet is their profit small;
         These things shall vanish all:
The City of God remaineth!

At first sight it may seem strange to find Martin Luther topping the bill in a focus on well-known English hymnwriters. But Luther's name appears in lights because of his massive contribution to hymnody as a whole, a legacy all too rarely recognized. The crisis in Christendom that was the Reformation of the sixteenth century transformed popular worship, and Luther in particular gave such priority to music that he placed it 'next to theology' and afforded it 'highest praise'. In an age of sound, heat, fury and all too little light, Jesuits concerned for traditional ways found themselves implacably opposed to so notorious a heretic and all his works. Yet it was difficult for the Order to deny the effectiveness of 'the new religion', and the hostile witness of one Jesuit father – namely that Luther's hymns 'killed more souls than all his books and speeches' – suggests an acute awareness of the pastoral challenge Wittenberg presented to Rome. It also underlines the undoubted fact that the so-called 'protestant' faith was spread by hymn-singing, if only because, set to memorable tunes, such hymns were precisely the kind of sermons ordinary folk could grasp. Some challenging words from Luther's *Table Talk* are relevant, for in 1540 the Reformer was clear, as a busy parish pastor, that

> Christ could have taught in a profound way but wished to deliver his message with the utmost simplicity in order that the common people might understand. Good God, there are sixteen-year-old girls, women, old men, and farmers in church, and they don't understand lofty matters! ... Accordingly, he's the best preacher who can teach in a plain, childlike, popular and simple way.
>
> [*LW* 54. 383–4. No. 5047]

The genius of Dr Martinus certainly enlivened countless aspects of contemporary worship; and many a composition on simple gospel themes made real impact as homespun hymns, invariably transposed from psalms, became powerful homilies.

In a quite remarkable way, Luther's interest anticipated the development of the hymn not only as central to Christian worship, but also as an invaluable way of spreading the faith in teaching and evangelism. Psalms had been said and chanted for centuries. But it was the merit of Martin Luther to relay the traditional worship of synagogue and church, and by a clever transposition of hallowed Old-Testament language, fashion the 'psalm-hymn'. From his days as postulant and novice, professed religious and ultimately Prior of the Erfurt house of the Augustinians, Luther had been nourished and reared on psalms which continued to supply a rich source of his devotional life. He termed them his 'Little Bible' and prized the way they inspired him to enter the very heartland of the faith. This was because, as if in anticipation of the work of Isaac Watts in late seventeenth-century England, Luther's prophetic use of Old Testament worship christianized the Book of Psalms. In short, if Erasmus chose to enlighten the world of learning by sanctifying Socrates, Luther preferred to relay the work of David whose music-making and prophetic vision pointed people to Christ as Lord.

An important, but neglected, *Treatise on the Last Words of David* (1543), highlights Luther's mature defence of the psalter as a proclamation of Christian truth:

> David boasts of being *the sweet psalmist of Israel* ... [but] ... he did not keep this certain promise of Messiah to himself ... For faith ... bursts into action, speaks and preaches of this promise and grace of God, so that others may ... come up and partake of it. Yes, his great delight impels him to compose beautiful and sweet psalms and to sing lovely and joyous songs, both to praise and to thank God in his happiness and to serve his fellowmen by stimulating and teaching them.   [*LW* 15. 273]

When persecution came, Luther joined the long tradition of those who upheld the power of the psalms to console and re-assure in times of trial and temptation. Indicted for following the Reformer's teaching, Henricus Vos and Johannes van den Esschen, both members of the Augustinian Order, were burnt at the stake in the Bruxelles Grand Place for their refusal to recant (1 July, 1523). Welcoming them both to the noble army of martyrs, Luther responded with an imaginative composition based on Psalm 96, and commemorated the rôle of 'two boys' in whose life and death

God's Word has re-appeared.

In short, what began as a traditional psalm to

> ... sing unto the Lord a new song,

Luther extended to embrace the cause of Reformation itself in this his first composition.

With its original first line

> *Eyn newes lyed wyr heben an,*

the hymn had all the appeal of the ballad or folk song. Making full use of such sources, Luther's writing proved altogether memorable because it combined musical and mnemonic skills of a high order. And later that same year, a second hymn,

> Dear Christians, let us now rejoice
> [his *'Nun freut ich ...'*],

appeared in unmistakable form, Luther anticipating in verse a long tradition of evangelical testimony to reach its zenith with the Wesley brothers, John Newton and Charlotte Elliott. For with real feeling, Wittenberg's Reformer witnessed to the God whose tender mercies in Christ

> Be the poor man's salvation.

Containing his characteristic emphasis that

> ... good works ... were worthless quite

before

> ... God's judging light,

it was a simple gospel sermon intended to implant 'good cheer' and 'sweet wonder' at the finished work of crucifixion and resurrection. A particularly revealing last verse (verse 10 – cf. *LW* 53. 220) explained the nature of the Lord's mission, Luther penning lines as if they were spoken by the very Spirit of God:

> 'What I have done, and what I've said,
> Shall be thy doing, teaching,
> So that God's kingdom may be spread –

All to his glory reaching.
Beware what men would bid thee do,
For that corrupts the treasure true;
With this last word I leave thee.'

The following year broadsheets containing printed versions of these compositions, and hymns based on Psalms 12 and 14, were in circulation. It was the prelude to an intense hymn-writing phase in his ministry as, between 1523 and 1524, Martin Luther wrote twenty-four of the thirty-seven hymns that have survived. Although he both paraphrased well-known Latin hymnody and versified familiar psalms, his work had unique appeal because it combined simple vigour and moving music. Writing to enlist the help of Spalatin in the cause, Luther informed the Chaplain to Ernestine Saxony's Elector of his plan

> to follow the example of the Prophets and the ancient
> Fathers of the Church, and to compose psalms for the
> people in their own tongue, that is, spiritual songs, so that
> the Word of God may be among the people also in the form
> of music.   [*LW* 49. 68]

Determined to minimize the impact of pirated versions of his work – with the help of Johann Walter, he was already perfecting the chorales that would later have such appeal for Schütz and Bach – Luther contributed a careful *Preface* to the *Wittenberg Hymn Book* of 1524. Terse but trenchant, his words enshrine the Reformer's commitment to hymns as homilies. Deferring to the Psalms of David and 'Saint Paul himself' as primary authorities, Luther made clear that by singing spiritual songs 'heartily unto the Lord, … God's Word and Christian teaching' can be 'instilled and implanted'. Accordingly it was his modest aim 'to make a start and to give a lead to those who can do better' so that

> the holy gospel which now by the grace of God has risen
> anew may be noised and spread abroad.
>
> [*LW* 53. 316]

That it was seems clear enough from a poem of *Meistersinger* Sachs of Nürnberg (1523) and its tribute to Luther as 'the Wittenberg nightingale now heard everywhere'. Yet if the reference indicates that real headway was being made, a cautious Luther remained on guard lest his grasp of 'a pure gospel' suffer dilution. Introducing the *Wittenberg Hymnal* of 1528, the Reformer duly inveighed against 'blunderheads' who had 'corrupted and adulterated' his earlier work 'until the true gospel was all but lost among so many gospels'. Ever the realist, he was aware of such commercialism and identified the phenomenon as

> ... the same thing that happened to the books of Saint Jerome, Saint Augustine, and many others.
>
> [Ibid p. 318]

In fact, the words of a contemporary Saxon proverb, 'there must be mouse dirt with the pepper', rang true. For Luther well realized the value of such a peppering process, and set to music compositions he was confident would not only blind Satan, but also disperse spiritual anxieties with the proclamation of divine truth. If temptations frequently beset such a warm mass of human emotions, laying siege to his very soul, Luther rapidly rallied to these *Anfechtungen* convinced that the power of evil itself gave him the resolution both to fear and to love God in Christ. The year 1527 proved peculiarly depressing. As he took stock of its devastating impact on the gospel cause, a sorely dejected Reformer deplored the aftermath of the Peasant uprising of 1525 and wrote that 'Christ was wholly lost to me'.

Although the precise date of the composition remains unknown, it was at about this sombre moment that Luther first conceived his most enduring and triumphant hymn. The opening verse of Psalm 46:

> God is our refuge and strength, a very present help in trouble,

comforted the Reformer so much that, whenever he had to face trials and tribulations, it was his custom to recite or sing the whole of the psalm with his University colleague Philipp Melanchthon, Wittenberg's professor of Greek. His composition of a psalm-hymn on assurance was no mere paraphrase of words attributed to David, and 'A mighty fortress' is justly revered as Luther's unique battle cry for the reformation of the Western

Church. Yet the hymn clearly gains immense strength from the psalm's first verse, just as recollection of a meditative gem in verse 10 – 'Be still and know that I am God' – reinforces conviction. A lofty sounding board too, Luther's allusive verse echoes forth teaching he derived from the apostle Paul, as well as much powerful apocalyptic resonating the Book of Revelation. For it would be difficult to deny that the whole teaching impact of *Ein feste Burg* stemmed from an idiosyncratic Luther whose very lyrics strove to let God be God! Nothing if not a great idealist, Luther's pastoral concern prompted him to set about a task of reformation the popes of Rome had singularly failed to tackle, to give the late-medieval Church of the West the initiative and lead many hoped for. Through a rousing hymn like this – invaluable for its transformation of a particularly apt psalm – Wittenberg's Dr Martinus thus strove to bring the Lord's own consolation back into the frustrated lives of ordinary people. No wonder he wanted to 'encourage any German poets to compose evangelical hymns for us', hymns of the quality of a composition which has been termed a sixteenth-century *Marseillaise*, because it chanted his message all round Europe.

> I wish that we had as many songs as possible in the common tongue which the people could sing during Mass, immediately after the *Gradual* and also after the *Sanctus* and *Agnus Dei*. For who doubts that originally all the people sang what the choir alone now sings? We need poets, poets as yet unknown, who can compose evangelical and spiritual songs, as St Paul calls them (Colossians 3.16), worthy to be used in God's Church.

A popular cause from the start, it should surprise no one nowadays that many good Lutherans hold this most symbolic of hymns so dear as to afford it status as something of a 'National Anthem of Heaven'! And however such spiritual charts fire the imagination, to rise and fall with the fashions in worship to be focused in this little book, Martin Luther's stunning composition demands the most serious consideration.

First of all, it is rewarding to focus attention on the leading idea of 'A mighty fortress', or what Thomas Carlyle translated for English consumption as 'A safe Stronghold'. But the romantic tale

that the Reformer sang the hymn to summon up courage before he
appeared at the Worms Parliament in the presence of the Emperor
Charles V (1521) is pure fantasy. Much ink has been used by those
trying to date the work, but few now doubt that it first appeared
during the late 1520s. Accordingly, it follows that in something of
a Sellars and Yeatman '1517 & All That' vein, any earlier dating
simply has to rank as 'wrong but wromantic'! For this would link it
with a comment made by Luther *en route* for the Imperial *Diet* at
which, despite the fate that had overtaken Jan Huss on a similar occasion (Huss was summoned to the Council of Constance and
condemned in 1415), he would face the implications of his protest
and go in person to Worms:

> though there be as many devils in that city as there are tiles
> on the roofs of the houses.

The link is of course to be found in words of the third verse:

> And were this world all devils o'er,
>   And watching to devour us,
> We lay it not to heart so sore;
>   Not they can overpower us.

Clearly then 'The mighty Fortress' referred to was not the forti-
fied entrance gateway of the walled city of Worms. But it could
well have been the imposing entrance to Schloss Coburg where,
in 1530, Luther, because of the ban confining him to Ernestine
Saxon territory, was obliged to wait while Melanchthon bar-
gained with imperial and papal counsellors, as both sides in the
great dispute dividing Christendom met at Augsburg to consider
his confession of faith. Ever since, the people called 'Lutheran'
have associated that creed – the celebrated *Augsburg Confession* –
with the hymn, as if rejoicing at the simultaneous impact of Word
and worship. And as Julius Köstlin wrote in a nineteenth-century
biography of the Reformer:

> This hymn is Luther in song. It is pitched in the very key
> of the man. Rugged and majestic, trustful in God and con-
> fident, it was the defiant trumpet blast of the Reformation,
> speaking out to the powers of the earth and under the earth

an all-conquering conviction of divine vocation of empow-
ering. The world has many sacred songs of exquisite ten-
derness and unalterable trust; but this one of Luther's is
matchless in its warlike tone, its rugged strength and its
inspiring ring.

Few members of the human race have had to face the full panoply
of power that withstood Luther when, at Worms, he sought to
defy both papal and imperial authority and teach a gospel that, in
his own way, he had by divine grace 're-discovered'. The opposition he depicts, in a first verse of almost combative engagement,
uses truly forceful lines memorably translated to read:

> The ancient prince of Hell
> Hath risen with purpose fell;
> Strong mail of craft and power
> He weareth in this hour;
> On earth is not his fellow.

Man cannot hope to get the better of Satan by force of arms. Yet
because the Lord is a refuge and strength, and in words of the
psalmist 'a very present help in trouble', the Christ can conquer
on behalf of believers. And Luther's vision of victory proves more
striking because of his use of martial language and the way it glo-
ries in ultimate triumph. The 'ancient foe' is not to be overcome
by striving, because such battles encourage dependence on 'good
works', not faith. So men and women must learn to trust 'the
proper Man' – the Christ who alone can bring victory against
impossible odds.

> With force of arms we nothing can,
>   Full soon were we down-ridden;
> But for us fights the proper Man,
>   Whom God Himself hath bidden.
>   Ask ye: Who is this same?
>   Christ Jesus is His Name,
>   The Lord Sabaoth's Son;
>   He, and no other one,
>   Shall conquer in the battle.

When the concluding line of verse 3 stresses that

A word shall quickly slay him,

this is of course Luther shorthand for the 'Word of God'. Left alone with his thoughts in the Coburg – a fastness he termed his 'wilderness' – the Reformer knew that the whole cause of the gospel for which he had laboured between 1517 and 1530 was under threat. In truth, his very life was more than ever at risk. Imperial Edict restricted his movement, and if Melanchthon had gone to Augsburg in his place to speak up for the faith of 'protestants', could such a mild, quiet-spoken, even timid colleague be trusted to stand firm? It was a cruel dilemma, and one of those moments in history when he who has pioneered a crucial cause finds it difficult to delegate. In the balanced judgement of Roland Bainton, late-lamented doyen of Luther scholars:

> The hymn to the end strains under the overtones of cosmic conflict as the Lord God of Sabaoth smites the prince of darkness grim and vindicates the martyred saints.
> [*Here I stand!* (London, 1951), p. 346]

Martin Luther married in 1525 – he had children, a home and a growing reputation. But now in the isolation of his wilderness he felt everything to be at stake, and the whole cause at risk. This is precisely the background to controversial lines in the hymn's fourth verse:

> And tho' they take our life,
> Goods, honour, children, wife,
> Yet is their profit small;
> These things shall vanish all!

Because he must have been fearful and in grave doubt, some have interpreted the stanza as demeaning family links, even that true Christians should be prepared to sacrifice all in the cause. But explanations that allow Luther to abandon his family so readily fail to understand a man whose teaching always spanned the whole range of human activity in the divine economy. Again and again Luther stressed the transitory nature of the kingdom of this world compared with the enduring plan of a God who, as *Alpha* and *Omega*, the beginning and the end, was the Creator inhabiting eternity. Such is the conviction of true perspective; and when

> These things shall vanish all:
> The City of God remaineth!

Truly, the vision is profound; and one as deep in theology as it is inspiring musically. Luther certainly realized the force of music in divine worship to make much of the unique way David had chosen to praise the Lord. He also knew (as the 'Devotional Treasury' of gleanings from some of his other compositions will illustrate below) how such hymns, when set to music of the compelling kind, could move men and women to piety, disciplining and training them from early days in a Christian life of service to God and their neighbours. It was a considered way of training the faithful to grow in faith, their grounding in 'the new religion' nurturing them to live out the gospel of Christ. For:

> ... the young must be trained and educated in the Scripture and God's Word daily so that they may become familiar with the Bible, grounded, well-versed, and skilled in it, ready to defend their faith and in due time to teach others and to increase the kingdom of Christ. For such, one must read, sing, preach, write and compose. And if it would help ... I would have all the bells pealing, and all the organs playing, and have everything ring that can make a sound ...
> [LW 53.62]

If *Ein feste Burg* thus has an anthem-like quality, Luther's sheer teaching achievement in both words and music simply has to afford him a high place in the charts of Christendom. 'A safe stronghold' may not be the 'National Anthem of Heaven', but it is surely a strong candidate for serious consideration! For wherever the heritage of the Reformation of the sixteenth century is recalled, Martin Luther's great hymn provides genuine inspiration and serves to remind faithful people that, whatever doubts and dilemmas confront them,

> The City of God remaineth!

A LUTHER DEVOTIONAL TREASURY

Luther's early hymns familiarized faithful folk with the best-known psalms, and the 1524 *Preface* clearly focused his concern to follow

> the example of the Old Testament prophets and kings who praised God with song and sound, poetry and psaltery.

Such psalm-hymns are not as well known in the United King-dom as in Germany, Scandinavia and especially the United States of America. But based as it is on Psalm 130,

> From Trouble deep I cry to Thee

provides a good example of one that is far from unfamiliar.

In many respects, Luther modelled his ministry on that of the apostle Paul, and the *Preface* duly noted not only 'the ancient custom of the Christian Church to sing Psalms', but made particular reference to Corinth and Colossae where believers received apostolic encouragement to adopt such worship. Above all, by avoiding any kind of literal translation, his renderings recognized the need for vigorous communication of the psalms for their Christian meaning. The Reformer therefore sought to popularize a hidden gospel in his psalm-hymns, and urged people to sing of 'Jesus Christ as Saviour'. If he likewise abandoned love ballads and lewd ditties, Luther could neverthe-less use contemporary newsmongering in song (*Zeitungslieder*), and many a market place resounded to gospel snatches as the faithful vied with hawkers, proclaiming the Word of God as more relevant than any of the food and drink on offer!

Two well-known compositions with central gospel themes are the Christmas hymn

> From Heaven on high I come to you,

and the hymn celebrating the Lord's resurrection and ascension:

> Christ Jesus lay in death's strong bands.

Examples of his 'catechism hymns' both illustrate the teaching emphasis Luther's hymnody handed down in a great tradition.

The second verse of 'From Trouble deep' (1523) simply has to be recalled in such an evangelical context, for here is a succinct summary of the gospel 're-discovery' Luther cherished:

> With thee counts nothing but thy grace
> To cover all our failing,
> The best life cannot win the race,
> Good works are unavailing.
> Before thee no one glory can,
> And so must tremble every man,
> And live by thy grace only.

No wonder the Lübeck authorities were obliged to take action when, in 1530, cathedral sermons urging traditional Catholic doctrine prompted a divided response as elements of the congregation tried to offer impromptu descants of Lutheran hymns during the singing of *Salve Regina*.

For inspiration and meditation, however, these samples represent the Reformer's true worth, and merit the appreciation of Christians from other traditions. Such verses can afford assurance and solace to all who seek to walk in the Way that is spiritual life.

Based on Psalm 12, and published in 1523, the fifth stanza of

> Ah God, from Heaven look down,

contains in concentrated compass the pre-eminence Luther afforded the Word:

> Silver that seven times is tried
> With fire, is found the purer;
> God's word the same test will abide,
> It still comes out the surer.
> It shall by crosses proved be;
> Men shall its strength and glory see
> Shine strong upon the nations.

Inspired by Psalm 67, 'Would that the Lord would grant us Grace' has been described as 'the first missionary hymn of Protestantism'. Published late in 1523, the opening verse is vintage Luther and altogether memorable:

Would that the Lord would grant us grace,
And with clear shining let his face,
With blessings rich provide us,
To life eternal light us;
That we his gracious work may know,
And what is his good pleasure,
And also to the heathen show
Christ's riches without measure
And unto God convert them.

In 1525, the insistence of the remarkable Katherine von Bora converted Luther from celibacy to the married state; and the Reformer's hymn on Psalm 128 contains stanzas that provide the perfect antidote to the controversial third verse of *Ein feste Burg*. The contrast is so striking that parallel quotation can help to take it in:

And tho' they take our life,   So shall thy wife be in thy house
Goods, honour, children, wife   Like vine with clusters plenteous,
Yet is their profit small;   Thy children sit thy table round
These things shall vanish all!   Like olive plants all fresh and sound.

In 1524, Luther's 'Let God be blest' effectively revised a Corpus Christi chant as a hymn for Holy Communion. The second verse provides a fine illustration of the Reformer's understanding of the eucharistic presence, to offer believers a humbling challenge for meditation:

The holy body is for us laid lowly
Down in death, that we live holy;
No greater goodness He to us could render,
To make think of his love tender.
Kyrieleison.

In 1538, Martin Luther gave 'Dame Music' herself doggerel that aptly summarized his commitment to the spreading of gospel 'good news' in spiritual songs. Such sentiments speak volumes about the effectiveness of a Reformer whose re-ordering of so much in public worship affords all faithful people an incomparable bequest and heritage.

> There cannot be an evil mood
> Where there are singing fellows good,
> There is no envy, hate, or ire,
> Gone are through me all sorrows dire;
> Greed, care, and lonely heaviness
> No more do they the heart oppress.
>   [Lw 53.319–320]

And after allusions to David pacifying Saul on the lyre, Luther gives thanks to the Almighty for creating 'Dame Music' by his Word, and extols her as a singularly effective songstress:

> For our dear Lord she sings her song
> In praise of him the whole day long;
> To him I give my melody
> And thanks in all eternity.

Chapter 2

THOMAS KEN

and

'Awake, my soul, and with the sun'

1 Awake, my soul, and with the
  sun
Thy daily stage of duty run;
Shake off dull sloth, and joyful rise
To pay thy morning sacrifice.

2 Thy precious time mispent
  redeem,
Each present day thy last esteem;
Improve thy talent with due care,
For the great day thyself prepare.

3 In conversation, be sincere,
Keep conscience as the noon-tide
  clear:
Think how all-seeing God thy
  ways
And all thy secret thoughts surveys.

4 By influence of the light divine,
Let thy own light to others shine,
Reflect all heaven's propitious rays,
In ardent love, and cheerful praise.

II

5 Wake, and lift up thyself, my
  heart,
And with the Angels bear thy part,
Who all night long unwearied sing
High praise to the eternal King.

6 I wake, I wake! ye heavenly
  choir,
May your devotion me inspire,
That I like you my age may spend,
Like you may on my GOD attend.

7 May I like you in GOD delight,
Have all day long my GOD in
  sight,
Perform like you my Maker's
  will –
O, may I never more do ill.

8 Had I your wings, to heaven I'd
  fly –
But GOD shall that defect supply;
And my soul, wing'd with warm
  desire,
Shall all day long to heaven aspire.

III

9 All praise to Thee, Who safe hast
  kept
And hast refresh'd me whilst I
  slept;
Grant, LORD, when I from death
  shall wake
I may of endless light partake.

10 I would not wake, nor rise
  again
E'en heaven itself I would disdain,
Wert not Thou there to be
  enjoyed,
And I in hymns to be employed.

11 Heaven is, dear LORD, where'er
  Thou art:
O, never then from me depart;
For to my soul, 'tis hell to be
But for one moment void of Thee.

12 LORD, I my vows to Thee
  renew:
Disperse my sins as morning dew;
Guard my first springs of thought
  and will,
And with Thyself my spirit fill.

13 Direct, control, suggest, this day
All I design, or do, or say;
That all my powers, with all their
  might,
In Thy sole glory may unite.

Doxology
14 Praise GOD, from Whom all
  blessings flow,
Praise Him, all creatures here
  below,
Praise Him above, ye heavenly
  host,
Praise FATHER, SON, and
  HOLY GHOST.

                    A M E N

Sublime focus of the Cathedral Church dedicated to the Holy Trinity and Saints Peter, Paul and Swithun at Winchester was a glorious late fifteenth-century screen that, providing inspirational setting for celebrations of the eucharist, surmounted the high altar. Sadly pillaged during the English Civil War, angels and apostles, saints and kings were defaced, but by good fortune, Oliver Cromwell's soldiery did not destroy the massive stone reredos itself. More than two centuries passed before a modern restoration fashioned new sculptures to fill the empty niches, and among these stands Thomas Ken, the Caroline divine who gave six years' selfless service to the neighbouring diocese of Bath and Wells before his deprivation as bishop in 1691. Sometime Fellow of the College and Prebendary of the Cathedral, the saintly Ken's *Manual of Prayer for Winchester Scholars* (1675) more than justifies his presence in such a holy place. Thomas Ken's hymns did not appear in the *Manual's* first edition and were published as an appendix to a 1700 reprint. But it was an eighteenth-century musical setting that gave the celebrated 'Morning Hymn':

> Awake, my soul, and with the sun
> Thy daily stage of duty run

a far wider appeal in Christendom at large than when merely recited by 'good scholars' whom Ken hoped would be 'brought up in a perpetuity of prayer.' His doxology in particular occupies high and holy ground of near perfection for its very simplicity as an enduring homily of Christian praise in the worship of Almighty God:

> Praise God, from Whom all blessings flow;
> Praise Him, all creatures here below;
> Praise Him above, ye heavenly host;
> Praise FATHER, SON and HOLY GHOST.

*

In many respects, Thomas Ken's 'Morning Hymn' is best seen as a commentary on his own spiritual pilgrimage. Once linked to the disciplined approach of the *Manual* and his later *Catechism* or *Practice of Divine Love* (1685), it has a wider application and an assured place in popular pastoral literature. From first to last, his stanzas have a compelling 'New-Every-Morning' imagery. As the rising sun heralds a new day, it just as surely summons the dutiful to attend to the next stage of their pilgrimage. 'Look on your soul as still undressed, till you have said your prayers', Ken's *Manual* informed his young Wykehamists and, by an extension set out on the title-page, 'all other <u>Devout</u> Christians'. The ancient practice of faithful folk – Jewish as well as Christian – had been to begin each day by reciting selected Psalms of David; and this was a discipline Ken's hymn attempted to extend to wider groups of individuals and congregations by the use of simple language to teach practical piety. Carefully chosen words counsel regular meditation and recovery of 'precious time mispent'. If the emphasis is demanding, and one that almost parallels the commitment of those in religious Orders, it shines with a pious vision to place human existence in divine perspective. Because life is God-given, solemn obligations follow, not least among them improving discipleship. Just as Thomas Ken's *Manual* offers an ideal introduction to his later *Practice of Divine Love*, so that tract is best understood as a catechism unique in its period plea for a belief that behaves. The lines:

> Improve thy talent with due care,
> For the great day thyself prepare

make the point with all possible clarity. And focus on the importance of 'sincere' conversation is echoed in a petition for 'particular graces'. Vigilance Ken commends as essential to ongoing witness in the life of faith. His allusion to judgement (verse 2) embraces not only 'the great Day' itself, but the kind of dutiful commitment that radiates conviction. Some condemn the lines

> Think how all-seeing God thy ways
> And all thy secret thoughts surveys,

fearful that they inculcate the worst kind of subjective piety. The couplet has been held to encourage either religiosity and an arrogant assurance, or nervous decline in breakdown and the awful anguish and anxiety that can submerge young and old alike in a slough of despond. Such psycho-assertion is unworthy, unhistorical and clearly calculated not merely to spurn but blatantly to destroy any kind of spirituality. It totally fails to respect the context of Thomas Ken's tract, for the real significance of this period piece of a *Catechism* lies in the emphasis it places on the need to control the tongue:

> Lord, purify my Thoughts, bridle my Tongue, guide all my Actions, guard all my Senses, stop my Ears, and turn away my Eyes from sin and vanity.

In fact, a singular feature of the hymn is the balance Ken achieved between practice and praise in the Christian life. For there is here a devout concentration and resolution to join the worship of the 'heavenly choir' which clearly stems from his own practice in private prayer. Originally verse 6 retained its authentic personal repetition ('I wake, I wake!'), but was soon revised for congregational use to read 'Awake, awake!' Similarly, verse 7, another original no longer included in the standard hymnals, read:

> May I like you [viz. the angelic choir] in GOD delight,
> Have all day long my GOD in sight,
> Perform like you my Maker's will –
> O, may I never more do ill.

Such stanzas effectively illuminate an English saint kneeling in the footlights, for Ken's principled resignation to the will of God proved a characteristic posture, prayerful but defiant, many crises colouring a career that repeatedly brought him into conflict with the State. Like others before and since, he could covet wings to fly him to heaven, yet he nevertheless remained steadfast in the face of reality and the knowledge (verse 11) that:

> Heaven is, dear Lord, where'er Thou art;
> O, never then from me depart:
> For to my soul, 'tis hell to be
> But for one moment void of Thee.

It is a demanding aspiration that not only makes divine praise the primary human duty but also has solemn obligations for a life of responsible witness. The *Catechism* certainly considers the Ten Commandments in a depth of meditative detail well reflected in verse 12:

> LORD, I my vows to Thee renew:
> Disperse my sins as morning dew:
> Guard my first springs of thought and will,
> And with Thyself my spirit fill.

A powerful prelude to his doxology, Ken's last verse is one of supplication and commitment with all the dedication of the psalmist:

> Direct, control, suggest this day,
> All I design, or do, or say;
> That all my powers with all their might
> In Thy sole glory may unite.

Just as *Book of Common Prayer* services concluded the Psalms with the traditional *Gloria*, so Ken's doxology provided the hymn's climactic paeon of praise. Quite apart from the personal dedication this enshrined in an important link with the liturgy, Ken's work did much to revitalize the public worship of the Church of England. The titles he gave his hymns related to services people knew, the intention being that those who recited verses in private would come and join together in the public worship of 'Morning' and 'Evening Prayer' in their parish church. The Restoration of Charles II in 1660 also restored the Church of England. But the outward restoration of fabric and ritual that pleased the King and Clarendon by no means satisfied Ken. With a physician's finger on the patient's pulse, he well knew the inner state of the church and regularly bemoaned an incidence of ignorance and irreligion that altogether appalled him. Nor was he, by seventeenth-century standards, a man of limited experience or clouded judgement. William Hawkins, his first biographer, records that on a holiday pilgrimage to Italy and the Rome of Clement X's Jubilee in 1675, Ken

> was often heard to say, that he had great reason to give God thanks for his travels, since (if it were possible) he returned rather more confirmed of the purity of the Protestant religion than he was before.

Yet such exposure in no way softened his criticism of 'the squalid sluttery of the fanatick conventicles', and rather confirmed his determination to play the pastor. A considerable advance on his embryo *Manual*, the *Practice of Divine Love* was thus the *Exposition of the Church Catechism* clearly phrased in the subtitle, neglect of which in his view accounted for the sad state of the diocese of Bath and Wells entrusted to Ken when he was consecrated bishop by William Sancroft in 1685. Not since the elevation of John Hooper to Gloucester in Tudor times had a prelate been so outspoken about the failure of his flock to grasp Christian fundamentals. Hooper had chosen to criticize shepherds more than sheep, fascinating period statistics finding no fewer than 171 of his 311 clergy unable to number the Commandments, others who could not recite the Lord's Prayer, and a number of bright sparks who volunteered the view that it was so called after 'the Lord the King'! As events transpired, Ken had little more time than Hooper in pastoral office as bishop, and the dedication of his *Catechism* 'To the Inhabitants within the Diocese of Bath & Wells' clearly indicates his determination as one caught 'up from among the meanest herdmen into the pastoral throne' to accept the responsibility he 'ought to pay to the Chief Shepherd ... to feed all His lambs and His sheep' and 'to teach them the knowledge and the love of GOD, and how they may make them both their daily study and practice'. Carefully '*contrived*' (his own word), Ken's *Catechism* addressed questions designed to shock penitents with the realization that any lapse amounted to 'violation of baptismal vows'.

Although it might be recalled that C.S. Lewis once used the imagery of caterpillars in a cabbage garden to describe the grovelling attitude required of sinners, Ken's precisely-worded, oft-repeated, 'Woe is me, wretch that I am!' is another period piece. For in the *Catechism* he effectively countered the Seven Deadly Sins with the demands of Mosaic Law to reclaim the spirit of many medieval primers for Protestant piety. Careful counsel he offers on preparation for the eucharist likewise gives his work a timeless reference. It leaves his reader in no doubt about the value Ken placed on Confession for those who lacked assurance of salvation. Here, in short, is a purposeful objectivity that gives the lie to many a carping criticism, and advice once offered to Winchester schoolboys is now extended to the people of his diocese. Let them be 'not ashamed to unburthen' their souls and secure 'ghostly Counsel', but in doing so secure 'the Benefit of Absolution'. In plain language based on the Prayer-Book rubric

Ken made it clear that

> though Confession of our Sins to God is only Matter of
> Duty, and absolutely necessary, yet Confession to our spiri-
> tual Guide also is, by many devout souls, found to be very
> advantageous to true Repentance.

The vital heartbeat of late-Caroline spirituality instilled such
piety, and Ken did not hesitate to urge use of the *Book of Common Prayer* for that purpose, his *Catechism* declaring it to be:

> very advisable, that persons, before they communicate,
> should read over the whole Communion office, or at least
> the exhortations there, which they will find to contain very
> proper, and plain, and excellent instructions.

Loyalty to the Stuarts had raised such a man to high office in the
English Church, just as that same loyalty brought about his
deprivation and decline in wilderness years. A Roman Catholic
by conviction, Charles II had, quite literally, played along with
the Church of England. But the King and Queen had no prince,
and as he prepared for the succession of James, Duke of York, his
unashamedly papist brother, Charles used Archbishop Sancroft
and a Commission of 1681 to strengthen a company of 'catholic'
sympathisers at Court who above all would be loyal to the House
of Stuart. Vacant 'royal' appointments in the church were made
on the recommendation of Commission members – Compton,
Bishop of London, as well as Sancroft, Viscount Hyde (the all-
important Rochester), Halifax, Radnor and Seymour – who
consistently forwarded politically 'suitable' candidates.

   No Mr Facing-both-Ways, Thomas Ken's Standfast quality was
recognized as much as his overall loyalty to the Supreme
Governor of the Church of England. Charles II even admired the
man's principled refusal to accommodate a well-known mistress
in a house owned by the Dean and Chapter on a royal visit to
Winchester. At the same time, the scruples which afforded Ken
patronage and the episcopate prevented his taking the oath to
William and Mary. The 'Glorious Revolution' thus obliged him
to keep company with those like Frampton, Lake, Lloyd and
Turner – all of whom had been promoted prelate by the 1681

Commission – in the grievous ecclesiastical bloodletting now known as the Non-Juring Schism. Caroline piety had henceforth to be practised in the wilderness, and a church that lost its Primate, eight diocesan bishops and some four hundred parish priests was never quite the same again. Some telling words of Ken's most recent biographer have relevance:

> It is one of the minor tragedies of English History that this man who seemed under the Providence of God destined to exercise so salutary a spiritual influence over his fellow countrymen, should have been so consistently baulked in his endeavours by secular crises beyond his control.
> [H.A.L. Rice, *Thomas Ken, Bishop & Non-juror,* p. 79.]

A THOMAS KEN 'SPIRITUAL TREASURY'

If Thomas Ken's 'Evening Hymn' is well enough known, it will come as no surprise that the 'Midnight Hymn' that completed his sacred trilogy has enjoyed strictly limited appeal in popular piety. At the same time his achievement as a devotional poet – Hawkins edited four volumes of poems and hymns on the gospels and major festivals in 1721 – deserves to be more widely known. The dedicated life that spanned such a fascinating period of English history certainly offers an inspirational quality to the faithful of any generation.

In their *Preface* to the *Book of Common Prayer,* 1662, the revisers made all too gracious allusion to 'the late unhappy confusions' that had besieged the Church of England. It was a reference Hugh Rice's exuberant biography took up, this notable single-sentence judgement recapturing much of the period context:

> A remarkable phrase as applied to a revolution, a civil war, the judicial murder of a King, a Viceroy, and an Archbishop, the imprisonment or exile of a whole Bench of Bishops, the ejection and deprivation of an entire parochial clergy, the abolition of all religious feasts and the proscription of the Church's Book of Common Prayer.   [op. cit. p. 36.]

Ken's 'Evening Hymn' closely parallels the 'Morning Hymn' in a majestic simplicity of wording that affords it inspirational depth in abundance, not least in these well-known stanzas:

> Forgive me, LORD, for Thy dear SON,
> The ill that I this day have done;
> That with the world, myself, and Thee,
> I ere I sleep at peace may be.
>
> Teach me to live, that I may dread
> The grave as little as my bed;
> To die, that this vile body may
> Rise glorious at the awful day.
>
> O, may my soul on Thee repose,
> And may sweet sleep mine eyelids close;
> Sleep that may me more vigorous make,
> To serve my GOD when I awake.

Later, the words:

> But though sleep o'er my frailty reigns,
> Let it not hold me long in chains;
> And now and then let loose my heart,
> Till it an hallelujah dart.

testify to the asceticism of a man who, when conscious that his life's end drew nigh, wore a shroud to prepare for the grave. Calculated to prevent his corpse being undressed, this could also have been the saintly Ken's way of depriving prying eyes a sight of any hair shirt he may have worn. It is an interesting speculation, and although in no way improbable, its truth will never be known. As for his reference to 'an hallelujah dart', this neatly complements Ken's recommendation of what he termed 'Ejaculations' or brief collects to be offered before reading Scripture or taking specific prayerful action. Typical of such was:

'Lord, make thy Word my Delight and my Counsellor,'

together with his much-used quotation from Psalm 119:

'Blessed be Thou, O Lord; O teach me thy Statutes.'

In much this context, another gem from the *Manual* deserves a place in the treasury Ken bequeathed his wider flock:

When you come into Church, or Chapel, not only on the Lord's Day, but on any other Day, use this short Preparatory Prayer at your first kneeling down:

O Lord, I humbly beg thy Holy Spirit to help my Infirmities at this Time and to dispose my Heart to Devotion, that my Prayers and Praises may be acceptable in thy Sight, through JESUS CHRIST, my Saviour.

Joy at the prospect of his last summons Ken does not hide in the wording of 'A Midnight Hymn'. Best described as an on-going choral experience, verse 3 itself provides a most moving homily for those who rate exposure to music high among the soulful moments in life. Once more use of the first person strengthens the intercessory plea of verse composition:

I with your choir celestial join,
In offering up a hymn divine;
With you in heaven I hope to dwell,
And bid the night and world farewell.

My soul, when I shake off this dust,
LORD, in Thy arms I will entrust;
O make me Thy peculiar care,
Some mansion for my soul prepare.

Despite his disciplined piety and the wilderness experience of rejected ministry, Ken knew about mansions, his friend Viscount Weymouth placing an apartment at the disposal of his needy Wykehamist contemporary. By a barter arrangement, the Lord of Longleat also afforded Ken a small annuity so that he could continue to enjoy his books. The poem 'An Anodyne' offers a vision of frustration as the deprived prelate pores over learned tomes to make a monastic retreat in his library at the Thynne's stately Wiltshire home. There, as often as not immersed in the Early Fathers and writings of medieval ascetics and mystics, he nevertheless remained convinced of the catholicity of his beloved Church of England. The preamble to his Last Will and Testament makes clear his principles in the matter:

> As for my religion, I die in the Holy Catholic and Apostolic Faith professed by the whole Church before the disunion of East and West; more particularly, I die in the Communion of the Church of England, as it stands distinguished from all Papal and Puritan innovations, and as it adheres to the doctrine of the Cross.

In a credal context, his *Catechism* offers more on the rich meaning Ken afforded the Church by using the word 'catholic':

> I believe, Lord, this Church to be Catholic, or universal, made up of the collection of all particular churches: ... Catholic in respect of time, comprehending all ages to the world's end, to which it is to endure; Catholic in respect of all places, out of which believers are to be gathered; Catholic in respect of all saving faith, of which this creed contains the substance, which shall in it always be taught; Catholic in respect of all graces, which shall in it be practised; and Catholic in respect of that Catholic war it is to wage against all its ghostly enemies, for which it is called militant.

For Ken had no regrets:

> I never did any thing in my life more to my satisfaction than my seceding.

As for the treasures of this world, he had them weighed in a delicate balance that found them prone to 'so many Accidents, that they quickly wither and decay'. The examples provided in some posthumously published *Meditations* (1725) make an unforgettable impact:

> The Pain in one Tooth, the Cramp in one Joint, the Gout in

one Toe, the Megrim in the Head, the Collick in the Guts,
the Fever in the Blood, the Sciatica in the Thigh, the Fistula
or Hemorrhoids in the nether Parts, or any one of these, takes
away the Relish of our Pleasures, and imbitters all the Volup-
tuous Persons Enjoyments; turning his Singing into Sighing,
his Musick into Mourning, and his Riot into Rage.

'A Midnight Hymn' reveals a Ken both ready and waiting to
depart this life. But it should not be used to misinterpret the
message of a man who fully understood his stewardship and spent
his life in redeeming the time of what he believed to be a
divinely-allotted span. The careful balance he sought is nowhere
better appreciated than in this Collect for Health:

> O LORD, when I am Sick, let me think I may Dye; when I
> am in Health that I may be Sick; that I may not misspend
> the Stock of my Life, but do Thee honour with my Health,
> and thou may'st give me Comfort for it in my Sickness:
> Even this, that Sin hath not bound me to my Bed, but thy
> Providence hath cast me down, which can and will lift me
> up, to Health in this World, or to Happiness in a better.
> Such an Enjoyment of Health give me, I beseech Thee, for
> Jesus Christ his Sake.   Amen.

Above all, a vivid insight of Thomas Ken's disciplined dedication
is surely to be found in his poetic portrayal of the ideal priest.
Much the finest pastoral charge of its kind, it is framed in the
second volume of verse published by William Hawkins some ten
years after Ken's death, but will no doubt live for ever:

> Give me the priest these graces shall possess;
> Of an ambassador the just address,
> A Father's tenderness, a Shepherd's care,
> A Leader's courage, which the cross can bear,
> A Ruler's arm, a Watchman's wakeful eye,
> A Pilot's skill, the helm in storms to ply,
> A Fisher's patience, and a Labourer's toil,
> A Guide's dexterity to disembroil,
> A Prophet's inspiration from above,
> A Teacher's knowledge, and a Saviour's love.

Give me a priest, a light upon a hill,
Whose rays his whole circumference can fill,
In God's own Word and Sacred Learning versed,
Deep in the study of the heart immersed,
Who in such souls can the disease descry,
And wisely fair restoratives supply.

PHILIP DODDRIDGE D.D.

Chapter 3

PHILIP DODDRIDGE

and

'Hark the glad sound!'

1 Hark the glad sound! the Saviour comes,
  The Saviour promised long!
Let every heart prepare a throne,
  And every voice a song.

2 On him the Spirit largely pour'd
  Exerts its sacred Fire.
Wisdom and Might, and Zeal and Love
  His holy Breast inspire.

3 He comes the prisoners to release
  In Satan's bondage held;
The gates of brass before him burst,
  The iron fetters yield.

4 He comes the broken heart to bind,
  The bleeding soul to cure,
And with the treasures of his grace
  To enrich the humble poor.

5 He comes from thickest films of vice
  To purge the mental ray,
And on the eyeballs of the blind
  To pour celestial day.

6 His Silver Trumpets publish loud
  The Jub'lee of the Lord;
Our Debts are all remitted now,
  Our heritage restor'd.

7 Our glad hosannas, Prince of peace,
  Thy welcome shall proclaim;
And heaven's eternal arches ring
  With thy belovèd name.

In Cambridge, Advent Sunday is lauded with Carol Services; and in places where great choirs sing, the magic of music does much for worship in historic chapels that have become world-renowned. By contrast, a celebration of the coming of Christ in a simple country church or chapel can seem remote and even drab, however enthusiastic the village organist and vocal support. Yet a faithful word – particularly if it is re-echoed in song – can prepare those present for the Way of the Lord just as effectively as the choristers and choral clerks of King's or Trinity, or the massed concert choir of the Austrian City of Salzburg at *Adventssingen*.

It is certainly the case that one of the best-loved of all hymns sung at this season nowadays – namely Philip Doddridge's 'Hark the glad sound!' – was never intended as Advent praise at all. For the pastoral make-up of the good Northampton preacher who wrote it always set out such stanzas to stress points made in his sermons. Various sheets of Doddridge's remarkable output were regularly used in the Castle Hill Chapel where he ministered from December, 1729, for some twenty-one years of his life. But it was only after his early death in October, 1751, at scarcely fifty years of age, that his former pupil and friend Job Orton of Shrewsbury edited and published 370 Doddridge hymns between hard covers. The introduction to this volume has proved as fascinating as the *Hymns founded on Various Texts in the Holy Scriptures* it contained, for there Orton expressed the fond hope that the work of Philip Doddridge 'might be serviceable to the Interest of Religion by assisting the Devotion of Christians in their social and secret worship'. Apart from his brief preamble, Orton was determined that the reader should sample Doddridge for himself; and although his editorial guidance supplies a number of shrewd insights, the hymns that follow in biblical order are most usefully printed together with their subject and the Old and New Testament scriptures they illustrate. For example, to refer to Orton rather than to *Ancient & Modern Revised*, can be revealing, for as set out there, 'Hark the glad sound!' is listed *CCIII* and headed '*Christ's Message*' with a reference to Luke 4.18–19. The original intention of Philip Doddridge thus related to Jesus at Nazareth reading words from the prophet Isaiah in the synagogue on the Sabbath.

[18.]The Spirit of the Lord is upon me, because he hath anointed me to preach the gospel to the poor; he hath sent

me to heal the broken-hearted, to preach deliverance to the
captives, and recovery of sight to the blind, to set at liberty
them that are bruised, [19.] To preach the acceptable year of the
Lord.

It was, in short, the simplest gospel hymn intended as back-up
material for a Northampton minister's Sunday sermon; and Philip
Doddridge pressed home his homily in song. The congregation
was expected to memorize the themes of their pastor's preaching, Job Orton duly explaining that such hymns were

> composed to be sung, after the Author had been preaching
> on the Texts prefixed to them, [for] it was his Design, that
> they should bring over again the leading Thoughts in the
> Sermon, and naturally express and warmly enforce those
> devout Sentiments, which he hoped were then rising in the
> Minds of his Hearers, and help to fix them on the Memory
> and Heart.

In other words, Philip Doddridge, by writing 'devout Paraphrases
on the Texts', aimed to assist congregations 'of plain unlearned
Christians' in 'lively Acts of Devotion, Faith, and Trust in God'.
It is certainly far-fetched to suggest that Doddridge here linked
the first with the second coming of Christ – the incarnation of
Jesus with the return of the Lord in glory. Rather was the purpose of his lovely hymn a clause-by-clause commentary on the
verses from Luke, the lively language of the original seven
stanzas conveying a powerful impression of purposeful Puritan
preaching with all the inspiration of a truly dedicated poet.
    A dazzling display in its own right, the composition outlived
every sermon Doddridge preached. For such 'catechism-hymns'
not only preserved the gospel he expounded for his own people,
but endured to teach future generations 'CHRIST'S *Message*' (cf.
Orton's *CCIII* reference above) in language altogether
memorable for its scriptural simplicity. Nowadays, indeed, when
the pulpit means less and less to the average worshipper (perhaps
because a failure of nerve has resulted in most clergy spending
little time in sermon preparation?), the cold comfort of many a
contemporary church can be countered by concentration on
hymns as a focus of devotion. The briefest consideration certainly

shows the genius of Doddridge as a Christian educator whose simple choice of metre makes memorable the message of the gospel he preached.

In the first verse it is thus a 'glad sound' the people should hear as prophecy is fulfilled in that Nazareth synagogue when the Christ read from Isaiah. And in the lines,

> Let every heart prepare a throne
> And every voice a song,

the evangelical impact of the pastor's concern is clarity itself. Not that Doddridge could manage much of a song himself, Orton's honesty, from the first-hand experience of an Assistant, obliging him to reveal that the hymnwriter 'had no ear for Musick'! But if he was neither singer nor unable to 'change two notes', the traditional Puritans among his people, who did not take kindly to singing words other than those of Scripture, would not have thought less of him. They would have judged their minister's faithfulness by his loyalty to Holy Writ in the textual foundation of hymnody. His people invariably sang by dictation, and to a metre constantly in use for psalms or well-known hymn tunes. Summarizing the main points of the sermon 'to bring over again the leading thoughts', such hymns were given out a line or so at a time by a precentor. They were then sung 'by dictation' to familiar eighteenth-century melodies like Doctor Croft's 'St Anne' ('O God, our help in ages past'), Webbe's 'Rockingham' ('When I survey the wondrous Cross'), and Croft's 'Hanover' ('O worship the King'). To appreciate that fact is to treasure all the more the impact of hymns set to the wide range of moving melodies contemporary congregations are privileged to enjoy in their worship today.

Whether in music or words then, this hymn of Philip Doddridge continues to make a genuine impact. Luther always showed a special concern for 'Christ's poor'; and Doddridge here makes much of the Lord coming

> ... with the treasures of his grace
> To bless the humble poor.

These are important lines, indicating as they do the stirrings of social conscience in the best evangelical tradition. For although Doddridge made clear that the cure of souls constituted the

primary purpose of Christ's coming, the Saviour's very presence
on the planet served to release prisoners, enrich the poor and bring
more than a measure of social enlightenment. In consequence, the
hymn radiates joy and wonder on both spiritual and practical
planes, and when used in divine service has real power to uplift
congregations in their worship.

As sung today, the hymn has but four verses (*see* 1, 3, 4 and 7
above). The original Doddridge text provided seven. The Scripture made reference to a Spirit able to give 'recovery of sight to
the blind', and loyalty to Holy Writ therefore obliged the author
to use the couplet

> And on the Eye-balls of the Blind
> To pour celestial Day.

Doddridge the preacher likewise made much of the proverbial
allusion to Christ's prophetic utterance – namely that 'The Spirit
of the Lord is upon me'. And in the second verse of his original
– itself no longer printed in hymnals now in use – the point is
emphasized in words which can move those in the charismatic
movement:

> On him the Spirit largely pour'd
> Exerts its sacred Fire.
> Wisdom and Might, and Zeal and Love
> His holy Breast inspire.

Although unfamiliar, it is language brimful of poetic impact; and
in terms of devotional conviction, it has lost little of its original
power to express religious emotion. For despite his general
commitment to the faith of John Calvin, Doddridge did not
dogmatize but wrote from the heart. His seriousness of purpose
unquestionably communicates, as heartfelt piety gives his spirit
utterance. Like Richard Baxter before him (and in many respects
he tended towards 'good old Mr Baxter's divinity'), Doddridge
had such a passionate concern for Christian unity that he should
be seen in the widest context and by no means placed within
sectarian confines.

In company with most Dissenters, Doddridge was denied a
university education; but unlike many he politely held to his

principles and declined the Duchess of Bedford's patronage to send him to Oxford or Cambridge provided he would agree to ordination in the established church. Yet learning he undoubtedly gained from John Jenning's Academy at Kibworth in Leicestershire, a haven of godliness where he contributed much in later life. Intellectualism *per se* was never part of his make-up; and the delicate child who lovingly recalled pre-schooling from his mother Monica, who used the blue and white Delft tiles decorating the kitchen breast to illustrate many a bible story from the Old and New Testament, early experienced personal faith. Such faith bore fruit in a lifetime of service as Doddridge proclaimed the Christian gospel with genuine conviction, verse 6 of this hymn sounding forth what his Saviour had accomplished for humanity.

> His Silver Trumpets publish loud
> The Jub'lee of the Lord; +
> Our Debts are all remitted now,
> Our heritage restor'd.

The footnote reference [+] was to Leviticus 25, explaining the year of Jubilee as 'The acceptable Year of the Lord', a preacher's device intended to convey to the congregation the compelling urgency of the gospel message. The Old Testament allusion itself is typical, for as may be seen from the 'Treasury of Devotion' illustrating this chapter from other Doddridge hymns, Orton's 'Author' customarily drew on 'the case of the Israelites', in particular noting how Doddridge 'hath accommodated [them] to the Circumstances of Christians where he thought there was a just and natural resemblance'.

By hallowed custom too, Philip Doddridge concluded the hymn with a comforting reference to the glorious prospect of after-life awaiting the faithful.

> Our glad Hosannas, Prince of Peace,
> Thy welcome shall proclaim;
> And heaven's eternal arches ring
> With thy belovèd name.

It is a stanza which provides a masterly summary for praise and worship conveyed in the Greek of *Hosanna*, the original Hebrew word for deliverance. Here is the ultimate in recognition from the pen of an influential period preacher. The Christ has come; the Christ can deliver; and the Christ can bring peace. But the proclamation or *kerygma* of his gospel must precede that peace.

In such a brilliant, simple and essentially pastoral way, Philip Doddridge proclaimed the ministry of Christ in perceptive and poignant terms that remain forever meaningful. Truly, as Ernest Payne once observed, he 'who can write hymns and verses of this quality has won his place among the immortals'. Nor can it be doubted that the worldwide worshipping Church continues to gain inspiration from both the simplicity and sincerity of Doddridge's remarkable achievement.

A DODDRIDGE DEVOTIONAL TREASURY

The *Hymns founded on Various Texts in the Holy Scriptures* (1755) ranged widely, eighteen stemming from texts in the Pentateuch, ten from the Historical Books of the Old Testament, ninety-two from the Prophets, forty-five from the Psalms, eight from Proverbs, and four from the Book of Job. From the New Testament, seventy-five derive from texts in the Gospels, ten from the Acts of the Apostles, ninety-one from the Epistles, and twelve from the Book of Revelation.

First lines of other well-known Doddridge hymns still used in worship include 'JACOB'S *Vow*' (Genesis 28.20–22):

O God of Jacob by whose Hand,
Thine Israel still is fed;

'*The Active Christian*' (Luke 12.35–38):

Ye Servants of the Lord,
Each in his Office wait;

and No. 286 on Orton's list, the hymn later described by the redoubtable Charles Haddon Spurgeon as 'Our Tabernacle

National Anthem':

> Grace! 'tis a charming Sound
> Harmonious to my Ear!

★

Here for meditation are some other hymns of Doddridge, refer-
ring to texts in both the Old and New Testaments. The first one
is still in use, but the remaining examples are reprinted to illustrate the undiminished power of such popular poetry in the
pilgrimage that can enrich religious life. All reference numbers
and biblical texts relate to Orton's *Hymns founded on Various Texts*
... (1755).

CLXXI GOD's Name profaned, when his Table is treated with Contempt. Malachi i. 12.

1 MY GOD, and is thy Table spread?
  And does thy Cup with Love o'erflow?
  Thither be all thy Children led,
  And let them all its Sweetness know.

2 Hail Sacred Feast, which *Jesus* makes!
  Rich Banquet of his Flesh and Blood!
  Thrice happy he, who here partakes
  That sacred stream, that heav'nly Food!

3 Why are its Dainties all in vain
  Before unwilling Hearts display'd?
  Was not for you the Victim slain?
  Are you forbid the Children's Bread?

4 O let thy Table honour'd be,
  And furnish'd well with joyful Guests;
  And may each Soul Salvation see,
  That here its sacred Pledges tastes.

5 Let Crouds approach with Hearts prepar'd;
 With Hearts inflam'd let all attend;
 Nor, when we leave our Father's Board,
 The Pleasure, or the Profit end.

6 Revive thy dying Churches, LORD,
 And bid our drooping Graces live;
 And more that Energy afford,
 A Saviour's Blood alone can give.

Job Orton appended a note that this hymn Doddridge 'Applied to the Lord's Supper'.

★

Himself a man of prayer, Doddridge did not hesitate to commend such devotions to others. This exposition of a verse in the Gospel according to St Matthew indicates the importance he attached to a life of regular self-discipline. Closely following the Scripture and its apostolic precept, this is to be secret and soulful, a regular means of dedication and re-dedication both morning and evening.

CLXXVII *Secret Prayer*. Matthew vi. 6

1 Father divine, thy piercing Eye
 Shoots thro' the darkest Night;
 In deep Retirement Thou art nigh,
 With Heart-discerning Sight.

2 There shall that piercing Eye survey
 My duteous Homage paid,
 With ev'ry Morning's dawning Ray,
 And ev'ry Ev'ning's Shade.

3 O may thy own celestial Fire
 The Incense still inflame;
 While my warm Vows to Thee aspire,
 Thro' my Redeemer's name.

4 So shall the visits of thy Love
   My Soul in secret bless;
   So shalt Thou deign in Worlds above
   Thy Suppliant to confess.

In this hymn and the last example below, it is interesting to note
not only Philip Doddridge's grasp of Scripture, but also the
evident pleasure he derived from wild life and the natural
environment of the countryside. The language and imagery of
romanticism is not far distant.

CCXXXVII. *Abiding in* **Christ** *necessary to our Fruitfulness.*
John xv.4

1 LORD of the Vineyard, we adore
   That Pow'r and Grace divine,
   Which plants our wild, our barren Souls
   In *Christ* the living Vine.

2 For ever may they there abide,
   And, from that vital Root,
   Be Influence spread thro' ev'ry Branch
   To form and feed the Fruit.

3 Shine forth, my GOD, the Clusters warm
   With Rays of sacred Love;
   Till *Eden's* Soil, and *Zion's* Streams
   The gen'rous Plant improve.

Chapter 4

ISAAC WATTS

and

'When I survey the wondrous Cross'

1 WHEN I survey the wondrous Cross,
   On which the Prince of Glory died,
My richest gain I count but loss,
   And pour contempt on all my pride.

2 Forbid it, Lord, that I should boast
   Save in the death of Christ my God;
All the vain things that charm me most,
   I sacrifice them to his Blood.

3 See from his head, his hands, his feet,
   Sorrow and love flow mingled down;
Did e'er such love and sorrow meet,
   Or thorns compose so rich a crown?

4 His dying crimson, like a robe,
   Spreads o'er his body on the tree;
Then I am dead to all the globe,
   And all the globe is dead to me.

5 Were the whole realm of nature mine,
   That were an offering far too small;
Love so amazing, so divine,
   Demands my soul, my life, my all.

Doc McGregor would have no secular music while he worked and had a preference for the metrical psalms whose lugubrious tempo tended to slow down the speed of the work as well as depressing the spirits.

[P.D. James, *Original Sin*, 1994]

The allusive quality of Lady James's prose invariably provides compelling reading. Although this fictional reference to the musical preferences of a pathologist engaged in macabre tasks may therefore seem remote from seventeenth-century religious practice, its unusual insight precisely recaptures the drear and shrouded situation facing Isaac Watts in his determination to stir, and no longer depress, the souls of the worshipping congregation in his charge.

When Minister of Mark Lane Chapel, it was certainly a lively twenty-eight year old who determined to wean his people from the inflexible orthodoxies of a period that prized metrical Psalms as the legacy an austere Calvinism decreed remain unaltered. Years earlier in his family circle, the young Watts had developed a real distaste for Sunday devotions at the Southampton Meeting House. Scant satisfaction came his way because humdrum, repetitive chants and the hour-long tedium of 'branching sermons' (when preachers transgressed the 'off-side rule' to extend any structured argument and make endless extra points!) altogether dominated the routines of spiritual life. Encouraged by a discerning father whose sensitivity recognized the heavy burden oppressing his son's very soul, Isaac tried his hand at hymn writing. As his brother Enoch noted, the hymns 'sung at the Dissenting meeting' were so far from his liking that

he could not forbear complaining of them to his father. The father bid him try what he could do to mend the matter.

It therefore seems that, between 1694 and 1696, snatches of Watts's hymns were sampled in Southampton some years before he directed his attention to metrical-psalter reform, just as the *Short Essay toward the Improvement of Psalmody* provides evidence enough that his work on the Psalms led directly to the provision of a new kind of song for use in Christian worship.

In effect, Watts campaigned to evangelize the Hebrew Psalter, and, just like Luther before him, devoted an intense phase of his early ministry to the writing of sacred songs. Whereas worship once involved people in the pew learning the Psalms of David well-nigh parrot-fashion, Watts, to quote R.W. Dale, 'redeemed the psalmody of the Congregationalists from Judaism, and made it Christian.' In *Musicks's Monument*, 1676, Thomas Mace had sadly observed much 'whining, toting, yelling, or screeking' in many a rural meeting, so when Watts attempted to check the dying devotion of Chapel life by paraphrasing the Psalms and writing innumerable hymns, he began to set in train a revival of English worship as a whole. Just as early-morning mists often have to burn off before summer days dawn in all their brilliance, Watts early realized that traditional psalmody blurred gospel truth. Too narrow an acceptance of David must shroud faithful hearts with 'the vail of Moses' when they ought to echo Jewish worship no longer and, instead, break through such haze to magnify the achievement of Jesus Christ in adoration and praise. Some words from the *Preface* to *Psalms of David Imitated in the Language of the New Testament* (1719) clearly indicate that he was concerned by the kind of congregational confusion that obtained:

> To see the dull Indifference, the negligent and thoughtless Air that sits upon the faces of the whole Assembly while the Psalm is on their Lips, might tempt even a charitable Observer to suspect the Fervency of inward Religion, and 'tis much to be fear[ed] that the Minds of most of the Worshippers are absent or unconcern'd.

Later the same *Preface* pinpoints with shrewd insight a pastor's unerring perception of the reason why. For as he chose to express himself:

> ... the Matter and Words ... are almost opposite to the spirit of the Gospel ... foreign to the State of the New Testament, and widely different from the present circumstances of Christians.
>
> [op. cit. xxvii–xxviii]

In contemporary parlance then, Isaac Watts had a dream, a dream that was to make him a great reviser simply because his vision was one that used Hebrew Psalms as a pattern for Christian praise. No longer sacrosanct in itself, Hebrew worship, however much it provided a prototype for the early Church, was nevertheless no Christian song. With acute pertinence, in a rhetorical question, Watts made the point precisely:

Where can you find a Psalm that speaks of the Miracles of Wisdom and Power as They are discover'd in a crucify'd Christ?

For should not Christians offer all worship 'in the Name of Jesus', and in 'the British Islands ... make their present Mercies under the gospel the subject of fresh Praises'? So the 'glorious work' that began with the psalms, Watts continued in the writing of hymns, convinced in conscience as he was that a pilgrim church must not be tied 'up to meer Forms of the Old Testament' but rather 'stand fast in the Liberty of the Gospel'. He worked on Psalms and hymns at much the same time, the law provoking him into the gospel experience he shared with all who had read the first edition of *Hymns and Spiritual Songs*, which appeared as early as 1707. For just as he was clear that the sermon was effectively the Word of God, Watts held hymn writing to be entirely in accord with the divine will as he argued the case for hymns as homilies. Although care had to be exercised lest the weaker brethren take offence, 'spiritual Songs' penned 'by humane Art' he insisted were in every way 'agreeable to the Sense of Scripture and the Christian Faith'. Likewise, should felicitous style not be achieved at the first attempt, a pleasing humility in Watts prompted him to note that 'The Blemishes ... may ... awaken some more pious and judicious Fancy to a more successful Attempt' anon.

Above all, it was the great doctrinal truths that concerned him most, and Watts strove to transpose the sacrificial language of the Old Testament into a clear New Testament emphasis on, and grateful affirmation of, the love of God in Christ. In his own words, he was determined to

Paraphrase dark Expressions enlighten'd, and the Levitical Ceremonies and Hebrew Forms of Speech chang'd into the Worship of the Gospel, and explain'd in the Language of our Time and Nation.

He made crucial clauses of ancient creeds, whether focused on the person of Christ, the divine work of his salvation or the mystery of the holy Trinity, intelligible in ways that gave new meaning to congregational prayer and praise. It was a remarkable achievement that used not only

> many parts of the Old Testament ... that have a reference to the Times of the Messiah [and] most of the Doxologies in the New Testament that contain any thing in 'em peculiarly Evangelical,

but was also notable because in his inimitable way, Watts rejoiced

> to see a good part of the Book of Psalms fitted for the Use of our Churches, and David converted into a Christian.
>
> [*Lyric Poems,* lv.]

He wrote in the four accepted metres of the period – a sensible attitude, and an approach that guaranteed his verse would relate to well-known tunes. For his times, such work certainly enjoyed sensational success and secured many a reprint. Broadly divided into three parts, the title-page of *Hymns and Spiritual Songs* set out what was 'I. Collected from Scripture'; then what Watts had 'II. Compos'd on divine Subjects'; and finally what had been 'III. Prepared for the Lord's Supper.'

An amazing compilation, using the fine language Watts was convinced was needed 'to save the ruin'd and degenerate World', the work first of all embraced paraphrases of Holy Scripture and drew freely on both Messianic proclamations from the Old Testament, and New Testament doxologies. Secondly, if there were many original compositions, Watts took good care that his poetry did not create hymns that might conflict with the great doctrinal truths of traditional Puritanism. Finally, a third section included hymns specially written for the celebration of Holy Communion, work of such superlative standard that, in the judgement of Harry Escott, it made Watts 'the first English hymn-writer of catholic importance just because he was a poet and pioneer prosodist as well' [*Isaac Watts Hymnographer* (1962), p. 17].

Over the years, almost seven hundred hymns resulted, hymns

of controlled composition and a high quality that guaranteed their widespread appeal and what may be termed institutional acceptance. For example, from Psalm 90 came

O God, our help in ages past,

a prayer of Moses so beautifully refashioned as to be recognized in recent years by Rupp as not only 'more than a hymn' but also 'an event in English history, and part of our very national existence' [*Six Makers of English Religion, 1500–1700* (1957), p. 115]. Then too, from universal and unqualified praise of the kind expressed in Psalm 117, Watts made David speak like a Christian in the doxology:

From all that dwell below the skies
Let the Creator's praise arise:
Let the Redeemer's name be sung
Through every land by every tongue.

That he could also make David hold forth as an Englishman, even as an eighteenth-century Whig, B.L. Manning did not doubt when describing the communication skills of a Watts able to equate 'Palestine, Judaea, Jerusalem, with Great Britain'. Aware that 'exquisitely sensitive commentators' criticized the approach as 'vulgar', Manning dismissed such objections, warming instead to the 'fascinating reflexions on English history' Watts offered, drawn as they were from a lifespan that, punctuated by the persecution of Protestant Dissent, had embraced events as significant as 'Gunpowder, Treason and Plot', the arrival of what Sellars and Yeatman termed 'an Orange' on the English throne, the Hanoverian Succession, and the defeat of the French – all of them crises which disconcerted Tories and upset Rome, polemicists pointing again to the deliverance of a chosen people. When his own father had suffered imprisonment for non-conformity, it is no surprise to find in Watts genuine feelings of relief when threats of renewed legislation against Dissent lapsed on the demise of Queen Anne. Later too, however much the largely unsectarian nature of his hymns has to be stressed, playful parodies are to be found in verse like

> Great William shall rejoice to know
> That George the Second rules below.

It is an impishness that demands digression and at least some reference to the little man (in stature Watts was barely five feet high) who did much to appeal to small children, albeit in a way now appropriately termed 'wrong but wromantic'. Specially written for the young, as for a rising generation of crucial importance, namely the young who must learn to fear both hell and the Lord as the beginning of any wisdom, his *Divine Songs* appeared in 1715. By 1810, the work had run into almost a hundred editions; but those who on that account have acclaimed *Divine Songs* as a children's original are altogether too generous to a volume that has to be seen in the clearly recognizable tradition of catechetical Calvinism. Its simple exposition attracted and charmed the young as much as it highlighted Watt's great gifts as an educator of children, and poems such as

> Let dogs delight to bark and bite,

and

> Birds in their little nests agree

made an impact on those whose parents were concerned that, as far as their offspring were concerned, there was a real possibility that

> Satan finds some mischief still
> For idle hands to do ...

Over the years, reaction to such ways of inculcating moral principles and training youngsters not only to be aware of the natural world, but also to learn to reason for themselves, has been varied. Lewis Carroll's Alice memorably misquoted words that 'did not come the same as they used to do', and to the reader's great amusement she found herself saying

> How doth the little crocodile

instead of

How doth the little busy bee.

In contrast, A.E. Housman, himself a poet of great distinction, commended this aspect of the Isaac Watts whose pleasing simplicity had also written:

> Soft and easy is thy cradle:
> Coarse and hard thy Saviour lay;
> When his birth-place was a stable,
> And his softest bed was hay.

An agreeable enough interlude in this context, Watts's work among the young is a much-neglected emphasis in an overall range of real accomplishments. For whatever high-flown philosophies were to involve the ageing Isaac as very much the period polymath, he was ultimately a man of simple faith moved by the Spirit. Everything he touched he simplified; and precisely because he did so, it tended to turn to gold. His so-called 'laboratory notebooks' clearly indicate such simplicity to be his consistent goal, this memorable passage from his *Preface* affording a personal plea real status as *apologia pro vita sua*:

> I have aimed at ease of Numbers and Smoothness of sound, and endeavour'd to make the sense plain and obvious; if the Verse appears so gentle and flowing as to incur the Censure of Feebleness, I may honestly affirm that sometimes it cost me labour to make it so.
>
> [*Hymns and Spiritual Songs* (1707), ix and x]

It was a shrewd observation of Dr Ernest Payne who argued that the five hymns of Isaac Watts which Lord David Cecil selected for the *Oxford Book of Christian Verse* actually represented him less than this single poem in a book of mystical verse:

> Far in the Heavens my God retires;
> My God, the mark of my desires,
> And hides His lovely face;
> When He descends within my view,
> He charms my reason to pursue,
> But leaves it tir'd and fainting in th'unequal chase.

Such humility and confession of frail humanity is fully realized in

> When I survey the wondrous Cross,

arguably the most moving, and even perhaps the greatest of the hymns of Christendom. It will come as no surprise to the reader to learn that Watts wrote the hymn for those who came to Communion to worship at 'the Lord's Board'; and here in the very fabric of Dissent are poignant words compelling soulful adoration of the Christ. For in the simplest language of thanksgiving, the author has framed the Passion and led faithful people to Calvary in a way that surely parallels the approach taken by the best of the Old Masters when they came to paint crucifixion scenes.

The hymn is certainly nothing if not a challenging homily on Paul's words to the Galatians when the apostle prayed that he be prevented from boasting 'save in the cross of our Lord Jesus Christ, by whom the world is crucified unto me, and I unto the world' (Gal. 6.14). Irresistibly powerful in clarity, such stanzas make a profound impression by their very simplicity. First, real genius is to be seen in the way Watts confronts his congregations with a lucid and staged sequence. At the outset, they are humbled before the Cross:

> My richest gain I count but loss,
> And pour contempt on all my pride.

Then follows a highly-charged middle section of carefully-crafted, emotional stanzas rallying the faithful to heartfelt realization of 'the death of Christ my God'. Medieval shrines, wayside Calvaries and meditation before the crucifix all have an abiding significance in prompting Christian worship, and here in words of Puritan spirituality is a legacy which, if it lacks visual impact, is nevertheless very similar:

> See from his head, his hands, his feet,
> Sorrow and love flow mingled down;
> Did e'er such love and sorrow meet,
> Or thorns compose so rich a crown?

A near miracle in itself, the last verse not only reaches a high plateau of consummate achievement, but can also plead in petition the ultimate appeal to ensure response to a Saviour's love. For with such a climax, Watts intends worship to mean the service of demanding discipleship:

> Were the whole realm of nature mine,
> That were a present far too small;
> Love so amazing, so divine,
> Demands my soul, my life, my all.

The hymn may lack the choral glory of many a setting of the Mass, but its very directness and candour, coupled with the way Watts invariably managed to write in unsectarian language, crowns its success as a challenge of simple piety. Again, it was Harry Escott who stressed a basic truth, namely, that a good hymn must have a beginning, a middle and an end; and there can be no denying the careful way Isaac Watts gave his work a structure that makes him such a great architect of English hymns. For he sought to focus worship in the congregation and avoid the age-old confusions that had frustrated worship for far too long. Sublime style is all very well, but Watts never made the mistake of sacrificing clarity to achieve it.

As a homily, moreover, this hymn generates all the humbling effect of real evangelism. Love conquers; Christ claims; and the only true response to such a burden of penitence and praise is a life of total commitment. In five brief verses Watts confronted his congregations with high drama. He has transformed Calvary's cruel gibbet into a 'wondrous Cross' from which the 'Lord' Christ reigns. If comparisons remain odious, a glance at the very different effect secured much later by Studdert Kennedy is altogether revealing.

> When Jesus came to Golgotha, they hanged Him on a
>   tree,
> They drave great nails through hands and feet and
>   made a Calvary;
> They crowned Him with a crown of thorns, red were
>   His wounds and deep,
> For those were crude and cruel days, and human flesh
>   was cheap.

When due allowance is made because of context – after all 'Woodbine Willie' wrote when changing times usually failed to move hardened hearts to heed gospel demands – his message to the new age nevertheless adapted Watts's vision of surveying the 'wondrous Cross'. With the people of Birmingham in mind, it is not service but apathy that dominates the poet's mind, with something of an after-taste in the hope that an overwhelming sense of pity might just manage to rally support.

> When Jesus came to Birmingham, they simply passed
> Him by,
> They never hurt a hair of Him, they only let
> Him die;
> For men had grown more tender, and they would not
> give Him pain,
> They only just passed down the street, and left Him in
> the rain.

The contrast is stark, and the reputation of Watts enhanced as 'the modest, self-forgetful but God-intoxicated saint of all his generation' [Erik Routley, 'The Bicentenary of Isaac Watts, 1948' in *HS of GB and I Bulletin*, Vol. 2, No. 5 (Jan. 1949), p. 70]. Truly, in the shrewd judgement of none other than the learned Dr Samuel Johnson:

> Few men have left behind such purity of character or monuments of laborious piety. He has provided instruction for all ages.

A WATTS DEVOTIONAL TREASURY

In the development of English worship, Isaac Watts holds a unique place. Before his time Church congregations were accustomed to psalm-singing, and it was largely through his initiative and influence that, on a scale unknown before, they were introduced to the singing of hymns as part of a fundamental redirection of reformed worship. The fact that gospel themes dominated the new hymns too will come as no surprise, for Watts appropriated every aspect of Christian faith in what rapidly became a renowned teaching ministry. In all he wrote no fewer than 697 hymns, most with the kind of Christocentric emphasis that afforded his verse real impact as homilies. As he expressed it in a tract of 1741, Watts was convinced that 'Fine Language is needed to save the ruin'd and degenerate World' [*The Improvement of the Mind*, p. 354], and he could certainly use poetry to preach with great power in challenging hymns like

> Alas! and Did my Saviour Bleed?
> And did my Sovereign die?
> Would he devote that Sacred Head
> For such a Worm as I?

Less forthright, but arguably of greater appeal to later generations, is Watts's fine exposition of part of chapter 5 of the Book of Revelation. A model of biblically-based praise, it is singularly compelling, the second verse in no way compromising the gospel Watts consistently sought to preach:

> 'Worthy the Lamb that died,' They cry,
> 'To be exalted thus;'
> 'Worthy the Lamb,' our lips reply,
> 'For he was slain for us.'

Much the same Revelation-based praise can be found in:

> Give me the Wings of Faith to rise
> Within the Vail, and see
> The Saints above, how great their Joys,
> How bright their Glories be.

Again, in the hymn's third verse, Watts clearly expounds his gospel emphasis:

> I ask them whence their Victory came,
> They with united Breath,
> Ascribe their Conquest to the Lamb,
> Their Triumph to his Death.

A committed labourer, Isaac Watts early determined to do everything possible to extend the frontiers of Christendom by hymnsinging, a vision readily appreciated in

> Jesus shall reign where'er the sun
> Does his successive journeys run;
> His kingdom stretch from shore to shore,
> Till moons shall wax and wane no more.

Once more too, much rejoicing in heavenly places brings such perspective that no worshipping communities can fail to be uplifted by the resounding climax:

> Let every creature rise and bring
> Peculiar honours to our King;
> Angels descend with songs again,
> And earth repeat the loud *Amen*.

In hymn after hymn to be sure, Watts repeats in verse the refrain of his *Preface*, namely that:

> While we sing the Praises of our God in his Church, we are employ'd in that part of Worship which of all others is the nearest a-kin to Heaven ... [for] ... The Gospel brings us nearer to the heavenly State than all the former Dispensations of God amongst Men.

Here too can be found the clear apocalyptic dimension that gave a genuine note of urgency to Watts's pastoral care. As he chose to express it himself in this same perceptive *Preface*:

> ... in these last Days of the Gospel we are brought almost within sight of the Kingdom of our Lord ... [even if] ... the Modes of Preaching in the best Churches still want some Degrees of Reformation.

A conviction that metrical psalmody was 'almost opposite to the Spirit of the Gospel' and as often as not 'foreign to the State of the New Testament' certainly fired his ministry with burning zeal. Old Covenant sacrificial emphases were transposed into a New Testament stress on love. And whatever the profundity, Watts strove for simplicity of style and a clarity of language in verse calculated to captivate the spirit. His congregations, in fact, all sang living hymns of praise to God, and sang them with conviction. If many a composition can illustrate the point, two sensational stanzas from another famed hymn must suffice to epitomize such work of dedicated sincerity and commitment to the cause:

> Before Jehova's awful Throne,
> Ye nations, bow with sacred joy;
> Know that the Lord is God alone:
> He can create, and he destroy.

> Wide as the world is thy command,
> Vast as eternity thy love;
> Firm as a rock thy truth shall stand,
> When rolling years shall cease to move.

C Wesley

Chapter 5

CHARLES WESLEY

and

'Love divine, all loves excelling'

1 LOVE divine, all loves excelling,
Joy of heaven, to earth come down;
Fix in us Thy humble dwelling,
All Thy faithful mercies crown;
Jesu, Thou art all compassion,
Pure, unbounded love Thou art;
Visit us with Thy salvation,
Enter every trembling heart.

2 Come, almighty to deliver
Let us all Thy grace receive;
Suddenly return, and never,
Never more Thy temples leave:
Thee we would be always blessing,
Serve Thee as Thy hosts above,
Pray, and praise Thee, without ceasing,
Glory in Thy perfect love.

3 Finish then Thy new creation,
Pure and spotless let us be;
Let us see Thy great salvation,
Perfectly restored in Thee;
Changed from glory into glory,
Till in heaven we take our place,
Till we cast our crowns before Thee,
Lost in wonder, love, and praise.

When recommending a range of hymns he published with his brother Charles in 1799, John Wesley termed the *Collection* 'a little body of experimental and practical divinity'. Conscious that nothing of its kind existed in the English language, he made much of the fact that his work embraced a 'distinct and full account of scriptural Christianity'. Firmly convinced of his case too, he unhesitatingly urged that the Hymn Book embodied 'a declaration of the heights and depths of religion, speculative and practical'. Such variety of composition commended itself to the full spectrum of a pastor's unique sensitivity, for Wesley was well aware that hymns could 'soon be worn threadbare' from overuse. With some *seven thousand* eventually to his credit, Charles Wesley took no such risk, but brother John played safe in an editorial rôle that made the '*Collection* not too large, that it may be cheap and portable; nor too small, that it may contain a sufficient variety for all ordinary occasions'.

In 1738, first Charles and then John Wesley experienced classic evangelical conversions, and, rejoicing in the new life they had found, ever afterwards treasured justification by faith *alone* as fundamental Christian teaching. Two brief lines from a hymn of Charles:

> Sinners of old Thou didst receive
> With comfortable words and kind,

show how he transformed the respectable religion implicit in the Prayer-Book into the good news of an explicit gospel. Missionary vision followed too, for all were changed who humbled themselves to accept Christ's sacrificial love on the cross. By repentance and faith, fallen sinners were saved by new birth both to be pardoned and to receive the spiritual power for growth in grace. Restored to favour, faithful folk could thus become saints in the image of God. Or, as John Wesley chose to express it in succinct terms:

> Justification ... is equivalent to pardon, and the very moment we are justified, sanctification begins. In that instant we are born again. [Quoted in V.H.H. Green, p. 111]

With all the force of sudden revelation, a message had been discovered that, unfolded over many years, became the mission of 'Methodism'. Methodical it certainly was too, for the creeds and catechisms of historic Christendom have only rarely gained such attention in teaching ministry as men, women and children were carefully instructed in the fundamentals of the gospel. Great themes were set out and simplified: the majesty and mystery of the Godhead; the fallibility of fallen, frail humanity; the incarnation and atoning love of Christ; the free gift of salvation so readily available; and the outworking of such doctrines for the holy life of the individual in righteousness and faith. Carefully related to worship, prayer and bible-reading, Christian behaviour became the pursuit of holiness, every theme being set out in the spirit of piety. Writing hymns to publish this godly devotion abroad, Charles Wesley's work raised poetry to exalted status as the handmaid of such piety, pleasing his brother by the genuine nature of careful commitment. John Wesley clearly made his choice of hymns resonant with 'the purity, the strength and the elegance of the English language', for his was an editor's selection which included neither 'doggerel', nor 'botches', nor 'patched-up rhymes'. Cherishing what they deemed common sense in prose as well as verse, the Wesleys would thus have no 'feeble expletives', no 'cant expressions', and 'nothing turgid' or by way of 'bombast'. Instead, in the knowledge that a direct appeal 'suited every capacity', they wrote with 'the utmost simplicity and plainness'.

If John's limited output was usually inspired translation, Charles showed real flair to prove himself a prolific lyricist, and certainly made his mark as a lyric poet. Yet his inspiration rarely encouraged flights of fancy because he knew these must devalue Christian fundamentals. For if he naturally rated sublime expression highly as an essential ingredient of idealism, he nevertheless shrank from giving rhythm priority over religion, and understood that poetry had to be kept in its place if devotion was to be quickened and faith confirmed, hope enlivened and love increased. Nevertheless, from his insight of the divine purpose, Charles Wesley also realized the limitless potential of poetry as the handmaid of piety, and his work did much to assist believers to attain 'not a poor perishable wreath, but a crown that fadeth not away'.

A poet with a musical ear, moreover, he rarely missed a trick of value in pastoral ministry; and if some readers may find the choice of

Love divine, all loves excelling

surprising as an illustration of his genius, it unquestionably sets the spotlight on a sensitive minister of the gospel who, like the Reverend Rowland Hill (1744–1833), could see no reason 'why the devil should have all the good tunes'. Later set to music by Henry Purcell (1761), Dryden's *King Arthur* included numerous highlights, none of them more appealing to enthusiastic audiences than the 'Song of Venus'. An impressive musical setting of warm romantic appeal, it rose to dizzy heights in the period hit parade of popular esteem. Realizing the potential of a piece that, by enshrining secular love, had become the talk of many a town, Charles Wesley boldy transposed the Dryden stanza so that:

> FAIREST Isle, all Isles Excelling,
> Seat of Pleasures, and of Loves;
> Venus here will chuse her Dwelling,
> And forsake her *Cyprian* Groves

became by brilliant parody:

> Love divine, all loves excelling,
> Joy of heaven, to earth come down;
> Fix in us Thy humble dwelling,
> All Thy faithful mercies crown.

Needless to state, the background was not quite so simple, and it is likely that more than a single experience lay behind the composition. For, deeply moved when his sister Kezia sought brotherly comfort and prayers for her conversion, Charles had written in his *Journal*:

> she ... believed now there was such a thing as the new creature. She was full of earnest wishes for divine love; owned there was a depth of religion she had never fathomed; that she was not, but longed to be, converted ...

And after his own conversion, such considerations added a uniquely personal dimension to re-wording the rest of Dryden's verse. If the poet originally penned this to read:

> Cupid, from his Fav'rite Nation,
> Care and Envy will Remove;
> Jealousy that poysons Passion,
> And Despair that dies for love.

Wesley, by skilful transformation, made it breathe:

> Jesu, Thou art all compassion
> Pure unbounded love Thou art;
> Visit us with Thy salvation,
> Enter every trembling heart

or what one writer has termed 'the essence of Methodism'.

When published (1747) in a collection of *Redemption Hymns* – 'Hymns for Those who seek, and Those who have, Redemption in the Blood of Jesus Christ' – a second verse, no longer used by congregations, conveyed all the urgency of evangelical campaigning:

> Breathe, O breathe Thy loving spirit
> Into every troubled Breast,
> Let us all in Thee inherit
> Let us find that second Rest.
> Take away our power of sinning,
> Alpha and Omega be,
> End of Faith as its Beginning,
> Set our Hearts at Liberty.

The third verse highlights religious experience, probing the mystery of the Godhead and responding to such new-found grace with the loving commitment and service of enduring, endless praise:

> Come, almighty to deliver,
> Let us all Thy grace receive;

Suddenly return, and never,
Never more Thy temples leave:
Thee we would be always blessing,
Serve Thee as Thy hosts above,
Pray, and praise Thee, without ceasing,
Glory in Thy perfect love.

Continuing the celestial vision too, the hymn's final verse is of particular interest, focusing as it does on a passion for perfection. For with the 'legal night' of his pre-conversion life in the past, Charles Wesley longed to achieve a sanctity and Christlikeness in his earthly life which his brother John recognized as a heavenly aspiration:

Finish then Thy new creation,
Pure and sinless let us be;
Let us see Thy great salvation,
Perfectly restored in Thee;
Changed from glory into glory,
Till in heaven we take our place,
Till we cast our crowns before Thee,
Lost in wonder, love, and praise.

No wonder 'sinless' was soon exchanged for 'spotless', however much the original wording best expressed the spiritual striving of one whose discipleship, if it began with the changed relationship of justifying faith, bore as fruit new birth, adoption, assurance and increasing sanctification. It is no exaggeration to style such stanzas a veritable cornucopia of evangelical theology, for in a mere thirty-two lines the Christian gospel is symbolized with the fulness of its 'great salvation' and love freely given, received and reciprocated.

The continuing quest for such love consumed Charles Wesley for the rest of his days as a life-long aspiration. Ever conscious of the apostolic emphasis 'We love Him, because He first loved us' (1 John 4.19), he struggled hard and long to achieve Christian perfection. In consequence, he was sorely troubled by moods that, though they could make him buoyant with hope, could also bring despair when meditation prompted him to recognize peccadilloes of anger, pride or selfishness crowding daily routines. Many a line from his hymns can provide such autobiographical insights, and two in particular indicate the godly priority of the saintly individual who, conscious of being

> Pardoned, yet still, alas, unclean

could feel such a failure that he could at times actually plead for a shortened pilgrimage:

> Do not let me live to sin,
> Waft me to the silent grave.

Needless to state such depths of despair were rare, and moments of intimate introspection far removed from the disciplined day-to-day quest of love in a life of witness elsewhere described in the well-known words:

> Forth in Thy name, O Lord, I go
> My daily labour to pursue.

For many a disciple, routines of this kind have proved little more than the tyranny of the trivial. But so inspired was Charles Wesley by biblical religion that regular early-morning meditations served to feed the prolific composition of his hymns. If the sixth chapter of the Book of Deuteronomy urged on the Lord's people a solemn responsibility of teaching divine precepts 'diligently unto thy children' (Deut. 6.7), Charles Wesley readily rallied and penned the lines:

> ... let me live to preach Thy Word
> And let me to Thy glory live
> My every sacred moment spend
> In publishing the sinner's Friend.

Like Luther before him, he conceived it to be his life's work to surround frail, faltering and fallen humanity with divine love; and for that basic reason Charles Wesley provided his congregations with countless hymns simply focused on Calvary as the Cross radiated the work of God in Christ to sinful men and women. The couplet:

> The immortal God for me hath died
> Jesus the Lord is crucified

affords challenging illustration and its message could hardly be expressed more succinctly. Then too, whether the chosen theme rejoiced in salvation, or shepherded converts along the road to sanctification, there to 'taste and see the riches of His grace', the composition was so carefully couched in Scripture that the very cadences of the English Bible and the *Book of Common Prayer* Psalter remain. In short, when he dealt with Holy Writ, the poet proved himself a dedicated pastor pledged to the promise that, faithfully set forth, the Word of God would by no means return void but accomplish the divine purpose.

When controversy came, and the great orator-preacher George Whitefield upheld Calvinist notions of a God who could even predestine selected sinners to eternal damnation, the Wesleys certainly did everything to counter such teaching with a renewed missionary zeal that stressed the free grace available to all. Emphatic refrains in hymns as renowned as 'Wrestling Jacob' witness to the way Charles Wesley nailed his colours to the mast and did much to encourage the evangelical cause through stormy seas of deep, depressing dogma. The hymns of the 1740s were consciously given a kind of 'U certificate' so universalist was the application the poet intended. Charles Wesley thus capitalised a key line of 'Wrestling Jacob' to read:

PURE UNIVERSAL LOVE THOU ART

but also damned as blasphemy what a key sermon his brother John delivered on 'Free Grace' (1740) rejected as 'the horrible decree' in the verse:

Good God! that any child of Thine
So *horribly* should think of Thee!
Lo! all my hope I here resign
If *all may* not find grace with me.

Such was his conviction in the matter that Charles did not hesitate to convey the truth he felt with all possible force:

O for a trumpet voice
On *all the world* to call
To bid their hearts rejoice

In Him who died *for all*!
For all my Lord was crucified;
For all, for all my Saviour died.

In short, both Wesleys were adamant that, in Christ, God's love reached out to the whole human race; and if, despite that truth, some were still lost, such an abuse of free will could only be laid at their own door. As Charles chose to stress it himself:

I this record leave behind –
Though damned, I was forgiven;
Every soul may mercy find,
Believe, and enter heaven.

A WESLEY DEVOTIONAL TREASURY

To provide readers with an adequate Devotional Treasury from the hymns of Charles Wesley would distort the proportions of this little book to such an extent that it could well strain the good relations between an author and his publisher. For the full range of Wesley's hymns is such that few seasons of the Church's year can ignore his significant contribution to Christian worship. Some years ago now, I attended a country chapel in Cambridgeshire where the musician in charge of a singular 'wheeze-box' instrument led the singing with no fewer than eight of Charles Wesley's hymns he deemed appropriate for 'Morning Worship'! If that experience would be difficult to match nowadays, it remains a commonplace in church or chapel, and many a cathedral besides, to hymn praise and prayer in Wesley's verse. And no wonder when you pause to recall a range of composition that embraces not only grateful words Charles wrote to celebrate his conversion:

O for a thousand tongues to sing
My great redeemer's praise

but many a hymn without which worship at sacred festivals from Advent to Whitsun would be the poorer. Examples are essential, but need not be laboured, so well-known is the work of Wesley.

Few will need to consult a 'General Index' when *first lines* are as
well known as:
For Advent:

> Lo! he comes with clouds descending

and

> Come, thou long-expected Jesus;

For Christmas:

> Hark! the herald angels sing

and

> Hark, how all the welkin rings!

For Lent:

> Still nigh me, O my Saviour stand,
> And guard in fierce temptation's hour

and

> O for a heart to praise my God,
> A heart from sin set free;

and, with 'Bible Sunday' particularly in mind,

> Come, divine Interpreter,
> Bring us eyes Thy Book to read.

In Passiontide:

> O Love divine! what hast Thou done?
> The immortal God hath died for me!

and:

> All ye that pass by
> To Jesus draw nigh:
> To you is it nothing that Jesus should die?

At Easter:

> Christ the Lord is risen to-day:
> *Hallelujah!*

At the Ascension:

> Hail the day that sees him rise,
> *Alleluia!*

and:

> God is gone up on high,
> With a triumphant noise;

And at Whitsuntide:

> Come, Holy Ghost, all-quickening fire

and:

> Away with our fears,
> Our troubles and tears:
> The Spirit is come!

At the same time, when the Wesley brothers arranged hymnals more to illustrate the Christian life than the Church's year, this is an imperfect way to sample the work of Charles. For his poetry glossed themes like adoration and love. The sacred persons of the Trinity revealed in Scripture were used to teach his people, a regular swing of the pendulum familiarizing the faithful, and indeed the not so faithful, with the fulness of a gospel ministry rarely equalled in the long history of Christendom. So no selection, however brief, can fail to mention the powerful conviction of:

Soldiers of Christ, arise;

the simple piety of:

Gentle Jesus, meek and mild

(a hymn of poignant emphases yet as profound as anything in Luther's children's *Catechism*, 1529); the direct challenge of:

Christ, whose glory fills the skies;

the prayerful petition and dedicated quest of holiness enshrined in:

O for a heart to praise my God

or in:

O Thou who camest from above

(a hymn so wide-ranging in its scriptural sources that it well compares with the richest of gems and their crafted settings in royal regalia).

Faithful to the end, Charles Wesley is well commemorated in the sublime tune Sir Hubert Parry later set to the last of all his hymns:

Ye Servants of God,
Your Master proclaim.

For his was a truly great poetic gift, and such elegance in verse did much to

... publish abroad
His wonderful name.

Examples of poor composition are rare, however much some might nowadays criticize instances of emotional evangelicalism. Curiously enough, the epitaph Charles Wesley composed for his mother Susanna's tombstone – including the lines

> True daughter of affliction she,
> Enured to pain and misery,
> Mourn'd a long night of griefs and fears,
> A legal night of seventy years

– arguably ranks as low as anything he ever wrote. All of which would confirm the view that the unique quality of most verse was firmly founded in the sublime source of its very inspiration. The point was nowhere better made than by F. E. Rattenbury who once argued that:

> ... a skilful man, if the Bible were lost, might extract it from Wesley's hymns. They contain the Bible in solution.
> [*The Evangelical Doctrines of Charles Wesley's Hymns*, p. 48]

How apt then the Memorial in Wesley's Chapel on London's City Road, and the tribute of these lines:

> As a Christian Poet he stood unrivalled;
> And his hymns will convey instruction and consolation,
> To the faithful in Christ Jesus,
> As long as the English language shall be understood.

Penner & Co sc. Paternoster Row

Augustus Toplady, July 25. 1761

Chapter 6

AUGUSTUS MONTAGUE TOPLADY

and

'Rock of Ages'

1 ROCK of Ages, cleft for me,
  Let me hide myself in Thee;
  Let the water and the blood,
  From Thy riven side which flowed,
  Be of sin the double cure,
  Cleanse me from its guilt and power.

2 Not the labours of my hands
  Can fulfil Thy law's demands;
  Could my zeal no respite know,
  Could my tears for ever flow,
  All for sin could not atone:
  Thou must save, and Thou alone.

3 Nothing in my hand I bring,
  Simply to Thy Cross I cling;
  Naked, come to Thee for dress;
  Helpless, look to Thee for grace;
  Foul, I to the fountain fly;
  Wash me, Saviour, or I die.

4 While I draw this fleeting breath,
  When my eyelids close in death,
  When I soar to worlds unknown,
  See Thee on Thy judgement-throne:
  Rock of Ages, cleft for me,
  Let me hide myself in Thee.   Amen.

He was an injudicious man, hasty in forming conclusions, and intemperate in advancing them: but his intellect was quick and lively, and his manner of writing, though coarse, was always vigorous, and sometimes fortunate.

Southey's judgement of 'the ever-memorable Toplady' affords admirable analysis. For if this 'proud Vicar down in Devon' penned one of the finest hymns in the English language, his preaching ministry, coloured as it was with uncompromising Calvinism, numbered Toplady among a group of really controversial eighteenth-century divines in the evangelical revival of religion.

It was in the early 1730s that Oxford's 'Holy Club' first welcomed George Whitefield into membership; and later, during John Wesley's Georgian missionary tour, Whitefield was given pastoral oversight of Oxford converts. But the rustic West-country deference that initially prompted Whitefield to acknowledge Wesley as 'spiritual father in Christ' was not to endure. Phenomenal success as a preacher – in particular the way Whitefield found himself able to move the masses, as the unchurched poor of Bristol and London flocked to hear him – led to embarrassing rivalries among the revivalists. A certain hard-hearted failure to heed their gospel had long troubled evangelists. Calvin, for example, when unnerved by a dissolute dimension among the citizenry of Geneva (in his day something of a Naples of the North), had reluctantly recognised a reprobate element. Disinclined to repent and seek heaven, such evidently preferred hastening on to hell. Explained in theological language, this kind of human indifference to, and even shunning of, gospel proclamation, gave doctrines of divine predestination new meaning and real force as the reason for such devil-may-care attitudes. Two centuries on, too, despite great success as a preacher, Whitefield in his turn failed to complete his mission and took comfort from a Calvinist theology the Wesley brothers deplored as akin to fatalism.

A principal route focus of reformed Christendom, this was also a sad parting of the ways because it did much to disperse the force of a great revival. After his impassioned sermon on 'Free Grace' (John's classic defence was delivered in March 1739), the Wesleys led a cause that came to be labelled 'Arminian' after a furore over free will and predestination had divided religious opinion in the so-called 'United Provinces' in the early years of the seventeenth century. This was a neo-scholastic debate that had raged between the liberal Calvinist Jacobus Arminius (Jakob Hermandszoon), whose piety owed much to the great Erasmus, and Franciscus Gomarus whose strict orthodoxy held that God had even ordained the Fall in Eden. Whitefield, albeit by no means so extreme, chose to disagree with Wesley, to find Calvinist doctrines of grace more convincing; and in a tract of December 1740, he commended covenant theology to Wesley together with a compelling doctrine of grace which exalted 'divine sovereignty' as much as it deplored all 'carnal reasoning'. An illustration from United Kingdom politics in contemporary times offers an analogy in the rivalry of 'the two Davids', Steel and Owen, for the leadership of a third political party. For once the Wesleys and their followers based on the London 'Foundery' (and backed up by 'United Societies' throughout the land) were ranged against Whitefield's 'Tabernacle' (and a parallel network of 'Calvinistic Methodist' Societies), battle lines were drawn that not only divided the leadership but dissipated the strength of what had once been acclaimed as a great awakening of the faith outside the somnolent Anglican establishment. In precisely this context and great divide the work of Augustus Montague Toplady has to be seen, for the 'Arminian' *versus* Calvinist controversy provides the key to any real grasp of a much-misunderstood ministry.

By the time Toplady was made deacon and licensed to a title at Blagdon, Somerset, on Trinity Sunday 1762, the feuding of Wesley and Whitefield had grown less intense. But although conflict between such patriarchal revivalists had declined enough within a decade to suggest at least a measure of agreement to differ, some of their second-generation *dévots* were to prove decidedly partisan. In consequence, the 1760s and 1770s witnessed a bitter renewal of hostilities. Confronted by the ministry of the simple Methodist lay preacher James Morris in Co. Wexford, Toplady recorded that

> Under that sermon [based on Paul to the Ephesians, 2.13] I was, I trust, brought nigh by the blood of Christ, in August, 1756.

Four years later, he proceeded B.A. at Trinity College, Dublin.

Then, to prepare for ministry, Toplady returned to London to find himself deeply moved by the preaching not only of Whitefield, but also by that of another moderate Calvinist, the Reverend William Romaine of New Way Episcopal Chapel. Curate of Farley Hungerford to the south of Bath in 1764, Toplady secured his first living at Fen Ottery in May 1766, by which date he was himself a convinced upholder of reformed doctrines of predestination. A letter of 8 July 1774, written after he had moved to Devon by presentation to the parish of Broad Hembury, indicates the vocational setting of such belief. Toplady thus noted that:

> With Him all events must be ultimately rested ... nor would I have a single incident removed out of His hand.

Despite poor and ever-declining health, the ministry of Augustus Montague Toplady was both active and vital as he proved himself a remarkable preacher-poet. Convinced as he was that, in the Church of England, ministry of the Word invariably concerned itself with moralizing rather than the serious business of gospel exposition, Toplady strove to make preaching a strength. In 1769, a number of Oxford undergraduates were sent down from St Edmund Hall for 'attending conventicles, meeting, praying, expounding Scripture, and singing hymns in private houses'. They dared to fulfil lay preaching commitments instead of dutifully attending College Chapel. 'Methodists' with Calvinist leanings, the celebrated 'Six' were first defended by Richard Hill, and then attacked in an 'Arminian' tract penned by the Principal of St Mary Hall. In *The Church of England vindicated from the charge of Arminianism* (1769), Toplady, styling himself *Clerus*, drew on the *Book of Common Prayer*, the *XXXIX Articles* and the *Book of the Homilies* to argue that Anglican doctrine was nothing if not Calvinist. For him, it thus not only followed that 'Arminians' had no right to authentic membership of the English Church, but also that Kay, Jones, Grove, Matthews, Middleton, and Shipman had fallen foul of Vice-Chancellor Durrell and Proctorial authority in the University for

> attachment to the doctrines of predestination unto life, regeneration by the Spirit of God, and justification by faith alone ... [that is] ... for believing and asserting the leading

truths of that very Church which the expellers, no less than the expelled, profess to agree.

Toplady certainly held fast to faith as the fruit, and in no way the cause, of election; and asserted of 'absolute predestination' that

> If faith or works were the cause of election, God could not be said to choose us, but we to choose Him; contrary to the whole tenor of Scripture.

In the context of a work of Jerôme Zanchius (1516–1590), Toplady had been plumbing the doctrinal depths of providence since 1760. After preaching in many a Meeting House and London Chapel where 'churchmen upon principle, are forced to go ... to hear the doctrines of their own Church preached', he published in 1769 what 'in great measure' was a free translation-cum-paraphrase of Zanchy's *Doctrine of Absolute Predestination*. Clear that 'We have generally forsaken the principles of the Reformation', Toplady's *Preface* confidently stated that 'Never was a Publication, of this kind, more *seasonable* than at present' for '*Arminianism* is the grand Religious Evil of this Age and Country'. In a phrase, Toplady damned 'Arminian' ideas because such conceived God as 'a Being of Infinite Wisdom' acting '*without a Plan: for which plan, Predestination is only another name*'. Or, expressed in the form of a rhetorical question:

> What, indeed, is *Predestination*, but God's *determinate plan of action?* and what is *Providence*, but the *evolution of that plan?*

Alarmed by the way Toplady had rekindled the flames of his earlier controversy with Whitefield, John Wesley did his utmost to discredit 'that lively coxcomb' in a twelve-page precis of Zanchius. He concluded a clever parody with this wicked spoof:

> The sum of all this: one in twenty (suppose) of mankind are elected; nineteen in twenty are reprobated. The elect shall be saved, do what they will; the reprobate shall be damned, do what they can. Reader, believe this, or be damned. Witness my hand, A _T_

In no time, a frenetic pamphlet war of sixteenth-century proportions resulted. Toplady's *Letter to the Rev. Mr John Wesley* rapidly denounced the 'flimsy, partial compendium' drawn up by an unscrupulous adversary 'to make the ignorant believe that the whole, with your omissions, additions, and alterations, actually came from me – an instance of audacity and falsehood hardly to be justified'. Particularly infuriated by the 'Satanic shamelessness which dares to lay the black position at the door of other men', Toplady at once set about exposing his opponent's theological ineptitude. It was a course of action which soon rallied a number of local preachers to the cause of the Methodist pope. Led by Walter Sellon who wrote numerous anti-Calvinist pamphlets, another active campaigner was that stalwart of the publishing house of early Methodism, Thomas Olivers. Best known as author of 'The God of Abraham praise', his dedication to the cause can be seen in the hymn's ninth verse, where a characteristic 'Arminian' emphasis reads:

> Before the great Three-One
> They *all* exulting stand,
> And tell the wonders He hath done,
> Through all their land.

Toplady, who held such doctrine to be 'red and venomed pestilence', not only decried John Wesley as 'a low and puny tadpole in divinity', but also roundly dismissed both Sellon – a mere 'pygmy on stilts' – and Olivers the publisher as 'Cobbler Tom'. For these years saw a stance similar to the bulldog defiance Winston Churchill would later flaunt in the face of what he believed to be really evil. Toplady, in short, had resolved to hold the line against 'Arminianism', determined as he was to mete out to its leaders more than the measure they had meted out to the Calvinist cause. His unrelenting ridicule and vicious vituperation by no means assisted the Methodist agenda and whether in private correspondence or published sermons Toplady used every opportunity to attack 'the inveterate troubler in Israel, Mr John Wesley'.

Once aware that Toplady's opposition had made him a 'flaming Calvinist' vilified in Methodism, Whitefield pursued a policy of 'outing' a confederate

> My good Sir [he wrote], why do you not come out? You
> might be abundantly more useful were you to widen your
> sphere and preach at large, instead of restraining your min-
> istry to a few parish churches.

In his last years Toplady did precisely that, and from December
1775 was often absent from Devon to divide his time between
editorial work for the *Gospel Magazine* and Sunday duty in the
Orange Street pulpit of London's French Reformed Church.
Something of a Cox and Box, and Knox and Foxe situation, these
years worked Toplady hard at his Knightsbridge publishing desk
and in his regular possession of the pulpit. A productive spell, it
also generated his brief lives of Knox and Foxe. Sermons that
appeared as 'sixpenny pamphlets' made no mean impact and
served to prolong the argument about grace and free will.
Toplady esteemed the sermon highly, a view derived directly
from John Calvin who, in his celebrated *Institutio Christianae
Religionis*, held preaching to be as much the Word of God as if a
congregation 'heard the very words pronounced' by the deity.
The Genevan patriarch argued that God adds 'the power of the
Spirit Himself' to the spoken word, a conviction Toplady chose
to forward with added Scriptural emphasis:

> A minister without the written Word would bid fair to be
> a false guide, a mere will-of-the-wisp ... and the Word
> itself without the Spirit, is but as a dial without the sun, a
> dead letter, and a book sealed.

When he turned to hymn writing – and his *Psalms and Hymns
for Public and Private Worship* was issued in July 1776 – Toplady's
Preface stressed that a perfect hymn 'could only be written by a
spiritual person under the impressions of spiritual influence'. Just
like the prophetic quality of preaching made for ever memorable
in the assertion that 'a mincing, timid, partial declaration of the
Gospel is a virtual denial of Christ Himself', Toplady's verse
invariably contained the imaginative, even impulsive, ingredients
so crucial in direct communication. His work was
confrontational and nothing if not intense, its devotional fervour
comprising the obverse of the militant Calvinism to be seen in
his anti- 'Arminian' campaigning. Writing to William Tucker of

Chard, Somerset, on 20 August, 1776, Toplady rejoiced that 'the good Spirit' had directed his friend's thoughts 'so greatly and so deeply to the grand Article of Predestination', convinced as he was that 'the denial of which' doctrine 'is neither more nor less than absolute and essential atheism'. Without predestination, he continued, 'no grace, no happiness, no holiness, no salvation' might be found; and significantly there followed a peroration with the plea that

> The Lord enable us to extract more and more honey from this precious rock ...

The wording is important, even autobiographical; for since Dublin days Toplady had treasured such biblical metaphors as truly supportive of the spiritual life. Of particular relevance here is the Isaiah reference (26.4) which, far more than any tradition of shelter in an awesome ravine while a storm raged in the Somerset region of the Mendips known as Burrington Gorge, spelt out the safe stronghold available to those whose lives were supported by God-given faith and free grace in Christ. Joyful at such indisputable grounds for praise, Toplady had composed over twenty hymns down in his Devon retreat since the early 1770s. But with the publication of 'Rock of Ages' – first of all in the *Gospel Magazine* (March 1776) and then, with minor modification in his *Psalms and Hymns* (July) – he achieved what his biographer Thomas Wright chose to term 'by general consent' the 'greatest hymn in the English language'. [*The Life of Augustus M. Toplady* (London, 1911), p. 1.]

From the outset, the underlying, unexpressed contrast between those who build life on shifting sands and the faithful who find their strength in the Lord Jehovah, afforded Toplady's composition a rich and dramatic quality. It is an effect heightened for the individual by the way the first verse is replete with a refrain of personal reference – '... cleft for me' (line 1); 'Let me hide' (line 2); and 'Cleanse me ...' (line 6). The same emphasis is continued in verses 2, 3 and 4, which contain many 'free-grace' allusions:

> Thou must save, and Thou alone (verse 2, line 6).
>
> Nothing in my hand I bring,
> Simply to Thy Cross I cling (verse 3, lines 1 & 2);

Foul, I to the fountain fly;
Wash me, Saviour, or I die (verse 3, lines 5 & 6).

Such imagery makes the hymn a most powerful homily and one brimful of real resonances for the Calvinist *versus* 'Arminian' contest which for so long had dominated its author's ministry. 'Rock of Ages' nevertheless achieved a distinction that was to set it high on the honours' board of Christian praise and way beyond such petty party strife. For not only was it accorded a respected place in *The Methodist Hymn Book*, but received the attention of a leading politician and future Prime Minister when, in 1848, William Ewart Gladstone chose to translate the hymn into Latin verse of great dignity:

Jesus, pro me perforatus,
Condar intra tuum latus,
Tu per lympham profluentem,
Tu per sanguinem tempentem,
In peccata mi redunda,
Tolle culpam, sordes munda.

Coram te, nec justus forem
Quamvis tota vi laborem,
Nec si fide nunquam cesso,
Fletu stillans indefesso.
Tibi soli tantum munus:
Salve me, Salvator unus!

Nihil in manu mecum fero,
Sed me versus crucem gero;
Vestimenta nudus oro,
Opem debilis imploro.
Fontem Christi quaero immundus;
Nisi laves, moribundus.

Dum hos artus Vita regit;
Quando nox sepulchro tegit;
Mortuos cum stare jubes,
Sedens Judex inter nubes;
Jesus, pro me perforatus,
Condar intra tuum latus.

The penitential character of Toplady's verse

> *Nil in manu mecum fero,*
> *Sed me versus crucem gero;*

undoubtedly struck sensitive chords for such a high Churchman; and there is a real power in these stanzas to arouse deep remorse in all but the most insensitive souls. Even those who find revivalist hymns repellent for their spurious sentimentality and pretty jingle-jangle rhymes that demean rather than dignify the Lord's Passion, value the composition for the underlying scriptural truth its verses contain. 'Rock of Ages' thus scores highly as a gospel homily of focused meditation. Written to make Christ's crucifixion real in popular worship, Toplady's very descriptive range dramatically depicts a sanctified spectrum. Jehovah still stands rock-like to uphold the full rigour of divine law, but in the finished work of Christ can offer gospel grace to those who, through faith, can hide in his 'riven side'. An early sermon indicated imagery that remained real for Toplady some years before the hymn was written. Faced with another exposition of the prophet Isaiah from their parson, the village congregation was exhorted to rely on the Word, the Rock, as Toplady argued that

> ... chiefly may they sing who inhabit ye spiritual Rock of Ages. He is a Rock 3 ways; as a <u>Foundation</u> to support: a shelter, to screen; & a <u>Fortress</u>, to protect.

Coupled with this extract from the Farewell Sermon he preached as curate of Blagdon (22 April 1764), Toplady's whole conception has to be seen in a context of covenant relationship. For as he left to minister in pastures new not far from Bath, he bade his flock to

> Stand upon a Foundation that cannot fail, even Jesus, the Mediator and Surety of the covenant, Christ, the Rock of Ages. He died for such, their sins.

No wonder Nehemiah Curnock, Editor of John Wesley's *Journal*, could write that:

> In life [Toplady] achieved fame as a ruthless controversialist on behalf of extreme Calvinism; in death he is honoured as the writer of one of the most popular hymns in the English language.

A TOPLADY SPIRITUAL TREASURY

Nowadays, when much theology seems increasingly suspect and is held in no mean measure of derision, hymn singing remains surprisingly popular and in itself enjoys something of a come-back. The media welcome every Sunday that dawns with selected sound-bites, just as, on vision, later programmes like *Songs of Praise* celebrate the fading light of the Lord's Day once dismissed in the traditional office of *Book of Common Prayer* Evensong. For the men, women and children who can no longer cope with doctrine care a great deal about hymns, however much most of them fail to realize that, in such carefully-contrived compositions, authors who lived in very different periods of history from the present, effectively condensed the peculiarities of their preaching in precisely the kind of prayer and praise deemed appropriate to the effective communication of their gospel message. Arguing in the *Preface* to his *Psalms and Hymns* (1776), Toplady expressed the case in succinct terms:

> ... what is a *Psalm*, or *Hymn*, strictly taken, but *prayer*, or *praise* ... occasionally [such can be] fraught with Doctrin [sic], Exhortation, and Instruction in righteousness; tending as the Apostle [Paul *To the Ephesians*, 5.19, and again *To the Colossians*, 3.16] expresses it ... to 'teach', to 'admonish', and to build up one another on our most holy faith.

As ever determined to make an impact, there is a piercing, well-nigh magnetic quality about the opening lines of many Toplady hymns which leaves an unforgettable impression. Think, for example, of:

> Your harps, ye trembling saints;

of the 'Chamber Hymn':

> What, tho' my frail eye-lids refuse;

and of course his extraordinary

> Deathless principle! arise.

And when it came to doctrine, what hymn is more exotic as a veritable Calvinist cornucopia than Toplady's 'Method of Salvation'? It is a work that analyses five principal points attributed to the Genevan Reformer, heads of proposals expounded in five verses of concentrated composition with all the insistent pleading of a catechism. First, the divine salvation of 'The Father we bless' confronts original sin head on. Secondly, the 'Father's most gracious design' is set in lights with a dramatic focus on Christ's love and the idea of election. The third verse proclaims 'glory' to be the end of creation, and so makes a reality of redemption. Fourthly, 'The sweet Spirit of grace' receives due praise in a properly vocational context. And the fifth stanza argues for the kind of perseverance and thankfulness to God for love that will endure 'to the end of our days.' Finally, from the doctrinal depths such theology breaks the surface in this climactic doxology:

> Father, Spirit and Son
> Agree thus in One.
> The salvation of those He has marked for His own;
> Let us too agree
> To glorify Thee,
> Thou ineffable One, Thou adorable Three!

Although none of Augustus Montague Toplady's other hymns can compare with such close Calvinist exposition, many moving passages from a provocative preaching career mirror the colours of reform in terse verse. One example is to be found in the hymn

> Compared with Christ, in all beside
> No comeliness I see;

where the subject comes under the spotlight in the wording of verse 4:

> Loved of my God, for Him again
> With love intense I burn;
> Chosen of Him ere time began,
> I choose Him in return.

Then too, the context of a composition published in the *Gospel Magazine, or Treasury of Divine Knowledge* (December 1774), sees lines of meditation, in the hymn 'What though my frail eye-lids refuse', yield to surging Calvinism:

> Bright seraphs, despatched from the throne,
> Repair to their stations assigned;
> And angels elect are sent down,
> To guard the elect of mankind.

Toplady never moves far from the doctrinal high ground what-ever his chosen subject. Arguably his most theological hymn, 'A Debtor to Mercy alone' is a classic of its kind, particularly to an author so well assured that 'Of Covenant-Mercy I sing'! Here the last four lines of the first verse assert:

> The terrors of Law, and of GOD,
> With me can have nothing to do;
> My SAVIOUR's Obedience and Blood
> Hide all my transgressions from view.

Moreover, when the Psalmist chose to wax eloquent, Toplady could follow his lead, the verse 'We hanged our harps upon the willows in the midst' ('of the rivers of Babylon' ... Psalm 137.1–2) when transposed, becoming the challenging:

> Your harps, ye trembling saints,
> Down from the willows take,
> Loud to the praise of Love divine,
> Bid every string awake.

With much of the composition at least reminiscent of pilgrim themes in John Bunyan, this is verse that also conveys the 'songs of expectation' of those who

> Through the night of doubt and sorrow

are clearly

> Marching to the promised land.
> [Baring-Gould's translation of the hymn by Ingemann]

As Toplady expressed it with all the appeal of simple piety:

> Though in a foreign land,
> We are not far from home;
> And nearer to our house above,
> We every moment come.
>
> ...
>
> When we in darkness walk,
> Nor feel the heavenly flame,
> Then is the time to trust our God,
> And rest upon His name.
>
> Soon shall our doubts and fears
> Subside at His control;
> His loving-kindness shall break through
> The midnight of the soul.

If Holy Scripture and the English religious tradition moved Toplady, liturgical orthodoxy in the established church also made its impact. For 'We sing to Thee, Thou Son of God' is a composition clearly inspired by, and much indebted to, the hallowed Morning Prayer canticle Te Deum Laudamus. If Dr Erik Routley found this a 'rather trivial' piece – even 'pointless' as a 'distortion of the theology of the Te Deum' [*I'll Praise My Maker* (London, 1951), p. 271] – his was a harsh judgement. In Toplady's own times such popularisation of ecclesiastical solemnity in the *Book of Common Prayer* had undoubted pastoral appeal, stanzas like these successfully simplifying a dignified approximation to Litany with lines unmistakable in their gospel proclamation and praise:

We sing to Thee, Thou Son of God
Fountain of Life and Grace;
We praise Thee, Son of Man, whose blood
Redeemed our fallen race.

Thee we acknowledge God and Lord,
The Lamb for sinners slain;
Who art by earth and heaven adored,
Worthy o'er both to reign.

To Thee all angels cry aloud,
Through heaven's extended coasts;
Hail, Holy, Holy, Holy, Lord,
Of glory and of hosts.

Toplady used his editorial rôle to publish most of his hymns in
the *Gospel Magazine*; and when presented with the opportunity
in 1776 to bring out *Psalms and Hymns* and draw sacred verse
from 'no fewer than between forty and fifty' volumes, a pleasing
modesty in the man not only included 'the very few hymns of
my own which I have been prevailed with to insert' [*Preface*], but
did so with a humble anonymity. By that date Toplady had in any
case barely eighteen months to live. His 'brilliant spirit in a
brittle frame' [Routley], already on the wane, is well captured in
a posthumously-published composition:

When languor and disease invade
This trembling house of clay,
'Tis sweet to look beyond the cage,
And long to fly away.

If an engraving of 31 March 1777, now in the safe-keeping of
Whitefield's Tabernacle, shows a profile of some immaturity and
physical distress, the man's determined features show no sign of
the sloth suggested in such an autobiographical aside. His young
life very much an unfinished symphony, Toplady's brief span
nevertheless achieved much. For too long now controversy has
been allowed to cloud his reputation, a renown recognized many
years later by a like-minded spirit when the redoubtable John
Charles Ryle, consecrated first Bishop of Liverpool in 1880, gave

his opinion in the same forcefully effective terms that:

of all English hymn-writers, none perhaps has succeeded so thoroughly in combining truth, poetry, life, warmth, fire, depth, solemnity and unction ...

Painted by J.Russell R.A.   Engraved by J.Collyer A.R.A.

REV.ᴰ JOHN NEWTON.

late Rector of the United Parishes of S.t Mary Woolnoth & S.t Mary Woolchurch Haw.

Born at London 24.th of July 1725 O.S. Died 21.ʳ Dec.ʳ 1807.

London Published as the Act directs 1.st Jan.y 1808 by J. Smith Coleman Street Buildings.

Chapter 7

JOHN NEWTON

and

'*How sweet the Name of Jesus sounds*'

1 HOW sweet the Name of Jesus sounds
   In a believer's ear!
It soothes his sorrows, heals his wounds,
   And drives away his fear.

2 It makes the wounded spirit whole,
   And calms the troubled breast;
'Tis manna to the hungry soul,
   And to the weary rest.

3 Dear Name! the Rock on which I build,
   My shield, and hiding-place,
My never-failing treasury, filled
   With boundless stores of grace!

4 By Thee our prayers acceptance gain,
   Although with sin defiled;
Satan accuses me in vain,
   And I am owned a child.

5 Jesus, my Shepherd, Brother, Friend,
   My Prophet, Priest, and King,
My Lord, my Life, my Way, my End,
   Accept the praise I bring.

6 Weak is the effort of my heart,
   And cold my warmest thought;
But when I see Thee as Thou art
   I'll praise Thee as I ought.

7 Till then I would Thy love proclaim
   With every fleeting breath;
And may the music of Thy Name
   Refresh my soul in death. Amen.

The navy ... is offensive to me ... as being the means of
bringing persons of obscure birth into undue distinction,
and raising men to honours which their fathers and grand-
fathers never dreamt of ...   [*Persuasion ch. 3*]

Words Jane Austen gave Sir Walter Elliot of Kellynch Hall,
Somerset, admirably introduce John Newton, whose father, himself a naval commander, early took his son to sea. The boy's subsequent career placed him high as a leader of religious revival within
the Church of England. Those who led the evangelical cause in the
eighteenth century preached for conversion. In their own lives, the
Wesley brothers and George Whitefield duly stressed the importance of such an experience in understanding Christ's gospel. Yet
before 'seeing the light' such men had by no means been numbered among the dissolute of the period. Rather were they, by
their own admission, decidedly dutiful in outward religious observance, and merely undiscerning in the doctrinal terms their later
preaching and teaching upheld as *sine qua non* of true faith. By contrast, John Newton's remarkable life, if it began at the knee of a
mother he described as 'a pious experienced Christian' [*A(uthen-
tic) N(arrative)*, p. 12], had a genuinely degenerate dimension about
it. When his mother died, the boy was only seven; and although his
father took him to sea as an eleven-year-old, John's early life was
that of a disinterested drifter convinced that nobody cared for him.
For even if, by Captain Newton's influence, he began 'upon the
quarter deck as a midshipman' [*A. N.* p. 36], desertion and recapture degraded him to serve 'before the Mast' with the riff-raff
rejects of a sordid society.

As a common seaman, John Newton was certainly well-versed
in the seamy side of life. An infidel who proudly proclaimed himself 'a Free-thinker', he revelled in the profanities for which he
became renowned:

my whole life ... was a course of most horrid impiety ... I
know not that I have ever since met so daring a blasphemer
[for] not content with common oaths and imprecations, I
daily invented new ones.

If he had any ambition in the 1740s, it was to realize a boyhood in-
fatuation and return to Kent to marry the eldest daughter of

'distant relations, but very intimate friends of my dear Mother' [*A. N.* p. 22]. In his own words, Mary Catlett of Chatham 'had been often considered by her mother and mine, as a future wife for me from the time of her birth' [Ibid.] For the rest, demanding service in 'the triangular trade' claimed Newton, and his *Journal*, a work its modern editor declares to be 'unique as a complete day-to-day record of the negro slave trade at the middle of the eighteenth century, from the point of view of a slave ship's captain' [Bernard Martin, p. xv], sets out regular routine. In later life, this time persuaded by William Wilberforce to write for a wide abolitionist public, Newton's *Thoughts upon the African Slave Trade* paraded the evils he encountered in 'a succession of difficulties and hardships' which 'for about the space of eighteen months' made him 'captive and a slave myself ... depressed to the lowest degree of human wretchedness' [op. cit. p. 2]. It was an existence that made 'the English and the Africans ... consider each other as consummate villains ... always watching opportunities to do mischief' [p. 24]; and in detail embraced not merely deception in commerce so that no 'article, that is capable of diminution or adulteration, is delivered genuine, or entire', but also much cruelty and repression. Given his own ship from 1750, Newton was 'absolute in command', and few lines are more devastating than the response 'a Black' charged for 'unfairness and dishonesty' and 'able to clear himself' gave 'with an air of disdain':

What! do you think I am a White Man? [op. cit. p. 24]

Ultimately, however, both Captain and crew were themselves ruled by the natural elements of wind and waves, for those who pursued careers of commerce on the ocean had much to reckon with in a period when seafaring was still a very risky business. Confronted by climatic extremes or plagued by deadly disease, many a 'Free-thinker' had his doubts. No exception to the general rule, this was precisely Newton's lot when the failure of a great Atlantic storm totally to shatter and swallow up the frail timbers of the battered *Greyhound* conjured up fleeting visions of a caring Providence. Leaving Newfoundland and 'the banks <u>March</u> 1 [1748], with a hard gale of wind westerly, which pushed us fast homewards ...', he 'carelessly took up' Thomas à Kempis 'to pass away the time ... as if it was entirely a romance' to combat the tedium of the voyage. The artistic verisimilitude of a mid-ocean swell doubtless added a full measure of persuasion to the narrative, for 'an involuntary suggestion arose in my mind: What if these things should be true?' [*A. N.* p. 82]. On the eve of the storm, one passage from *Imitatio Christi* certainly made profound impact:

> Since Life is of short and uncertain Continuance, it highly concerns you to look about you, and take good heed how you employ it.

When the tempest tore the ship apart on 10 March '(that is in the present stile the 21st)', Newton, 'spent with cold and labour of manning the pumps' dwelt on the cry of a fellow crewman:

> it is too late now, we cannot save her or ourselves.

A brief conference with the Captain followed:

> ... and just as I was returning from him, I said, almost without meaning, 'If this will not do, the Lord have mercy on us'. This (though spoken with little reflection) was the first desire I had breathed for mercy for the space of many years.
> [*A. N.* p. 85]

In recollections of later years, this chequered history of near disaster assumed providential proportions, or as Newton expressed it himself:

> Taken in all circumstance, it was astonishing, and almost miraculous, that any ... survived to relate the story.

But re-live it he did, again and again, as 'a day much to be remembered' for:

> On that day the Lord sent from on high and delivered me out of deep waters. [*A. N.* p. 87]

Allusions in hymns, sermons and tracts indicated the indelible impression of what Newton termed 'an awful dispensation'. In consequence the whole episode has been exaggerated almost as much as the heart-warming experience John Wesley underwent at that celebrated religious-society meeting in Aldersgate Street, London, on 24 May 1738. For Newton, however, conversion was neither so sudden, nor so readily achieved. He 'could not utter the prayer of faith' nor 'draw near to a reconciled God and call him Father'. Instead, 'on every ... side [he] was surrounded with black unfathomable despair.' Autobiographical lines of the hymn

'A Word from Jesus calms the sea' (Matthew 14. 28–31)

later set out his situation in verse 6:

> The storm increas'd on ev'ry side,
> I felt my spirit shrink;
> And soon, with Peter, loud I cry'd,
> 'LORD, save me, or I sink.'

In 'Approach, my soul, the mercy-seat' too, the sixth verse conveys similar sentiments, albeit now with definite commitment:

> 'Poor tempest-tosséd soul be still,
> My promised grace receive'.
> 'Tis Jesus speaks – I must, I will,
> I can, I do believe.

And in *A Review of Ecclesiastical History*, a gloss on Paul's voyage to Italy along the windswept Cretan coastline described the distressed situation of an apostle

> expecting every hour to be either swallowed up by the waves, or dashed to pieces against unknown rocks or shores ... almost worn out with hardship and anxiety ... [yet with] ... no human probability of deliverance the Lord manifested the care he had of his servants.   [p. 220]

For Newton, Paul thus provided a pattern from the primitive church which not only paralleled his own exposure to the elements, but also afforded compass bearings for spiritual salvation in genuine perception of divine providence – for 'what can disappoint the purpose of God?'

Despite much common assumption to the contrary then, John Newton's evangelical conversion, described in a wide range of primary sources that focus spiritual autobiography, was a faltering, gradual progress and by no means instantaneous. Sailing back to the Sierra Leone coast as Mate of the *Brownlow* – a measure of modesty coupled with uncertainty made him decline command of the slave ship owned by the Liverpool magnate Manesty – he had soon to face the old temptations and 'again returned for a season like a dog to my vomit'. Physically weakened too, and ravaged by the occupational hazard of swamp fever, his self-respect was low enough to make subsequent restoration to normal health seem providential. Such a boost, if it encouraged morale, also convinced Newton of his need to 'make no more resolves but cast myself before the LORD, to do with me as he should please'. The 'Middle Passage' duly completed, Newton's mind focused on speedy return to England and marriage to Miss Catlett. But uncompleted business in Antigua caused the slave ship to make an unscheduled stop at Charlestown on the North American mainland, and there he gained some new religious insights. First, perplexed by news of mounting rivalry between the Wesley brothers and George Whitefield, he altogether failed to grasp divergent emphases in doctrine:

> I supposed that all who attended public worship were good Christians ... I was much in the dark about preaching, not doubting but whatever came from the pulpit must be very good.

And secondly, although at the time in no way opposed to the institution of slavery itself, Newton found himself fascinated by the attitude different owners took to the elementary catechism of slaves they had prepared for baptism that merely promised heavenly bliss but no relief from earthly bondage.

Nuptials celebrated at St Margaret's, Rochester, in February 1750 duly linked the lonely Newton to the family who, through his beloved Mary, he had long valued for the warm friendship it had extended to him. Correspondence with an intelligent brother-in-law – for Jack Catlett was in pupillage to a London attorney at the time – clearly indicates new links in a pilgrim's progress:

It is not the Christian Religion merely as by Law established, nor as deliver'd by any collective body of Churchmen under the Sun that I would in all points vindicate to
you, but the Religion which every impartial Free-thinker
may deduce from the plain literal text of ye new testament
...

Such scriptural emphasis proved fundamental to Newton's
increased grasp of a gospel which, if tinged with continuing
respect for providential guidance in a context of moderate Calvinism, strengthened commitment to the evangelical cause. A
backward glance at this early stage of his quest prompted reference
in the *Authentic Narrative* that:

the wise and good providence of God watches over his
people from the earliest moments of their life, overrules and
guards them through all their wanderings in a state of
ignorance.   [*A. N.* p. 4]

After his first voyage in the *Duke of Argyle*, young Captain
Newton, recuperating with his wife at Chatham, was deeply
moved by Doddridge's graphic account of the vanquished Gardiner. For although the 'Forty-Five' ended a brave military
career at Prestonpans, the Colonel had years earlier turned his
back on a dissolute life and committed himself to Christ. In a
commentary in his diary, Newton wrote that such episodes so
'correspond with my own case' that 'I burst 2 or 3 times into
tears ... from sincere repentance and shame' [quoted in B.
Martin, *John Newton*, p. 123]. It was this repentance and a heartfelt sense of deliverance from sin that finally enabled Newton to
claim the forgiveness freely given by Christ, and to recognize the
'glorious change' wrought in him by the work of the Holy Spirit.
It gave him confidence, and after years of aimlessness, contributed
a new sense of purpose. Counselled by Dr Jennings, a dissenting
minister known to his mother, he compared notes with Alexander Clunie, a commander friend he had met in the West Indies,
and began to acquaint himself with the state of English church
life. In 1754, some incidence of epilepsy gave him more time for
such surveys by ending his sea-going days. Once again, Newton's
diary related his reaction to deplore 'the melancholy conditions'

that obtained in parishes where divine service had degenerated into dull and dreary routines to send him 'almost asleep in prayer time'.

Widening this sample of market research with a visit to London, Newton indulged the period fashion of 'gadding to sermons'. With an introduction from Clunie's pastor, he both visited Whitefield, and used the ticket he secured to hear that controversial evangelist preach at the Moorfields 'Tabernacle'. If Dr Johnson informed James Boswell that he judged Whitefield an 'egotist' to be rated with 'a thousand other old women and fanatick writers of memoirs and meditations' [Boswell's *Life* (ed. Rodney Shewan for The Folio Society, 1968), II. 166], Newton clearly received a blessing:

> Never before had I such an idea and foretaste of ye business of heaven. Mr Whitefield made use of ye office of ye Church of England, interspersing exhortations encouragements etc: occasionally all along: and it seemed as tho' that composure that elevation and assurance of faith which shone in his frame and discourses was in some measure diffus'd over the whole assembly: he made many little intervals for singing hymns, I believe near 20 times in all ... we were about 3 hours in ye ordinance, at the end I went away rejoicing. [Quoted in Martin, op. cit., 148]

When Samuel Johnson thus attributed such popularity 'to the peculiarity of [Whitefield's] manner', clear that he 'would be followed by crowds were he to wear a night-cap in the pulpit, or were he to preach from a tree' [Boswell, *Life*, op. cit., I, 357], altogether innocent of such critique, Newton took the man's message to heart convinced that:

> all the dark parts of ye 7th of Romans belongs in an eminent manner to me ... If notwithstanding all my vileness I was made free from sin by the spirit of Life in Jesus Christ, what a wonderful instance am I, both of the riches and the freedom of Grace. [Quoted in Martin, op. cit., 150]

It is a clear indication that he had already grasped the law-gospel antithesis in what his *Review* later termed the 'pure religion of

Jesus' [*Ecclesiastical History*, p. vii].

These were also years that assisted Newton, appointed by 'particular providence' Tide Surveyor at Liverpool, to ponder vocation to ministry. His preparation dictated the study of New Testament Greek in the off-peak moments of this new shore career, just as much as it also afforded more time 'to wait in prayer and meditation upon the Lord'. Various friends encouraged Newton to seek Holy Orders, but six years elapsed before he could secure episcopal agreement and a title to ordination. This eventually came through the good offices of Lord Dartmouth who, like the redoubtable Selina, Countess of Huntingdon, made it his business to get to know bishops prepared to promote suitable candidates who would serve the 'evangelical cause'. Both Primates had succeeded in blocking Newton, arguably because his past was becoming as well known as his readiness to act as minister to a dissenting Meeting in Warwick. It was a tricky time, for in correspondence with a Congregationalist admirer, he had himself made clear that he had

> quite done with the Established Church, so called – not out of anger, or despair, but from a conviction that the Lord has been wise and good in disappointing my views in that quarter; and I believe if the admission I once so earnestly sought was now freely offered, I could hardly, if at all, accept ...
> [Ibid, p. 195]

Other friends remained supportive, and the intercession of an Oxford graduate, the Reverend Thomas Haweis, Rector of Aldwinckle, persuaded Lord Dartmouth to offer the self-taught Newton the curacy of Olney in Buckinghamshire. A small lace-making town in 'country low and dirty', Olney was then in the diocese of Lincoln, whose bishop somehow endured an hour's interview with a candidate whose 'only difficulty' was 'to subscribe, *ex animo*' to the *Book of Common Prayer* 'as to sum and substance'. It was Newton's fond hope that the liturgy contained 'not a line contrary to the Word of God', a pious thought he chose to elaborate with the conclusion he believed '... indeed, that there are not many ...'. And although, as he put it, 'to avoid the character of a dissembler, I could not but dissent with his Lordship in some things' – in particular a few expressions in *The*

Ministration of Baptism, in *The Order for Burial of the Dead* and the *Catechism* – 'he kindly accepted me & was satisfied with the examination I went thro'.'

Ordained deacon on 29 April 1764, Newton was made priest on Trinity Sunday that same year, and remained curate of Olney until 1780. It was to be a memorable ministry, not least for pastoral skills that used hymns to teach the faith. In the estimation of Erik Routley, John Newton became:

> a strongly evangelical clergyman who preached and taught with great fervour the theology of sudden conversion, of hell fire and the need for immediate repentance; his gospel, which came from his stormy and battered life, was grim and apocalyptic.
>
> [Erik Routley, *I'll Praise My Maker*, p. 64]

That such a gospel was much indebted to Pauline theology is evident from the emphasis Newton placed on Christ as the Saviour who alone could remove the stranglehold of sin. He seized every opportunity to noise abroad his own sense of deliverance 'from the power and domination of sin', and to the last followed the apostle who, when writing to the young church at Corinth, remained conscious of the frailty of the human situation. Invoking Paul's own words, Newton did not cease to recall 'the effects and conflicts of sin dwelling in me' to 'groan, being burdened' (2 Cor. 5.4). This message most of his hymns hammered home, even his '... mercies, countless as the sands' deploring, in verse 2, the fact that

> My best is stained and dyed with sin,
> My all is nothing worth.

Accordingly, in what is surely a text-book presentation of the gospel set out for the Church of England in the evangelical revival of the eighteenth century, Newton's contribution to the celebrated *Olney Hymns* which he wrote with the poet Cowper stressed the shortcomings of sinful humanity to such an extent that all might see in clear relief their need of salvation in Christ. Devotional verse like

> Come, my soul, thy suit prepare

is thus deepened and given precisely this gospel perspective in the context of verse 3:

> With my burden I begin:
> Lord, remove this load of sin;
> Let Thy blood for sinners spilt,
> Set my conscience free from guilt.

Universally acknowledged as John Newton's most successful hymn,

> How sweet the Name of Jesus sounds
> In a believer's ear ... ,

even has a verse consistent with such emphasis. Although found in the hymnals of almost all Christian denominations nowadays (but interestingly enough *not* in the *New Catholic Hymnal* which only makes use of Newton by including a 'slightly adapted' form of his superb doxology), verse 4 is invariably omitted by editors fearful of those darker tones of doctrine deemed outmoded. Be that as it may, the hymn writer did not himself shrink from forthright proclamation of the whole gospel as he understood it from Scripture, and for Newton this meant forceful exposition of the kind that took account of the serious blemish sin and Satan had wrought in the divine economy. In short, a stanza like:

> By Thee our prayers acceptance gain,
> Although with sin defiled;
> Satan accuses me in vain,
> And I am owned a child

simply would not allow the faithful to forget their flawed past, and rather reminded them that both sin and Satan remained to weaken life in the Spirit. Composed on the same cautionary lines, verse 6, by stressing praise far more than blaming blemish, strives to redress the balance and succeeds with the sustained sound of the sanctuary:

> Weak is the effort of my heart

And cold my warmest thought,
But when I see Thee as Thou art,
I'll praise Thee as I ought.

That sound, the subject of Newton's brilliant offering, is of course praise. Entered in Book I of his *Olney Hymns in Three Books* (London, 1779), the composition was intended as commentary 'On select Texts of SCRIPTURE', in this case 'SOLOMON's SONG', ch.1. 3, 'HYMN LVII, *The name of* JESUS'. Likening the sweet savour of good ointments in the love poem of Solomon to the way the very name Jesus attracts all who have found fulfilment in his finished work, this is a hymn overflowing with Christian joy. A perfect homily of heartfelt praise and thanksgiving, it admirably accords with the plea Newton made in his *Preface* to the *Olney Hymns*. For there he urged that 'Perspicuity, simplicity and ease ... be chiefly attended to', just as in 'public worship ... for the use of plain people' he made it clear on a personal level that 'doctrines of grace are essential to my peace' (op. cit., p. viii). How apt then that from a 'never-failing treasury' such 'boundless stores of grace' are available. If there is sadness, Jesus consoles; if there is injury, healing is at hand; if there is anxiety, fear is dispelled. Bruising no longer disfigures; troubles are calmed; and just as manna fed the children of Israel in the wilderness, so grace sustains spiritual hunger and eases the fatigue of those enduring life's pilgrimage. Brimful of autobiographical reflection, this particular couplet

'Tis manna to the hungry soul,
And to the weary rest,

provides a powerful parallel between the way Israelites, bound for the promised land, and dependent on daily dispensations of manna, were kept humble, and the personal custom Newton outlined in correspondence daily to recall the achievement of the Christ whose deliverance from sin demanded a humble walk with God.

It is indeed 'Dear name!' For what a wealth of biblical imagery Newton's composition used to proclaim the gospel. Jesus is thus not only a rock, a shield and a shelter, but the well spring and fountainhead of a full range of divine attributes used in the

Scriptures. These the hymn's fifth verse rehearses in a packed profile of prophetic proportion and personal piety. The allusive quality of a name so meaningful not only conveys deep truths like a
clever sermon on scriptural synonyms, but is also pastorally compelling in the way it heightens personal praise in public worship.

> Jesus! my Shepherd, Husband, Friend,
> My Prophet, Priest, and King,
> My Lord, my Life, my Way, my End,
> Accept the praise I bring!

Such lyrical power is made especially effective by the note of
penitence struck in the next verse. For Newton is clear that just
as the full glory of God must partially be obscured to those who
worship on earth, so the quality of the praise they offer is bound
to be limited and unworthy. Anyway, the faithful have no excuse
for inactivity, but bear a solemn responsibility to preach the coming of the Kingdom. In a remarkable way, the last lines of this
stunning composition convey an almost magical momentum. For
they sum up the central message of the eighteenth-century evangelical revival reflected in dedicated pastoral ministry of the kind
which consumed Newton throughout his Olney period and
beyond:

> Till then I would Thy love proclaim
> With every fleeting breath,
> And may the music of Thy Name
> Refresh my soul in death.

In his time at Olney, John Newton confronted every issue with
growing confidence. Of his conversion he now had no doubt,
and as his struggle to gain acceptance in the ordained ministry of
the Church of England receded into the past, so his commitment
to his people increased. That he impressed his flock need not be
doubted, for the limited sum of £60 per annum paid to him as
perpetual curate (the vicar's stipend was drawn by an absentee)
was soon supplemented by John Thornton, a prosperous mer-
chant banker and convinced supporter of the 'evangelical' cause.
Inspired by a copy of the *Authentic Narrative* Newton had sent
him, Thornton not only advanced Olney's curate £200 p.a. for

work among a poor community of cottagers struggling to eke out their living by making pillow lace and straw plait, but also funded the erection of a fine gallery in the parish church and effectively doubled the seating available to a vastly-expanded congregation for worship. With other clergy – prominent among them Adam in Lincolnshire, Berridge at Everton, Grimshaw at Haworth, Milner, first at Queens' College, Cambridge, and then at Carlisle Cathedral, Simeon, also at Cambridge, but at King's and Holy Trinity Church, father Venn at Huddersfield, his son at Clapham, and Walker in Truro – Newton successfully channelled the revival stirred up by the Wesleys and Whitefield into England's parochial system. Such dedicated pastors challenged the complacency of a life of ease in Sion to urge what, in his *Review of Ecclesiastical History* (1770), Newton termed 'a second reformation' (p. xv). He certainly intended 'to attempt the apology of Evangelical Christianity' and 'vindicate the doctrines of the Reformation, or, in other words, the main doctrines taught in the articles and homilies of the Church of England' (op. cit.). Now his life's mission, it was a work he continued when Thornton presented him to the living of St Mary Woolnoth, Lombard Street, a parish he made a centre for the new evangelicalism in London, and a haven that gave spiritual shelter to a considerable congregation of artisans, merchants, shopkeepers and strangers from as far afield as Holborn or from the south bank of the Thames.

In the big city, Newton's ministry proved both influential and, for an Anglican rector, idiosyncratic. Rigid denominationalism he had long deplored, being approached in 1782 to sponsor a Dissenting Academy at Newport Pagnell. His brotherly attitude to Olney Free Church evangelicals is clear from the way he not only attended Baptist and Independent Meetings for worship, but actually suspended and re-scheduled prayer meetings in the parish when these clashed with those timetabled by Mr Drake, the Independent Minister. This entry from the *Diary* for Tuesday, 26 September 1765, is typical:

> Omitted our prayer-meeting to-night and attended Mr Bradbury, who preached a very good sermon at Mr Drake's. I am glad of such opportunities at times to discountenance bigotry and party spirit, and to set our Dissenting brethren

an example, which I think ought to be our practice towards all who love the Lord Jesus Christ, and preach His Gospel without respect to forms or denominations.

By definition, Newton held dissenting teachers to be 'only Ministers of independent congregations'. In consequence it was 'Independent Ministers' like himself who, albeit with reservations on matters like the baptism of infants, nevertheless served the establishment in their ministry. Altogether averse to the Prayer-Book rubric that:

> *It is certain by God's Word, that children which are baptized, dying before they commit actual sin, are undoubtedly saved ...*

he made clear his own conviction that

> ... they may be and are saved whether baptised or not; for I cannot think that the salvation of a soul depends upon a negligent or drunken minister, who cannot be found when wanted to baptise a dying infant.

Equally, when dissenters chose to denounce the restrictive or repetitive nature of worship based on the Church's liturgy, Newton was not slow to answer in kind:

> Crito freely will rehearse
> Forms of pray'r and praise in verse:
> Why should Crito then suppose
> Forms are sinful when in prose?
> Must my form be deem'd a crime
> Merely for the want of rhyme?

From the start of his London ministry, Newton commanded the crowds from the pulpit of St Mary Woolnoth, his Sunday sermon on 19 December 1779, 'the Day of his First Public Service in that Church' setting the style as he strove with the apostle to speak 'the truth in love' (Ephesians 4.15). Published as *The Subject and Temper of the Gospel Ministry*, after characteristic acknowledgement that 'the Providence of God has placed me in this City, and in this Church' (p. 6), his address outlined a ministry altogether in line with his assent to the *XXXIX Articles of Religion*. 'Summarily contained in' that formulary of the faith of the Church of England, Newton thus conceived his care of souls on the basis of 'the truth as it is in Jesus, according to St Paul's expression ... to speak the truths of God'. His forthright approach and determination 'not to amuse ... with subjects of opinion or uncertainty, or even with truths of a cold, speculative, uninteresting nature' certainly made its mark, not least in the profound influence he exerted on those pioneers of social conscience, Hannah More and William Wilberforce. At the time of his conversion crisis in 1785, Wilberforce sought the rector's spiritual counsel; and in the intervening years before, with active help from Mr Pitt and Charles James Fox, the Abolition Bill passed the Commons in 1804, Newton did much to throw his 'mite into the public stock of information'. The cool objectivity of his *T[houghts upon the] A[frican] S[lave] T[rade]*, 1788 – a pamphlet Cowper commended for its 'conscientious candour and moderation' when all London was as divided for and against a commerce supported or denounced as by apartheid issues in 20th-century Commonwealth affairs – undoubtedly helped Wilberforce. Clear that he was himself 'a competent witness upon this subject', Newton also appreciated it to be no simple matter 'to write altogether with coolness ... and especially not easy to me, who have formerly been so deeply engaged'. Nonetheless he knew that the

> many things which I saw, heard and felt, upon the Coast of Africa, are so deeply engraven in my memory, that I can hardly forget, or greatly mistake them, while I am capable of remembering anything.   [*T.A.S.T.*, p. 40]

Such experience he witnessed before the Privy Council in 1788, Hannah More judging his *Thoughts* and evidence to be 'sensible, judicious, well-timed, and well-tempered'.

That he kept up such outward appearance when deeply saddened that his beloved Mary was slipping away from him, provides further testimony to both the calibre and commitment of the man. Mrs Newton died on 15 December 1790, and fearful then, as on many earlier occasions, that his love for her 'stood in the way of his love for God', John chose to preach. He did so not only on that fateful day, but also on three other occasions before he committed Mary to the grave, likewise writing both the sermon and the supporting hymn for her funeral. Moreover, when sympathy came along and his people recommended remedies and rest for his grieving, Newton gave the terse rejoinder

> Dr Pulpit is my best physician!

And the London rector who in the mid-80s had taken exception to George Frederick Handel's abuse of scripture in *Messiah* – Newton did his utmost to rival a Westminster Abbey commemoration of the sacred oratorio with fifty examples of expository preaching on texts around which the renowned musician had merely scored *libretti* – continued to expound the scriptures for a further seventeen years. Even when he could barely see, with memory so weak that a day's activity he could not recall had actually been spent in the pulpit, Newton determined not to retire:

> What! Shall the old African blasphemer stop while he can speak?

A NEWTON SPIRITUAL TREASURY

Although for the present purpose the Christian fellowship Newton extended to William Cowper merits no more than *en passant* mention, seen in context the *Olney Hymns* were no mere collaborative effort. For all 'Three Books' reveal a true pastor's concern to involve one of the few really talented poets who have penned both paeans of praise and *cris de coeur* in moving English of real literary quality. Following a nervous breakdown brought on by failure at the Middle Temple, Cowper was cared for in convalescence by a Mrs Unwin whose rented property bordered Olney Green. Newton had first met Cowper at Huntingdon in 1767, and, aware of the poet's torment, went out of his way to counsel the educated newcomer of 'Orchard Side' who became his nearest neighbour in the village. For the curate, deep and soulful conflicts posed no new dilemma, and with all the confidence of a moderate Calvinist, Newton attempted to console his unstable parishioner as they toured the surrounding countryside together and disputed on every conceivable subject. By 1769, Cowper, now a regular worshipper at the parish church and indebted to preaching he adjudged 'plain and neat', started to contribute hymns. Newton chose themes for prayer meetings and bible studies, likewise making much of 'the Progress and Changes of the Spiritual Life'; and he and Cowper began to compose pieces for the inspiration of those parishioners who gathered together for prayer. It was a remarkable start too as Newton's gratitude for Dartmouth's gift of a room in the family seat – 'the Great House' – joined with a plea for prayerful fulfilment in the lines:

> Dear Shepherd of thy people, hear,
> Thy presence now display;
> As thou hast given a place for prayer
> So give us hearts to pray

provided the perfect complement to profound sensitivity in Cowper's

> Jesus, where'er thy people meet,
> There they behold thy mercy-seat.

When the *Olney Hymns* were eventually published in 1779, Newton's *Preface* referred to the fact that, for him, they 'perpetuate the remembrance of an intimate and endeared friendship' (p. vi). That he also alluded to Cowper's 'long and affecting indisposition', and took good care to make clear even to 'a good judge of composition' that he chose 'to preclude a misapplication by prefixing the letter **C**' to the work of his 'dear friend', showed him to be concerned for his colleague as a lost soul. If doctrinal considerations braced him to defend Calvinist orthodoxy, his commendable grasp of the gospel gave Newton an open, even an ecumenical, outlook and a real sense of pastoral priorities in Christian ministry.

> When a house is on fire [he wrote], Churchmen and Dissenters, Methodists, Papists, Moravians and Mystics are all welcome to bring water. At such times nobody asks, 'What do you think of the five points?'

Moderate discipleship of John Calvin as a mentor in Christian doctrine may not have been good for Cowper's emotional psyche – and Newton was adamant that 'What is by some called High Calvinism I dread.' But the poet clearly respected the curate's providential insights, parishioner being seldom separated from pastor for 'nearly 12 years ... for 12 hours at a time, when we were awake and at home'. Trying to imitate Cowper, Newton recalled the bouts of agonizing distress that beset his friend, a time when if he counted it a privilege to walk pensively 'in the valley of the shadow', Cowper pleaded for

... a closer walk with God

in a hymn that worried its way through three more verses before reaching its author's confident conclusion

So shall my walk be close with God,
Calm and serene my frame;
So purer light shall mark the road
That leads me to the Lamb.

Newton had clearly become sufficiently obsessed to read religion into everything. As expressed in one composition, country walks with Cowper made him rejoice at the way

Bleak winter is subdu'ed at length.

It was a hymn that welcomed the coming of spring in God's good time – a season as renowned for birdsong and the 'warbling thrush' as for fields ablaze with colour and the 'cowslip's sweet perfume' – to prompt from his pen 'one hymn a week to expound at the Great House.' If this was sometimes a word of rustic simplicity of which the creation hymn

XCI <u>The Spider and the Bee</u>

provides a good example, it could also prove as profound and powerful as his

LVII <u>Looking at the Cross</u>.

This contrast between simplicity –

> On the same flow'r we often see
> The lothsome spider and the bee;
> But what they get by working there,
> Is different as their natures are –

and doctrinal depth –

> In evil long I took delight
> Unaw'd by shame or fear;
> Till a new object struck my sight,
> And stopped my wild career –

became a pronounced feature of the way Newton hammered home, in hymns as homilies, a personal appeal designed to promote the Christian gospel. An entry in his *Diary* made this precise point when he wrote:

> ... most of the morning [spent] hammering at a hymn for tomorrow yet could not finish it.

For if he invariably preached six times in seven days, he customarily made but 'one hymn a week to expound at the Great House, and I seldom can do it very soon'. But if he personally deplored his 'poetical talent' as 'very slow', most compositions straightly challenged faithful and unfaithful alike with scriptural authority as they were confronted with what Newton termed 'Gospel Truth'. First, man's sinful nature was set out, usually in direct exposition of a text chosen from the Old or the New Testament. After all, Book I of the *Olney Hymns* was precisely focused on a whole range of relevant scriptures. For example, in the context of the Book of Genesis, ch.4.3–8, the fifth stanza of the hymn

> When Adam fell he quickly lost

embraced the lines

> Such was the wicked murd'rer Cain,
> And such by nature still are we,
> Until by grace we're born again,
> Malicious, blind and proud, as he.

Secondly, after Newton duly recognizes the sinfulness not only of mankind but of individual sinners – a trait some deplore as harping on sin – due emphasis is given to the mercies available to the penitent. Another commentary on the Book of Genesis, the hymn 'My name is JACOB', with its famed first line of providential reassurance that epitomizes moderate Calvinist conviction

> NAY, I cannot let thee go,

includes a typical fourth verse:

> Once a sinner near despair,
> Sought thy mercy-seat by pray'r;
> Mercy heard and set him free,
> LORD, that mercy came to me.

For the rest, Newton holds nothing back, unreservedly commending Christ and him crucified. Hymn LIV, 'CHRIST crucified', frames the message of evangelical revival in the first verse:

> When on the Cross, my LORD I see
> Bleeding to death, for wretched me;

and then goes on in verse 3 to commend faith in discipleship:

> Come, sinners, view the Lamb of God
> Wounded and dead, and bath'd in blood!
> Behold his side, and venture near,
> The well of endless life is here.

Hymn LVII, 'Looking at the cross', is a particularly powerful piece of work, not merely for these prefatory lines of autobiography:

In evil long I took delight,
Unaw'd by shame or fear;
Till a new object struck my sight,
And stopped my wild career ...,

but for the way the sinner is made to stand before Calvary's cross
and behold the Lord he had helped 'to nail ... there'.

I saw one hanging on a tree,
In agonies and blood;
Who fix'd his languid eyes on me,
As near his cross I stood.

Sure, never till my latest breath,
Can I forget that look;
It seemed to charge me with his death,
Tho' not a word he spoke.

If men like Newton deplored the crucifix, preaching conversion
as turning and the kind of moral change that, through faith in
Christ, and in the power of his death and resurrection to bring
new life, such intense scrutiny of the crucified certainly parallels
much catholic devotion.

A second look he gave, which said,
'I freely all forgive;
This blood is for thy ransom paid,
I die, that thou may'st live.'

Ultimately, however, it was not catholicism but a cautious
Calvinism which best recalls Newton's stand. The workings of
divine providence could alone explain the many mysteries and
mercies of a long life; and under the sub-heading, III PROVI-
DENCES, *Olney Hymn* LXXVII <u>Are there few that shall be saved?</u>
sheds much light on the mission of this extraordinary man.

Destruction's dangerous road
What multitudes pursue!
Whilst that which leads the soul to GOD,
Is known or sought by few.

And after an effective piece of symbolism in the great 'flood of waters' – surely another instance of autobiographical imagery – this couplet:

> A few were sav'd in Noah's ark,
> For many millions drown'd.

High drama to be sure, and in a context of revivalist preaching in the 'good old cause', two further verses succinctly summarize the pastoral idealism of John Newton:

> Obey the gospel call,
> And enter while you may;
> The flock of CHRIST is always small
> And none are safe but they.

> LORD, open sinners eyes
> Their awful state to see;
> And make them, ere the storm arise,
> To thee for safety flee.

The Scriptural standards Newton set himself throughout a prolific output certainly parallel his achievement as a preacher. For of supreme importance to John Newton's great gifts in the composition of hymns was a determination to commend the word of God to his people, rather than any compositions of his own. Achieved with a memorable clarity, this is nowhere better illustrated than in Paul's doxology concluding the apostle's Second Letter to the Corinthians (2 Cor.13.14), a text Newton invariably used to conclude worship in the Church of St Peter and St Paul, Olney, set out in Book III of the *Olney Hymns* as No. CI:

> May the grace of CHRIST our Saviour
> And the FATHER's boundless love,
> With the holy SPIRIT's favour,
> Rest upon us from above!
> Thus may we abide in union
> With each other, and the LORD;
> And possess, in sweet communion,
> Joys which earth cannot afford.

Chapter 8

JOHN KEBLE'S

'Bless'd are the pure in heart'

and

The Christian Year

1 BLESS'D are the pure in heart,
For they shall see our God,
The secret of the Lord is theirs,
Their soul is Christ's abode.

2 The Lord, who left the heavens
Our life and peace to bring,
To dwell in lowliness with men,
Their pattern and their King.

3 Still to the lowly soul
He doth Himself impart,
And for His cradle and His throne
Chooseth the pure in heart.

4 Lord, we Thy presence seek;
May ours this blessing be;
Give us a pure and lowly heart
A temple meet for Thee.

[From a poem composed for 'The Purification', first published
in *The Christian Year* (1827) and later revised by John Keble to
become one of his best-known hymns.]

There is a unique quality about the English countryside, and few fail to recognize the indefinable character that makes the Cotswolds its very heartland. By the standards of the British Isles, the area is large enough in scale. Yet if much of it is internationally known, picturesque market towns like Chipping Campden and Cirencester, Bourton-on-the-Water and Stow-on-the-Wold attracting innumerable tourists, secluded spots still exist where even American visitors have yet to penetrate. The valley of the River Coln is one such shrine, for although the road that links the Oxfordshire town of Burford to Bibury is well enough known, the gentle trout stream that meanders from that Gloucestershire village to Coln St Aldwyns runs into the comparative secrecy of Keble country. If the poverty of the parish and the size of his family obliged the Reverend John Keble, Senior, to live in a house of his own at Fairford three miles away, he was vicar of Coln St Aldwyns until he died in his ninetieth year. The old priest's son John regularly took Sunday duty there. In fact, when his father died in 1835, 'John the Good' moved his invalid sister Elizabeth to Coln parsonage and lived there for some months before he went to Hampshire. It was certainly here, and when he was curate of Eastleach and Southrop in 1823, that John Keble's relaxed and sunny strolls matured in the prayerful meditation that became spiritual poetry in *The Christian Year*. Recollection of a ramble from Bibury in the very year of his ordination (1815) shows Keble captivated by such countryside:

> Some of the spots which I passed on our jolly river Coln are quite beautiful enough to recompense one for a much longer walk.

And when he left the Cotswolds to become vicar of Hursley, his letter to Charles Dyson (12 June 1835) refers to separation from 'dear little Coln' as a 'melancholy reality.'

Keble's new cure took him to rural Hampshire, to a living in the gift of Sir William Heathcote, within six miles of the cathedral city of Winchester. If Oxford was some fifty miles away, John was never far from the former Oriel pupil who lived in style at Hursley Park. Between All Saints' parish church and his estate, the baronet found a house which Keble soon made into a parsonage home. Here with Charlotte Keble (for he married in

October 1835, a few months before being instituted), John and his dear, timid 'Bird' of a sister, Elizabeth, were to live for almost thirty years. Like the old house at Fairford, where he not only spent his own childhood but had been superbly tutored for Oxford by his father, Hursley Vicarage provided the focus of a wider family and witnessed another generation of Keble ministry. An open door welcomed all comers, and in what was effective household catechism, the seasoned godliness of an old-fashioned English clergyman patiently taught his village people, their sons and daughters, the high discipline of traditional Christian principles. In any age, local people are the mainstay of their church; and in nineteenth-century England the real strength of the so-called Tractarian Movement resided in parishes like Hursley where John Keble, the country vicar dutifully defended the faith once delivered to the Saints.

Historians have a lot to answer for, and in terms of the great tradition perhaps church historians have done the Tractarians grave disservice. For a start, most of the books concentrate almost entirely on the Oxford end of what has been termed a 'Movement'. Early luminaries of the celebrated Oriel College Common Room certainly held the University spellbound. John Keble's 'double first' placed him on a par with Robert Peel in terms of academic attainment; and John Henry Newman's brilliant sermons at St Mary's were neither parochial nor plain, but infected dons and undergraduates alike with an intelligent approach to the faith. If undoubtedly fervent, such 'New-mania' was also respectable and far removed from the enthusiasm of Evangelicals and Methodists. The flamboyant Froude also played a key rôle – Richard Hurrell Froude who stirred up the dialectic to give the Fellowship an ecclesiastical notoriety that almost parallels the literary and dramatic impact of an Oscar Wilde. And then there was Edward Bouverie Pusey. An Oriel Fellow by examination in 1823, he secured appointment as Regius Professor of Hebrew by the Duke of Wellington when still in deacon's orders (1838). Once ordained priest and installed in his canonry at Christ Church, Pusey remained in post until his death in 1882 to dignify cathedral and Oxford worship in general with such a combination of pedantry and ritualism that a later canon [the Regius Professor of Ecclesiastical History, Claude Jenkins] found so endearing he refused to walk in procession on the 'large white marble slab in the floor of the central aisle' (H.P. Liddon), placed over the Reverend Doctor's tomb.

Few Dons have gained more respect from Oxford than John Keble. When he died, funds for a College in his memory were raised on a scale and with a rapidity that surprised even his closest admirers. J.T. Coleridge recognized it as 'almost unprecedented'; yet the man himself was so much larger than the University he served, and demands national, even world-wide recognition. This is not for a moment to question the scholarship of one who, laden with University prizes, proved an invaluable, caring College Tutor and, in the undergraduate slang of the period, 'peculiar grinder' to Oriel men. It is not to doubt his contribution to Common Room or High Table where in Oxford, as he once wrote in a letter home, 'we go on much as usual, criticizing sermons, eating dinners and laughing'. Nor should it deprive him of prestige in the Chair of Poetry to which he was elected in 1831, any more than his celebrated 'Assize Sermon' on 'National apostasy' can fail to register a prophetic quality and scale of determined utterance in Keble that later characterized the *Tracts* themselves. After all, Newman made it known that he 'ever considered and kept the day of the publication of the sermon as the start of the religious movement of 1833' (*Apologia Pro Vita Sua*). But if John Keble was thus identified as the prime mover and remained in touch with many an Oxford attempt to condition the religious establishment of Victorian Britain, his true vocation was far removed from 'the dreaming spires' so that even much-loved Colleges like Corpus and Oriel had their place.

A modern writer, [Georgina Battiscombe], subtitled her fine biography *A Study in Limitations*; yet Keble's principal dilemma was arguably the parson's perennial problem of priorities. Priesthood was to him a clear vocation, and in such a context even his Oxford experience counted for little if it did not advance parish ministry. Early evidence of such conviction exists in a letter to Coleridge (29 January 1818) when Keble entertained doubts about accepting the Oriel Tutorship so soon after ordination:

> I thought at first it would be a very uncomfortable thing to me to give up my Cure, and become an Academic again; but I get more and more reconciled to it every day. You consider Tuition as a species of pastoral care, do you not?

otherwise it might seem questionable, whether a clergyman ought to leave a cure of souls for it.   [*Memoir*, p. 73]

In 1823 another letter points to pastoral priority in a life of dedication:

> I feel as if I should be very glad to get away to some country curacy.

And that Keble got away in spirit too is clear enough from the mounting evidence of romantic recollection in poetry soon to be published in *The Christian Year*. If Wesley read books on horseback, Keble meditated and set his meditations to verse as, during Long Vacation duty in his beloved Cotswolds, he rode to take Divine Service in the family parish. He certainly prized the Fairford link, and until his father died in 1834 remained in the closest contact with a family he cherished. As many a bereavement scarred him in these years, so grief in the fellowship of suffering increased his spiritual stature. Named after his mother, Sarah Keble, John's second sister, died of tuberculosis when only 18 years of age. 'That she is happy I have,' he wrote, 'the firmest faith.' In 1819, his younger brother Tom – Fellow of Corpus, but *en famille* the 'King's Fool'! – survived a serious bout of pneumonia 'almost like a resurrection'. The death of Mrs Keble herself on a Sunday morning in May (1823) – 'she fell asleep' and 'never did I see such perfect, such dovelike calmness' – ended her son's time as a Fellow resident in College. His father needed him, and Fairford claimed him – Fairford, where only two years later his favourite 'baby' sister, the darling Mary Anne, 'fell into her last sleep' and succumbed to meningitis. Thomas More's Chelsea family claimed Utopian strengths when sixteenth-century Europe fell apart; and there are surely domestic parallels to be found three centuries on in a letter John wrote from the Kebles' Fairford home:

> ... the separation is painfully trying: humanly speaking, irreparable; but the Almighty has mercies in store which we know not of, and they are both so calm and patient – my Father even cheerful – that I cannot, upon consideration, be uncomfortable ... My brother and Bessie are with us, and

are the greatest support to one another, and to us; and the
baby is like a little angel sent among us to shine in an over-
clouded place. Then we have our Bibles and Prayer-Books
at hand ...   [*Memoir*, p. 138]

This reference to the household's ultimate resource in time of need
– '... we have our Bibles and Prayer-Books at hand' –
provides useful focus on the relief Keble found in 'the Good
Book'. A well-spring of his spiritual life, it inspired a poetry of occasions – the Sundays and Festivals, Saints' days and sacraments –
that comprised the Church Kalendar. As is the way with
authors, and poets in particular, close friends had a sight of Keble's
stanzas from time to time. The gesture was a pastor's
attempt to share secrets of an inner life and by no means a
pre-publication sampling, for Keble was the humblest of men. He
had no plans for a book, and in the great tradition had tended his
own little garden of the soul over a number of years to keep a rare
devotional treasury for intimate moments of sacred meditation.

I mean to take plenty of time, to make out the ecclesiastical
year ... and I feel as if this could take up my life.

But Oxford friends, among whom Charles Dyson took the lead,
saw this as undue modesty; and it was ultimately John's aged
father who, in the hope of seeing the book in print before he
died, prevailed on his son's scruples. So James Parker of Oxford
printed *The Christian Year* in June, 1827, and even then 'John
Keble, Junr' insisted on the anonymity of his publication.

By any standards, *The Christian Year* is a spiritual classic, yet
few critics give a satisfactory explanation of the author's purpose.
All too often dons delight in making simplicity complex, and the
romantic nature of Keble's essentially religious verse – much of
which has little appeal to the matter-of-fact faithlessness of the
post-Victorian world – has been roughly handled by scholars
who completely ignore its context. The book has no preface; but
a page and a half of 'ADVERTISMENT' makes those who take the
trouble to read it well aware of a purposeful author:

The object of the present publication will be attained, if any
person find assistance from it in bringing his own thoughts

and feelings into more entire unison with those recommended and exemplified in the Prayer Book.

No reference is made to poetry, yet starting with Richard Hurrell Froude, almost all commentators have made a prime point of condemning stanzas for what might be termed the language of Wordsworth and soda. From Keble himself too, they have had their reply. He wrote, he stressed, for the plain man, and in a pun his pert but patronising pupil Froude was informed that the work was meant as 'pottery' and not poetry at all.

What then was the point of *The Christian Year*? The answer is simple: Keble intended his 'Thoughts in Verse' (words taken from the title-page) to be of use in 'practical religion' and so of value in promoting popular piety. In short, the 'Good Book' was as much the *Book of Common Prayer* as it was the Bible, for his commentary on the Kalendar related to texts from appropriate scripture passages selected as either 'Gospel' or 'Epistle' readings for the 'SUNDAYS AND HOLIDAYS' of the Church's year. A High Churchman himself, Keble well knew the supreme significance of the liturgical Kalendar in the historic Western Church, for at its heart the eucharist provided the very pulse of catholic spirituality. Accordingly, by encouraging the faithful and not-so-faithful to relate their devotions to 'successive portions of the Liturgy', even extending their prayers to 'the several Occasional Services', Keble sought to make congregations aware 'of that soothing tendency in the Prayer Book' and in effect provide a primer for Victorian people.

The poem Keble composed for 'The Purification' provides perfect illustration of precisely this purpose. Based on the blessing and promise of what is still best known as 'The Sermon on the Mount', the simplest verse applied and enlarged words from St Matthew's Gospel (5.8.):

> BLESS'D are the pure in heart,
> For they shall see our God,
> The secret of the Lord is theirs,
> Their soul is Christ's abode.

Successive stanzas sketched in the divine design of incarnation. Using all the skills the Electors recognized when they made him

Professor of Poetry at Oxford for a decade from 1831, Keble drew on rich veins of scripture, the Evening Prayer canticle Nunc Dimittis, and ores of contrasting imagery. In lyrical language he penned truly inspirational lines to link purity with praise. Mary and Joseph presented the Holy Child in the Temple; Simeon blessed God for his vision of the world's salvation; and the octogenarian Anna prophesied that Israel's long-awaited redemption was nigh. If the subject matter was similar to much current evangelical hymnody, Keble's treatment made a most significant advance. For instead of soulful, subjective concentration on the impending crucifixion of Jesus, his verse conveyed, with a marvellous objectivity, the miracle of incarnation:

> Give ear, ye Kings – bow down,
> Ye rulers of the earth –
> This, this is He; your Priest by grace,
> Your God and King by birth.
> [*The Christian Year*, p. 279, verse 4]

His verse he certainly intended for the encourgement of heart-felt meditation; but it also drew on a rich catholic heritage which church congregations invariably by-passed. The *Book of Common Prayer* made provision for what was termed 'THE PRESENTATION OF CHRIST IN THE TEMPLE commonly called *The Purification of Saint Mary the Virgin*'. Assigned by the Kalendar to February 2, the feast was rarely observed, at least by the people; and Keble therefore made it his mission to implement traditional catholic teaching. After all, a fine Collect enshrined that doctrine:

> ALMIGHTY and everliving God, we humbly beseech thy Majesty, that, as thy only-begotten Son was this day presented in the temple in substance of our flesh, so we may be presented unto thee with pure and clean hearts ...

On that foundation, Keble chose to build what for Bunyan was 'the house called Beautiful' and popularize a great tradition. Seventeen stanzas long in *The Christian Year*, his original poem had to be pruned. Yet it had served its initial purpose, and away from Oxford in the context of demanding parish routines, Keble refined his early composition to produce the famous hymn which remained faithful to his vision. A recent work dedicated to the memory of Michael Ramsey contains an essay by Dr Geoffrey Rowell who has shown how Keble made poetry 'the natural handmaid of religion' [C.R. Henery (Editor), *A Speaking Life: The Legacy of John Keble* (Gracewing, Leominster, 1995), p. 56]. An object lesson to be sure, but if four of the simplest stanzas can ever comprise a homily in the pursuit of holiness, these are they, the sublime counsel of Keble's last verse epitomizing far more than Tractarian spirituality:

> LORD, we thy presence seek;
> May ours this blessing be;
> Give us a pure and lowly heart
> A temple meet for thee.

No philosopher like Newman, Keble left Oxford to defend the faith as an English country parson. Catechism he regarded as crucial to teaching ministry, and under that heading a single stanza neatly summarized the whole purpose of *The Christian Year*:

> Was not our Lord a little child,
> Taught by degrees to pray,
> By father dear and mother mild
> Instructed day by day?

A University don who published such verse was bound to come in for criticism, and however successful his little book – over ninety editions went to press in the author's lifetime, and by the end of the century sales in Britain and the United States of America had exceeded a million copies – Keble was easily embarrassed as the author of a best-seller. Although never subjected to ordeal by autograph hunters as was Peter Mayle in Provence, visitations to Hursley frustrated him in later life. Paralleling the popularity of Sir Edward Elgar when that celebrated musician composed 'Pomp and Circumstance', the march that did so much for patriotism in time of war, Keble's *Christian Year* found him a hall of fame. His work of spiritual pilgrimage and parochial *pietas* certainly went a long way to defend the faith in a wider arena. Nevertheless, in perspective, it has to be assessed in the context of a simple parish priest's dedication and devoted ministry.

In terms of that wider vision, the lure of Oxford remained a great temptation at least until Keble was married and well settled in as Vicar of Hursley with Otterbourne. So when, in 1827, Oriel had to elect a new Provost, several Fellows were convinced that they had in Keble a most promising candidate for Head of House. But although he certainly found the prospect pleasing, Keble convinced himself that responsibilities to a fast-fading father and invalid sister (Elizabeth suffered from a disability and was obliged to wear an artificial limb) ruled out any 'clear call'. The election was also to prove a quite extraordinary episode insofar as division among Keble's friends sadly damaged his cause. If Hurrell Froude was thus passionate in his mentor's support, Newman's critical acumen – '… we are not electing an angel but a Provost' – made clear a reservation that claimed Pusey for the opposition, a manoeuvre he later deplored with genuine and deep regret.

For its part, the University decided on Keble for the Chair of Poetry. His election secured a decade's intermittent link and some forty Latin lectures he began in the Hilary [Lent] Term, 1832. Although Oxford undoubtedly valued the tenure, Keble found it 'uphill work' and vastly preferred a Clarendon Press assignment at Cardwell's invitation. This was a new edition of the *Laws of Ecclesiastical Polity.* Undertaken at much the same time, the task had its frustrations, and it is no surprise to find so fastidious a scholar informing Coleridge (May, 1832) that preparations for the poetry lectures 'have hindered me sadly in my Hooker.' If that was in fact the case, such neglect was nothing compared with the way historians have subsequently ignored the importance of the edition in assessing Keble's overall development. For by affording understanding of a reformation that went beyond the sixteenth century to renew apostolic links with the Church Fathers, Hooker provided a timely antidote that kept Keble loyal to a Church of England Newman was soon to leave for Rome. Quite apart from the learned apparatus and footnote details which adorned his three-volume work, John Keble prefaced the *Hooker* which Oxford University Press published in 1841 with more than one hundred pages of analysis. These not only highlight the editor's respect for a 'great and venerable writer' he found 'full of instruction, piety and eloquence' (p. xxxviii), but also shed invaluable light on Keble's grasp of authority in the history of Christendom. Albeit in different ways, both Roman claims and Puritan threats provoked controversy to focus on 'the question of church authority'. As convinced as Hooker himself in very different times, Keble thus favoured a religious Settlement by which 'the episcopal succession had been so carefully retained in the Church of England' that 'both her liturgy and ordination services [were] strictly conformable to the rules and doctrines of antiquity' (p. lxvii). He certainly realized that the Elizabethan church had to keep faith with 'foreign protestant congregations', and felt this explained why 'Jewel, Whitgift, Bishop Cooper and others' made a less than whole-hearted 'appeal to Christian antiquity'. In short, when the Tridentine Fathers did their utmost to

> obtain express declaration ... that no prelate had any power in the Church, except what he received through the successors of St Peter ...;

and Puritan divines pressed the battle forward on another front, Keble marvelled that 'anything like apostolical succession is left among us'. That it was, he attributed to Hooker, or more precisely to Divine intervention, because it pleased 'God in His mercy to interfere' through the judicious Richard Hooker who insisted on 'the divine origin and indispensable necessity of the episcopal order' (p. lxxvi). *Sine qua non*, the doctrine was to be proudly proclaimed by the Tractarians. But a tale reminiscent of the Murgatroyd ancestral gallery in *Ruddigore* is relevant. It relates to an observation of H.P. Liddon who, when he passed a portrait of Bishop William Jackson in Christ Church Hall, regarded that well-fed, pompous prelate with the remark:

> Is it not strange, dear friend, to reflect that *that person* should have been chosen, in the Providential order, to connect Mr Keble with the Apostles?
>
> [Quoted in Battiscombe, *Keble*, p. 40]

In short, the *Preface* to *THE WORKS of that learned and judicious divine MR RICHARD HOOKER* contains many a clue to John Keble's churchmanship. Before the *Tracts* were written to be sure, one of their authors had detected approval in Hooker for many a 'high Church' practice:

> ... we seem to discern a kind of theory, silently pervading the whole language and system of the Church ... certain actions of the body, such as bowing at the name of Jesus ... turning towards the east in prayer ... forms of matter ... the cross and ring ... ceremonies ... offering ... material objects ... tithes ... a specimen of our whole property and holy-days, of our whole time ... by devout using to bring own a blessing on the whole.   [pp.c–ci]

In turn too, the reference to tithes provides more evidence of the acute sense of grievance Keble felt against state secularization of church property. His celebrated sermon had been preached at the Summer Assize in 1833, but the wording of the *Preface* clearly had Irish Church disestablishment in mind and declared church property sacrosanct.

At much this time he wrote poetry for the *British Magazine*, work he republished with Newman and others in *Lyra Apostolica* (1836). The little volume contained a whole Keble section – 'CHAMPIONS OF THE TRUTH' (pp. 198–204) – in which he vehemently attacked sacrilege, broken vows and spoliation at a period when he considered restoration more appropriate to the needs of Holy Church. Including the line:

CHRIST'S charter blurred with coarse usurping hand,

his 'Church and King' was intended to bring a nation to its knees and

In fear and grief for Church and King [to] pray. [p. 203]

By logical argument, the church establishment ought therefore to be hallowed as very much a public sacrifice, and such catholicism seen to be 'a channel of supernatural grace'. If he admitted Hooker's recognition of 'gradual but decisive change', Keble was equally clear that the apologist's care for a cause later championed by Archbishop Laud enabled the Anglican Church to continue 'at such a distance from Geneva' that made it 'near to primitive truth and apostolical order'. The alienation of things once hallowed he held to be impiety, for 'by Hooker's own account, prayers, tithes, festival days, church ceremonies, are so many sacrifices, truly and properly so called' (p. cvii).

By his own standards then, John Keble was no innovator but firm in his stance against Rome, Protestantism and rationalism, and a consistent defender of the faith and apostolical succession into the bargain. If he wrote *Tract IV – Adherence to the Apostolical Succession the Safest Course* (September, 1833) – to remember him solely in the context of Oxford notoriety is to undervalue the roots of Keble's commitment to a great tradition of essentially pastoral ministry. No wonder that, as well as its primary subject, the *Tract* itself contained a formidable array of argument ('On Alterations in the Prayer Book') intended to protect the *Book of Common Prayer* against 'profane innovation'. So the Keble who read papers on mysticism in the Early Fathers to Oxford's newly-formed Theological Society was himself a parish priest who regularly catechized parishioners away from the University. And the Keble who kept his balance to retain perspective and hold the Anglican line after the 'catastrophe' (R.W. Church) of Newman's *Tract XC* had already set out in his letter to Pusey (19 April 1829) a responsible concern for weaker brethren in times of crisis.

> The persons first to be considered in all religious publications, I should say, are the unlearned good sort of people: and if the learned have doubts, why should they not correspond among themselves till they find answers, instead of disturbing the devotions as well as the opinions of their quiet neighbours?   [H.P. Liddon, *Life of Pusey*, Vol. I. p. 167.]

Contact by correspondence certainly kept Keble in touch with the Oxford leadership of a gathering movement he had done so much to inspire. When University reform loomed, and 'the terrible secular spirit which has come over the place' threatened to overwhelm an Oxford founded for religion and good learning, he was the first to argue the traditionalist cause against a secular establishment in both state and church. *Lyra Apostolica* carried Keble's poem on 'The Creed' (CXLVII, p. 199) and deplored the University's failure to forward its proud device *Deus illuminatio mea:*

If waiting by the time-crowned halls,
Which nurtured us for CHRIST in youth,
We love to watch on the grey walls
The lingering gleam of Evangelic Truth; –
If to the spoilers of the soul,
Proudly we show our bannered scroll,
And bid them our old war-cry hear,
'GOD IS MY LIGHT; whom need I fear!'
How bleak, that hour, across our purpose high,
Sweeps the chill, damping shade of thoughtless years
    gone by!

In no sense the hermit of Hursley, Keble was thus well aware of any threat to the faith, and very much a defender of the mid-nineteenth-century Church of England. Although he did not always trust W.E.Gladstone, he respected the greatness of the man almost as much as he deplored the liberalism of 'poor Arnold'. For with Dr George Moberly a regular holiday resident in his parish, the Vicar of Hursley kept abreast of the wider educational scene and vastly preferred the traditional ethos of Winchester College to dubious advances at Rugby. Dr R.D. Hampden was another liberal to incur displeasure. This was not because of Hampden's elevation to the Regius Chair of Divinity when some had hoped for the appointment of Keble himself, but because the professor subsequently became Bishop of Hereford. Very much a three-headed Cerberus ready to oppose any intrusion from Rome, Protestantism or rationalism, Keble rallied in defence of his principles. For him the move of such a well-known liberal to the eminence of episcopal office was no way to defend the faith, and prompt reaction saw Keble at work on the organization of protest by petition.

Any three-dimensional Keble portrait must therefore take account of far more than what Newman once termed the man's 'remarkable looks, so earnest and so sweet'. For behind the 'quiet unpretending form' which so impressed the congregation that beheld him at the opening of St Augustine's College, Canterbury, in 1848, was the firm resolve that held uncompromising views. This was the Keble who saw fit to petition the Court of Arches and the Judicial Committee of the Privy Council at the time of the Gorham Judgement and the Colenso crisis; and this was the

Keble who played an important part in reviving Convocation in 1852. Newman had early observed that 'Keble does not like to give his opinion <u>on a sudden</u>' (9 June 1843). But give it he did, and whenever he sensed that danger threatened the Church as a divine institution, Keble was well able to land letters on the right desks. If there are many who criticize his failure to comprehend Britain's transformation as the first industrial nation, the almost credal commitment to Christian outreach is nowhere better displayed than in this extract of a letter to Coleridge in 1862:

> ... apropos ... the South Pacific and South African Letters
> which have been so much of our reading of late [they help]
> ... in a very special way to realize the Communion of Saints,
> and to feel (D.V.) one not only with the distant living, but
> with the holy dead.

Nearer home, another great strength of Keble's parish ministry was to be found in the care he took in the preparation of candidates for confirmation. Coleridge's *Memoir* set out information he gleaned from the good Vicar's faithful assistant, the Reverend Peter Young, 'in regard to this most important pastoral duty' (p. 509). Keble devoted at least a year to a flexible course he shared with his wife. This began in Lent, and after some '20 or 30 lessons in the whole' concluded with 'the administration of the Rite' by the bishop at the end of Lent the following year. Children, boys and girls, came to him for regular Sunday morning classes when they first read selected scriptures together before proceeding to study

> ... first the Baptismal Service, then the Catechism, then the
> Confirmation Service, and, lastly, the Office for Holy Com-
> munion.   [Ibid.]

He did not mix age groups, but like the best of experienced teachers took 'those of different ranks' separately. Of particular note was the trouble he took over more senior boys who, Young reported, 'usually came to him each alone every week'. And if they could not do so because of pressure of work, Keble did not scruple to visit such 'farm lads' individually 'however far off'. As Coleridge wrote, the Vicarage team were 'substantially the servants of the parishioners'; and if, in his seventies, Keble found Hursley folk 'sadly disappointing' and declared that neither 'true religion nor useful learning' appeared to flourish and abound, that by no means stopped him insisting to the last that church-going was a catholic privilege. Nor did a slight stroke, followed by recuperation away in Penzance where he had charge of his ailing wife, prevent Keble posting an address 'To the Newly-Confirmed at Hursley' in prayerful recollection that 'March 28, 1865' was a special 'day of such good beginnings' for the cate-chumens of his flock.

The conscientious care that sent this 'Address' to far-away parishioners is eloquent testimony to the Keble who happily referred to himself as a 'country parson'. When his recent biographer described her subject as 'a lazy author' [Battiscombe, p. 236], the judgement is questionable because Keble's humility of expression frequently obscured his brilliance as a fully-stretched writer. For as well as the witness of a full spectrum of correspon-dence in the cause, he was pre-occupied with numerous Oxford projects. For example, when barely settled at Hursley he joined Newman and Pusey to promote, in a *Library of the Fathers* (1836), an edition of influential patristic authorities before the sad East/West Schism of 1054. If Keble's primary understanding was a translation of Irenaeus (the posthumous publication seen through the press by Liddon appeared in *The Library* as Volume 42), the wider editorial rôle he had assumed proved particularly burden-some after Newman's defection to Rome. For he also busied him-self with 'Works of the Standard English Divines' published as *The Library of Anglo-Catholic Theology*. Originally priced by James Parker of Oxford, and 377 Strand, London, at £25 the set, this made available the complete writings of bishops like Andrewes, Cosin and Laud to rival a Cambridge University Press promotion (at the behest of the Parker Society) printing works of prominent sixteenth-century divines who, in their day, had reformed the English Church. Keble's contribution was a two-volume life of Bishop Thomas Wilson. Hitherto virtually neglected, the books exposed rich seams of material to careful mining, and revealed measured re-emphasis of spiritual values Keble cherished most. In fact, the 'Memoir' showed such sympathy for Wilson's patient ministry in adversity precisely because Keble, its 'compiler', prized a similar set of principles himself.

Reference to the young priest's move from parish work

> for the next five years as wholly taken up with the chap-
> laincy and tutorship, in his mind eminently pastoral
> employments ...

surely has an autobiographical quality, Keble finding a parallel in
his Oxford experience with the Wilson who taught James, Lord
Strange, the Earl of Derby's son, at Knowsley. If a vacancy in the
see of Sodor and Man might seem fortuitous because Derby, as
Lord of the Isle, chose to nominate his Chaplain, Keble made
much of Wilson's scruples when he first felt bound to decline
preferment. Equally, when King William III chose to urge his
acceptance, Keble noted that Wilson was 'Forced to accept the
Bishoprick of Man' (p. 77). And so from 27 November 1697, to
7 March 1755, when he died at 93 years of age in the 58th year
of his consecration, Thomas Wilson upheld the kind of godly
discipline in the Church that prompted eulogies from his biographer. Keble was, for example, quick to remind his reader that

> the old notion so generally received since Hooker's time, of
> the identity of Church and State in a Christian country, was
> far from being worn out in the Isle of Man. [Op. cit., p. 165]

It followed that Manx people were accountable to the spiritual
power, and Bishop Wilson faced many a crisis as he strove to
maintain 'ancient discipline' [p. 202]. Ideal material for his narrative, Keble naturally drew on mounting friction in numerous
causes célèbres between the bishop and the Island's governor to
illustrate the nature of catholic commitment. Wilson's 'Ecclesiastical Constitutions', approved by 'a Convocation of the Clergy at
Bishop's Court, the 3rd day of February, 1703' were accorded
high praise because of the provision they made

> for enforcing ... the whole edifying system of the Prayer-
> book.   [p. 206]

And in like manner Keble applauded the evident esteem in which
Bishop Wilson held excommunication as a salutary sanction, his
sympathetic <u>Form for Receiving Penitents</u> 'back into the

Church', and his notable composition of a *Catechism* with the Manx and English languages in parallel columns. Even the bishop's last will and testament Keble chose to uphold as a pastoral document; and it was with real feeling that,

> on the basis of his veneration for the Universal Church and unreserved faith in the Bible,

Keble found Thomas Wilson worthy of comparison with St Augustine of Canterbury in the history of the British Church. No wonder he saw fit to add that, on Wilson's demise, the Isle of Man was 'left to cool down to the ordinary temperature of the British dioceses at the time' [Vol. II, p. 970].

The holy, disciplined life of Thomas Wilson can certainly be likened to a mirror in which Keble came to see himself. The parallels are pointed and poignant and need little elaboration. When presented for the Doctorate in Divinity, *honoris causa*, Oxford University's Public Orator, William Wyatt, had described Thomas Wilson as 'a stout High Churchman'; and so by eighteenth-century standards he was. But a century later, the Tractarians extended that ideal to include the discipline of confession to a priest as a key constituent of pastoral ministry. Keble himself encouraged the practice, finding it of real value to regulate the moral standards of his flock. And if in his early Oxford days he had been Richard Hurrell Froude's spiritual director, he later became confessor to Edward Bouverie Pusey. In perspective, such discipline was carefully related to the eucharist, and it is no surprise to find that the title-page of John Keble's *On Eucharistical Adoration* (1859) carried a quotation from Thomas Wilson's *Sacra Privata*:

> GRANT, O LORD, that in reading Thy Holy Word, I may never prefer my private sentiments before those of the Church in the purely ancient times of Christianity.

Written in careful theological language as shrewd and subtle as the very best among the long series of Oxford *Tracts*, this is a work of exemplary piety and does much to inspire devotion. Like George Richmond's missing portrait, it conveys the elusive character of the author. For there is an enduring quality of Christian commitment in the life and thought of John Keble which combined with the gentle popular appeal of his verse and made no mean impact on the religion and society of Victorian England.

A KEBLE DEVOTIONAL TREASURY

Although he was himself tone deaf and quite unable to set devotional verse to music, a number of well-known hymns derive from stanzas published in *The Christian Year*. 'Blest are the pure in heart', a spiritual gem if ever there was one, has already been considered in the context of this Keble chapter. Together with 'New every morning is the love', 'Sun of my soul, Thou Saviour dear', and 'There is a book, who runs may read', such hymns possess precisely the kind of inspirational quality that commends them as classics for meditation. It was certainly John Keble's purpose to encourage his people to undertake regular routines of private prayer and daily worship, convinced as he was that such exposure to Scripture and the liturgy would inspire them to love and serve the Lord. If his hymns still retain that appeal, most of Keble's poetry has long been forgotten, sadly ignored by a Christendom addicted to literary criteria far removed from the Victorian ideal. This is unfortunate because, once he had been persuaded to publish the work, *The Christian Year* undoubtedly drew on a deep well-spring of personal piety, a spiritual resource with a timeless quality.

It can certainly claim attention here, for, as composed, Keble's work has a catechetical character and continues to afford prayerful readers memorable commentary on the seasons of Advent, Epiphany, Lent, Easter and Trinity. His treatment of Saints' Days, the sacraments, and occasional offices, clearly contains much of immortal worth. For Keble sought to enforce the discipline of the *Book of Common Prayer* Kalendar with meditations in popular verse and, in an unfolding series of stanzas, prompted wider meditation from his reader. The subject for Advent III – when Christ demanded to know what the multitude expected of John the Baptist (Matthew 11.7–9) – admirably illustrates the point:

> What went ye out to see
> O'er the rude sandy lea,

> Where stately Jordan flows by many a palm,
> Or where Gennesaret's wave
> Delights the flowers to lave,
> That o'er her western slope breathe airs of balm?

By adding poetic colour to the gospel text, Keble's use of simple rhyming stanzas adds a new dimension to the matter-of-fact gospel record. His aim and object – to persuade the prayerful believer of doctrinal truth beyond his vision – is clearly expressed in verse 4:

> Here may we sit, and dream
> Over the heavenly theme,
> Till to our soul the former days return;
> Till on the grassy bed,
> Where thousands once He fed,
> The world's incarnate Maker we discern.

As a whole, the poem is certainly a period piece; yet by recalling the ministry of Jesus in the Holy Land it inspires contemplation of the work of Christ as God incarnate. And throughout *The Christian Year*, Keble delves into doctrine to set forth many a mystery of the faith in the kind of meaningful verse that moved Victorian men and women. A poem for Good Friday is typical, for these lines convey the divine message not only of a mission accomplished in the Lord's incarnation, but also in the work of crucifixion:

> Is it not strange, the darkest hour
> That ever dawn'd on sinful earth
> Should touch the heart with softer power
> For comfort, than an angel's mirth?
> That to the Cross the mourner's eye should turn
> Sooner than where the stars of Christmas burn?

Keble may have made little impact on his congregations, for his faint, gentle voice often went unheard. But just as the pen is mightier than the sword, so the tender feeling of his poetry stirred souls to strong emotions in the faith. Love of the *Book of Common Prayer* imparted a genuinely scriptural quality to many a verse, and any reader dipping into *The Christian Year* is soon aware of a skilled use of biblical language. Frequent allusion to Nature also serves to enhance what Keble's ADVERTISEMENT termed 'that <u>soothing</u> tendency in the Prayer Book'. That he was himself deeply moved by natural phenomena, by flora and fauna, is clear enough, many a line and allusion showing reverence for Wordsworth's sensitive approach to life itself. His was a romantic age, and Keble the poet made every use of creation in his determination to reveal the Creator God. For that very reason he was sad to record a complete absence of scenic reference in the writings of Thomas Wilson, and made particular note of the fact that his otherwise model 'apostolic bishop' failed to comment, in writings, prayers or sermons, on 'anything which indicates a taste for the beautiful and picturesque in nature'.

Altogether unlike Wilson, Keble, despite a characteristic reserve present in all his poetry, was well nigh overwhelmed by the impact of Nature. On almost every page, *The Christian Year* contains graphic descriptions of the changing seasons, and these invariably symbolize heartfelt spiritual truth. Ponder the opening of the poem set for 'The Circumcision of Christ':

> The year begins with Thee,
> And Thou beginn'st with woe,
> To let the world of sinners see
> That blood for sin must flow.

Less direct, and far more in keeping with Keble's customary reticence in composition, are lines written for Advent II:

> Why then, in sad and wintry time,
> Her heavens all dark with doubt and crime,
> Why lifts the Church her drooping head,
> As though her evil hour were fled?
> Is she less wise than leaves of spring,
> Or birds that cower with folded wing?
> What sees she in this lowering sky
> To tempt her meditative eye?

After Easter too, despite the warmth generated by seasonal advance, an important feature of this stanza for Easter I is its chill reminder of the Passion:

> For oft, when summer leaves were bright,
> And every flower was bath'd in light,
> In sunshine moments past,
> My wilful heart would burst away
> From where the holy shadow lay,
> Where Heaven my lot had cast.

Again, a universe inspired by love is Keble's autumn theme for the Second Sunday after Trinity:

> The clouds that wrap the setting sun
> When Autumn's softest gleams are ending,
> Where all bright hues together run
> In sweet confusion blending:-
> Why, as we watch their floating wreath,
> Seem they the breath of life to breathe?
> To Fancy's eye their motions prove
> They mantle round the Sun for love.

Throughout too, words and lines indicate with clarity his familiarity with the flora and fauna of a

> ... land with milk and honey flowing.

A captured glimpse of 'oak and cedars' in the English countryside he can project on far-off Palestine.

> Nor may our household vine or fig-tree hide
> The broken arches of old Canaan's pride.

Yet it is the Keble who can hear and observe the rural charm he knew so well who is properly at home:

> The low sweet tones of Nature's lyre
> No more on listless ears expire,
> Nor vainly smiles along the shady way
> The primrose in her vernal nest,

> Nor unlamented sink to rest
> Sweet roses one by one, nor Autumn leaves decay.

Evident ornithological interest embraces not merely the commonplace 'Red-Breast', 'dove' and 'blackbird's song', but can recognize the 'wheeling kite's wild solitary cry'. And reference to the dawn chorus just as surely paints a poet's early-morning praise. Not for him the crude territorial claims of 'Nature red in tooth and claw', but:

> In the low chant of wakeful birds,
> In the deep weltering flood,
> In whispering leaves, these solemn words –
> 'God made us all for good.'

Miracles of light and scenic splendour also move Keble. Sunshine transforms the fields into 'emerald meadows gay', just as its impressive glare not only lingers on 'snow-clad peaks of rosy light' but when

> High towers the rainbow arch

crowns 'joyous greeting' with a fleeting shower.

It is brilliant refreshment and a further reminder of the universe as the firmament of a Creator God. For Keble constantly made use of images that likened the Church to the reflected Moon, just as for him shining stars symbolized Saints in Heaven, and trees in Eden represented Saints on earth. These stanzas written for 'Septuagesima Sunday' clearly express a credal affirmation of the Communion of the Saints and their faithful commitment to the cause:

> The saints above are stars in Heaven –
> What are the saints on earth?
> Like trees they stand whom God has given,
> Our Eden's happy birth.
>
> Faith is their fix'd unswerving root,
> Hope their unfading flower,
> Fair deeds of charity their fruit,
> The glory of their flower.

Throughout *The Christian Year* too, the Church's solemn task and sacred mission is a paramount concern of poetry written to confirm the faith. Made plain by a mention on 'St. John Baptist's Day', pastors of old taught the world to learn 'by their speaking lives', and none of them more than Peter. It might be supposed that, on 'St. Peter's Day', Keble would laud a Pontiff Prince of Apostles. In fact, although his last verse used the Petrine devices, the emphasis is Prayer-Book and pastoral, and one that clearly parallels the discipleship of Thomas Cranmer's collect:

> The pastoral staff, the keys of Heaven,
> To wield a while in grey-hair'd might,
> Then from his cross to spring forgiven,
> And follow JESUS out of sight.

Accordingly, whatever the metre – for Keble evidently enjoyed the challenge of ringing changes in metrical complexity – mission remained the poet's overriding concern. Vocational verse 'Addressed to Candidates for Ordination' for the 'Tuesday in Whitsun-Week' starts with this frustrated pastoral soliloquy:

> 'LORD, in Thy field I work all day,
> 'I read, I teach, I warn, I pray,
> 'And yet these wilful wandering sheep
> 'Within Thy fold I cannot keep'.

Much the same emphasis can be found when, on the 'Fifth Sunday after Trinity', the poet urged the perseverance conveyed in Christ's command to keep on fishing (Luke 5.5–6). Simon was rewarded for such mission with the miraculous draught of fishes, and in his turn Keble is convinced that obedience can bring comfort and stir the soul to renewed effort:

> So day by day and week by week,
> In sad and weary thought,
> They muse, whom God hath set to seek
> The souls His Christ hath bought.

That Keble acutely felt the solemn responsibilities of priesthood, he demonstrated in the loyal service rendered to his family, flock and wider public over many years of Christian ministry; and this primary purpose of the Church's foundation crowns his poem for the 'Sunday after Ascension':

> Apostles, Prophets, Pastors, all
> Shall feel the shower of Mercy fall,
> And starting at th'Almighty's call,
> Give what He gave,
> Till their high deeds the world appal,
> And sinners save.

In the full realization that the history of Christendom had not always adhered to such priority in the preaching of the gospel, a High Churchman's stanza (written for the old Service of Commemoration for Deliverance from 'Gunpowder Treason') shows Rome every compassion when urging the faithful that they

> Speak gently of our sister's fall:
> Who knows but gentle love
> May win her at our patient call
> The surer way to prove?

Fully persuaded that doctrinal divisions and human failure have sadly limited the divine initiative – for

> In the waste howling wilderness
> The Church is wandering still,
> Because we would not onward press
> When close to Sion's hill

– the ultimate impact of Keble's verse is one of hope. And it was that hope and faithful commitment in a life lived a day at a time which gave an inspirational quality to his verse.

After his stroke, as his own life ebbed away at Bournemouth, Keble's concern was only for his wife. A letter to Coleridge indicates not only the measure of that care but overall awareness of a worsening situation that, despite frequent resort to 'brandy and turtle soup ... by day and by night', brought the realization that Charlotte was barely able 'to go on from day to day'. Fearful for her, Keble felt 'no new or special anxiety ... for his own

health'. Yet even after he had suffered a second stroke and subsequent paralysis, he was constantly at Charlotte's bedside for a
whole week before he himself died. For his first biographer and
'DEAR KIND FRIEND', Keble's very posture 'showed the habitual
prayerfulness of his heart'; and in the *Memoir*, J.T. Coleridge
noted that 'the Lord's Prayer he uttered most commonly'. It was
a philosophy of life that had been given perspective long ago in
verse composed for Trinity XV:

> 'Live for to-day! to-morrow's light
> 'To-morrow's cares shall bring to sight,
> 'Go sleep like closing flowers at night,
> 'And Heaven thy morn will bless.'

Years of disciplined devotion brought Keble real strength and the
sanctity which was his greatest contribution to the Church. As
he phrased it himself in a stanza for 'Holy Communion':

> Fresh from th' atoning sacrifice
> The world's Creator bleeding lies,
> That man, His foe, by whom He bled,
> May take Him for his daily bread.

So regular attendance at the eucharist was central to what he
once termed 'Natural Piety'. When the essay *On Eucharistical
Adoration* appeared in 1859, Keble's 'Preface' apologized to the
reader for dealing with 'His most holy and ineffable Mystery ...
in a controversial way'. And a Treasury that attempts to bring
some insight to bear on *The Christian Year* cannot hope to
recapture the real Keble without some reference to devotional
aspects of that tract.

Towards the end of his life, John Keble had certainly tired of repeated references to *The Christian Year* – references to what he had
come to term '*that* book' – and some of his own words urge a
wider view on those who made judgements. 'I wish ... people, instead of paying me compliments about what they call my poetry,
would see if there is not some sense in my prose.' In a devotional
context, few priests in the great Christian tradition have offered
such simple guidance on the way to enter a church. Once inside:

we bow our knees and pray ... breathe a short prayer when
we begin reading our Bibles ... as we read to recollect ourselves ...

And if that approach is commended to those in church for private prayer or divine worship at a Prayer-book office, with the
eucharist in mind

> ... there must be special adoration and worship in the heart of
> everyone seriously believing a special, mysterious presence of
> Christ, God and man, expressed by the words, This is My
> Body special [because of ...] the greatness of the
> benefit offered; next, its being offered and brought home to
> each one personally and individually; thirdly, the deep con-
> descension and humiliation on the part of Him Who offers
> the benefit.

Or as he wrote later in the same tract:

> God's holy Word from beginning to end abounds in
> examples to ... prompt ... deeper and more intense adora-
> tion ... and ... the gift in the Holy Eucharist is Christ
> himself ... to change us after His image, "from glory to
> glory" ....

Keble's central theme of ' "Christ in us", not only Christ offered
for us; a "divine nature" set before us, of which we are to be
made "partakers" ' is developed by means of a striking devotional
analogy with the thief on the Cross who recognized Christ's
innocence:

> The deep veneration he had conceived for our Lord, as for
> an innocent Man receiving the due reward of such wicked
> deeds as his own, was rewarded with an adoring faith in Him
> as Lord and Judge of the whole world; and he became the
> first example of those who should be saved by the blessed
> Cross. And ... what is it that we remember specially, and
> on which we fix our mind's eyes in Holy Communion, but
> the same which he then saw with his bodily eyes? – the
> Body and Blood of Christ, i.e. Christ Himself, offered up

by himself for that thief and for each one of us? And if he
worshipped, and was blessed, why not we?

Scripture provided the basic ground of Keble's argument, and
very much in line with the kind of reasoning he had used in the
Tracts themselves, he declared the *onus probandi* to lie with his
opponents:

> According to all sound rules of argument, it is rather our
> right to call upon those who censure the practice [viz. the
> practice of adoration] to cite some text forbidding it, than
> it is theirs to call upon us for one expressly enjoining it.

And in lines reminiscent of the rationale behind much medieval
piety and devotion, there comes this purple passage:

> From the beginning it has been understood that the blessed
> Angels are ever at hand attending on the Christian altar, tak-
> ing part in our hymns and thanksgivings, and wafting upwards
> in a mysterious way all our dutiful prayers and offerings.

Irrespective of the controversy behind it, many took heart
when reading such passages of Keble's prose. Whatever he wrote
came to be prized for a devotional content of real potential in
pastoral application. Even John Mason Neale, averse as he was to
the new-lamps-for-old approach that neglected long centuries of
traditional worship, warmed to Keble's skill as a hymn writer [cf.
Michael Chandler, *The Life and Work of John Mason Neale*
(Gracewing, Leominster, 1995), p. 185]. If there is a secret
ingredient in such successful compositions, it is surely to
be found in the fact that John Keble drew on enduring
Christian truths. Whether these were expressed in poetry or
prose mattered little, for when set out with such sincerity of
purpose, his writings could not fail to cheer and uplift the hungry souls he fed in a lifetime of dedicated ministry. Although
unmistakably the work of a Victorian poet, these 'Evening' lines
from *The Christian Year* enshrine the ageless appeal of the
simplest devotional instruction, just as they form a perfect hymn
and profound homily:

> Abide with me from morn till eve,
> For without Thee I cannot live:
> Abide with me when night is nigh,
> For without Thee I dare not die.

No wonder that a Hursley parishioner who had experienced John Keble's ministry recorded this cherished memory:

> Father and I do read *The Christian Year* every Sunday, and it do bring him out to us more than we knew even when he was alive.

Chapter 9

JOHN HENRY
NEWMAN

and

'Firmly I believe and truly'

1 Firmly I believe and truly
   God is Three, and God is One;
   And I next acknowledge duly
   Manhood taken by the Son.

2 And I trust and hope most fully
   In that Manhood crucified;
   And each thought and deed unruly
   Do to death, as he has died.

3 Simply to his grace and wholly
   Light and life and strength belong,
   And I love supremely, solely,
   Him the Holy, him the Strong.

4 And I hold in veneration,
   For the love of him alone,
   Holy Church as his creation,
   And her teachings as his own.

5 Adoration ay be given,
   With and through the angelic host,
   To the God of earth and heaven,
   Father, Son, and Holy Ghost.
                           Amen.

Strange to relate, contaminated Neapolitan oysters indirectly resulted in the composition of one of the most valued hymns in the English language. For, laid low with a serious attack of typhoid, John Henry Newman's Mediterranean tour nearly ended in disaster on the island of Sicily. Between 6 and 26 May 1833, he lay at death's door, inbuilt stamina alone enabling the patient to survive a primitive physician's remedies which did Newman almost more harm than the fever itself. Yet survive he did, and as he returned home, to be becalmed on board a cargo vessel transporting oranges from Palermo to Marseilles, it was a convalescent and trustful Newman who penned the truly inspirational 'lines, "Lead kindly light" … which (in the modest wording of *Apol[ogia Pro Vita Sua]*) have since become well known' (p. 30).

Three simple stanzas not only set in focus the way the God of the Old Testament provided by day a cloudy, and by night a fiery, pillar to lead Moses and the Israelites through the wilderness; but also invested Newman's verse with pregnant autobiographical symbolism. Conscious of the hymn's all-embracing nature, Louis Bouyer once chose to describe it as a 'long soliloquy' [*Newman, His Life and Spirituality* (1958), p. 149]. In the crowded context of Newman's Oxford career the judgement is both pertinent and imaginative. From the mid-1820s, College and University affairs – to make but *en passant* reference to the tragic early death of a favourite sister – had racked Newman close to breaking point. The scrupulous Tutor of Oriel was a natural Examiner for Schools in 1827; and on the election of Hawkins as Provost of his College, Newman was an obvious successor as Vicar of St Mary's, to be instituted and inducted to serve Oxford's University Church on 14 March 1828. Otherwise, Hawkins and Newman had their differences. When Sir Robert Peel deemed it expedient to revise his views on Roman Catholic emancipation, he inevitably tempered his support for church establishment. It was a situation that dictated responsible resignation from his parliamentary seat; and when the former Home Secretary then conscientiously sought a new mandate from his Oxford constituents, Newman's circle decided to oppose him while, for his part, Hawkins argued for Peel's re-election. Oriel's fellowship found itself deeply divided in consequence, and Newman indicated, in a letter of 1830, something of the tension that made

College politics

> a state of constant bickerings – of coldness, dryness, and donnishness on his [the Provost's] part, and of provoking insubordination and petulance on mine.
>
> [Ker, Gornall & Tracey (Eds.), *Letters and Diaries* (Oxford) II, 202.]

Worse, when Hawkins refused to assign new pupils to him, Newman's 'duties of Public Tutor' gradually lapsed as his men proceeded to degrees; and had he not busied himself in study of the Early Church Fathers 'with intensity and passion', likewise finding further fulfilment in a care for kinsfolk that moved his family from Brighton to live near him at Rose Hill, such a series of shocks could have destroyed him. As it was, the earth certainly shook. The year 1830 witnessed numerous revolutionary movements in continental Europe; and with the English Parliament the prey of liberal agitation in an acrimonious prelude to the great Reform Bill, it seemed as if the whole social and political fabric of the nation was under threat, and ecclesiastical stability itself at the mercy of *demos*. So when in December, 1832, Robert Hurrell Froude, a venerable Archdeacon of Totnes fearful for the increasingly consumptive condition of his son Richard, a young Oriel colleague whom Newman greatly admired, invited Newman to take a voyage and enjoy the winter warmth of the Mediterranean, such generosity was so well timed as to be irresistible.

It certainly proved a magical break. The Bay of Biscay blessed the party with calm seas and something of a prosperous voyage; and careful letters home logged the whole expedition. To view ancient sites and have time for reflection was an added bonus, so many a peaceful interlude in the progress from Portugal to Corfu, to Malta, Messina, Naples and Rome itself, served to inspire a full range of poetry. As he waited on home events like the worsening situation in Ireland too, distance gave perspective and Newman sent monthly contributions to the *British Magazine* – work later collected together with verse from Keble, Froude, Bowden, Wilberforce and Williams in *Lyra Apostolica* – a periodical founded in 1832 to resist Liberal interference with the church. When Harriett and Jemima informed their brother of 'all the mad schemes of Government, and of the despoiling of the poor Irish

Church' (21 Febuary. 1833), John Henry's published rejoinder gained wide circulation in a period when verse was a particularly appealing medium. In *Persuasion*, Jane Austen had noted that 'we are living through a great age for poetry'; and as if to make good use of that realization, here in verse was an effective commentary that contrasted early acceptance of Christian values with the way contemporary politicians lost no opportunity to marginalize the church establishment. Newman's mood is clearly indicated by the first, third and last stanzas of a poem that later found a place in *Lyra Apostolica* as part of a section headed 'Profaneness' and numbered CXXX with the title 'SACRED SEASONS' (pp. 174–5):

> WHEN first earth's rulers welcomed home
> The Church, their zeal impressed
> Upon the seasons, as they come,
> The image of their guest.
>
> ...
>
> But craving wealth, and feverish power,
> Such service now discard:
> The loss of one excited hour
> A sacrifice too hard!
>
> ...
>
> Where shall this cease? must Crosiers fall,
> Shrines suffer touch profane,
> Till, cast without His vineyard wall,
> The Heaven-sent Heir is slain.

When the Froudes took their leave in April, Newman stayed on to explore more of Italy. It was a mixed experience of peaks and troughs as ancient sights stirred his very soul, just as in Sicily sickness well nigh ended his days. No wonder such striking imagery shines forth from 'Lead, kindly Light'. For deeply moved to analyse events, and with time to consider his position, Newman knew he not only had 'work to do in England', but was also fully assured that even if the 'night is dark', he would find guidance. Such commitment was crucial for all that awaited him in Oxford and beyond:

So long thy power hath blest me, sure it still
Will lead me on.

Brimful of confidence, Newman noted that his 'health and strength came back with such a rebound, that some friends at Oxford, on seeing me, did not well know that it was I' [*Apol.* p. 43]. Shortly after his return on 9 July 1833, John Keble's Assize Sermon on the theme of national apostasy – which Newman 'considered ... as the start of the religious movement of 1833' [Ibid., p. 35] – quickened the pace of events. Briefly these centred on his own preaching from the pulpit of St Mary the Virgin, a teaching ministry which focused the Vicar's anxiety and concern to know how, or even if, it was still possible to come to terms with the Erastian policies of a government that had virtually transformed the established church into a sect. As he chose to express it:

the Apostolical Church in this realm is henceforth only to stand, in the eye of the State, as <u>one</u> <u>sect</u> <u>among</u> <u>many.</u>

The search for catholic purity was on, but, in the 1830s at least, Newman was clear, as the dedication of the second volume of *P[arochial and] P[lain] S[ermons]* to J.W. Bowden ('Feb. 21st, 1835') testifies

that the English Church amid many defections still holds her influence over an attached and zealous laity. [Op. cit., p. v]

And in the sermons themselves, Newman indicated again and again that worship was worship according to the *Book of Common Prayer*; and in particular, he preached '... on St Andrew' (Sermon I expounding John 1.40) of:

the Psalms ... the prayer-book of the Church ever since they were written.   [Op. cit., II, p. 7]

For him praise to the Almighty was best rendered in hallowed, traditional language. This gave priority to the Psalms, and if hymns figured for Newman, they did so largely as canticles and creeds. A Whitsunday Sermon on 'The indwelling Spirit' [*P.P.S.*, II, No. xix, p. 231] made clear to the University Church congregation that, for their Vicar, worship was to be seen as an offering to God:

> We must renew our confession, and seek afresh our absolution day by day, before we dare to call upon God as 'our Father', or offer up Psalms and Intercessions to Him.

And as the very model of catholic traditionalism, Newman reverenced the Athanasian Creed as the classic hymn of commitment and confession in words from another of his *Parochial and Plain Sermons* (on 'The Gospel, a Trust committed to us', Vol. II, p. 270) that shows his high regard for it as

> the most precise and systematic of all the creeds ... [which is] ... rather, as the form of it shows, a hymn of praise to the Eternal Trinity.

In another of his perceptive judgements, Louis Bouyer declared 'the real world of John Henry Newman' to be 'the world of the Scriptures'; and his view enjoyed particular validity in Newman's conviction that, to secure 'His Divine work in our hearts', the Church should never cease to make good use of

> the Psalms ... and ... the Creeds; all of which have become sacred, from the memory of saints departed who have used them, and whom we hope one day to meet in heaven.
>
> [Op. cit., I, No. xx, p. 263 and 269]

He found '... the *Te Deum* (with the creed) ... especially suitable in divine worship' and 'in as much as they kindle and elevate the religious affections', they are 'hymns of praise and thanksgiving'. Then too, coupled with his conviction that 'the Jewish Psalter has been the standard book of Christian devotion from the first down to this day' [III, p. 184], Newman's preaching made regular reference to 'the injunctions of the Apostles', namely those words of James – 'Is any afflicted? let him pray. Is any merry? let him sing psalms' – and Paul, who urged 'speaking to each other in psalms, and hymns, and spiritual songs'. Both insisted on the practice of sacred Psalmody as a duty, an obligation Newman did not hesitate to proclaim.

The priority he gave worship at the time he masterminded the celebrated *Tracts for the Times* is rarely recognized. But those who take time to delve into the veritable treasure trove of sermons preached at St Mary's in these same years can only marvel at the way Newman's spiritual stature increased even when he was most in doubt and turmoil at the state of the English ecclesiastical establishment. For by whatever standards he assessed it, Newman now found ambiguity in the Church of England. At best it seemed to represent a compromise between protestantism and acceptable catholic tradition. As he pursued his study of the Early Fathers, he tried to focus apostolic authority for the break with Rome, if only because he needed to convince himself that English Christianity possessed primitive integrity. Perhaps Cranmer's Reformation could be justified as a determined attempt to banish banality in worship – for rituals that venerated images, prayed for the dead, and honoured the Roman popes were unknown in the primitive church and surely inclined to a practice not far removed from idolatry? In a scrupulous search for compromise, Newman went to great lengths to conceive a *Via Media* of the kind that conducted a steady course between Roman error and a reformation doctrine like justification by faith *alone*. He was convinced that neither had support in Scripture or the Fathers, and that both needed a renewal of pristine purity to recapture the heavenly vision of true catholicism.

In his *Lectures on the Prophetical Office of the Church viewed relatively to Romanism and Popular Protestantism* (1837), Newman was fearful of criticism that he merely forwarded a paper 'theory' with 'no existence out of books'. His classic statements remain relevant, for as he wrote:

> Protestantism and Popery are real religions ... but the *Via Media*, has never existed except on paper
>
> [op. cit. p.20]

And again

> What is this but to fancy a road over mountains and rivers, which has never been cut? When we profess our *Via Media*, as the very truth of the Apostles, we seem to be mere

antiquarians or pedants, amusing ourselves with illusions or learned subtilties, and unable to grapple with things as they are. [op. cit. pp.20–21]

Regardless of such objections, he strove valiantly to give substance to 'the third system' in a bold attempt to determine 'whether what is called Anglicanism ... is capable of being professed'. At first he was clear that such a 'third system' did exist '... in all its parts, in the writings of our divines, and in good measure is in actual operation'. After all, evidence enough came to hand in a real 'inventory of our treasures', in the pastoral practice of worship and preaching the scriptures. But if Newman warmed to the Caroline divines, and especially to Lancelot Andrewes, further patristic study obliged him to face up to the strength of argument from the history of heresy and schism in the Early Church. For by analogy he found it

difficult to make out how the Eutychians or Monophysites were heretics, unless Protestants and Anglicans were heretics also; difficult to find arguments against the Tridentine Fathers which did not tell against the Fathers of Chalcedon; difficult to condemn the Popes of the sixteenth century, without condemning the Popes of the fifth. [*Apol.*, p.115]

Already the end was in sight as, *en passant*, something of an anti-litany Newman set out in what he headed a 'History of my Religious opinions' pronounced 'anathema to a whole tribe of Cranmers, Ridleys, Latimers and Jewels!' [*Apol.*, p. 116]. And with the publication of *Tract XC* (February, 1841), he highlighted a principled objection, namely that:

It is a duty which we owe both to the Catholic Church, and to our own, to take our reformed confessions in the most Catholic sense they will admit.

Despite the stark relief of such a setting, the Anglican bishops refused to recognize the implications of Newman's argument and dwelt instead on the debt the Church owed those who framed its formularies. If Newman then chose to withdraw from the glare of the footlights and leave his centre-stage rôle for the wings, his was no theological recantation but simply physical removal to the outskirts of his parish beyond Iffley. There, at Littlemore, with the fine personal library he brought with him from Oriel, he devoted himself, in the bosom of his family, to a ceaseless round of pastoral duties among a community of agricultural workers. Well aware that his brilliant Oxford career was over, these were years of gradual withdrawal as Newman prepared himself for a new allegiance. He had experienced conversion to God in his early evangelical days; and he was now to become a convert to Holy Church. Yet this was no simple step, for in some judicious words of Father C.S. Dessain, 'Becoming a Catholic in mid-nineteenth-century England was graver than becoming a Communist in the mid-twentieth century'. 'Kindly light' nevertheless led Newman on through sadness in 'the parting of friends', until a resolute line in a family letter of 15 March 1845, informed his sister Jemima of his conviction that

I am in a schismatical Church.

That sorry state lasted no longer than October when he was received by the Italian Passionist, Father Dominic. If fulfilment lay ahead in 'the one ark of salvation' that was the Catholic church, Newman never forgot his Anglican past. Far from it, for in 1850, *Lectures* he published *On certain Difficulties felt by Anglicans in submitting to the Church Catholic* viewed her from St Peter's bark as 'silent, ambiguous, unsympathetic, sullen, and even hostile'. There is even something of a contemporary ring about his insight and vision of a Church of England with

ritual mutilated, sacraments defective, precedents inconsistent, articles equivocal, canons obsolete, courts Protestant, and synods suspended; scouted by the laity, scorned by men of the world, hated and blackened.

But with the 'Branch Church' behind him at last, Newman flourished in the appealing tree of life at Rome where, with 'no bond but that of love', he was grounded in the ways of St Philip Neri before the return to England as an ordained priest of the Catholic Church in 1848. It was a labour of love he set up in the Birmingham Oratory that same year, with a second London house founded in 1849. Renowned for their life of prayerful meditation and teaching and skilled as confessors, those who practised the precepts of the saintly sixteenth-century Florentine were to be mirrored in Father Newman's ministry, their ideals nowhere better expressed than in two verses of a hymn or 'Song' entitled 'St Philip in his School' he included in his *Verses on Various Occasions* (CLXX, 306):

> This is the Saint of gentleness and kindness
> Cheerful in penance, and in precept winning;
> Patiently healing of their pride and blindness,
> > Souls that are sinning.
> > > …
> Thus he conducts by holy paths and pleasant,
> Innocent souls, and sinful souls forgiven,
> Towards the bright palace where our God is present,
> > Throned in high heaven.

Some years before too, in May and June 1865, a remarkable poem Newman had published in a new Catholic literary magazine *The Month*, sought to popularize the Roman doctrine of *purgatory*. Entitled *The Dream of Gerontius*, his cantos were themselves popularized even more when set to music by Sir Edward Elgar in 1900, a decade or so after their author, by then raised as John Henry, Cardinal Newman, had been laid to rest. From that setting stem two hymns prominently featured in the choral work: that of Gerontius himself, 'Firmly I believe …'; and that performed by the Choir of Angelicals, 'Praise to the Holiest in the height'. If the latter is surely one of the most sublime in any hymnal, the former deserves to be better known because of a series of stanzas Newman composed to illustrate the Catholic creed he had for so long struggled to believe, and at last held dear as the summit of sacred achievement.

The setting and subject of *The Dream of Gerontius* are somewhat remote when 'Firmly I believe and truly' is sung by a congregation in the regular round of Christian worship. But a background sketch can incomparably assist both the understanding and feed the meditation of faithful people. The Greek word *gerontion* means 'frail old man'; and in Newman's poetic vision the subject of *The Dream* is death itself. In short, the canvas is one that first depicts the homecall of Gerontius; and then portrays in a setting of angels and demons, the soul of the departed as he contemplates in turn purgatory, judgement and the 'After Life' of the 'Holiest in the height'.

Near to death, Gerontius is conscious that 'Jesu' and 'Maria' are calling him; and he asks that his friends pray for him as

> ... a visitant
> Is knocking his dire summons at my door,
> The like of whom, to scare me and to daunt,
> Has never, never come to me before:
> So pray for me, my friends, who have not
> strength to pray.

And it is then that, as his friends pray, and in turn invoke the prayers of 'Holy Mary', 'All holy Angels', 'All Apostles' and 'Disciples', as also 'Innocents', 'Martyrs', 'Confessors', 'Hermits', 'Virgins' and 'Saints', that Gerontius rouses his fainting soul to play the man and meet his God. It is thus in the context of an outpoured Litany that he makes the bold confession that has become this noble hymn of faith. Like the best of homilies, its theme is simple, and its message profound: simple in language, profound in doctrine. For in a mere twenty lines all the principal catholic emphases of Christian faith are affirmed.

The first verse is one of conviction in the Trinity and recognition of Christ's incarnation, the frail humanity of Gerontius clearly appreciating the meaning of the Lord's manhood as he meditates on eternity. Next the practical impact of the crucifixion comes into focus as the Christian's enduring hope – all unworthy thoughts and deeds receiving sentence of death 'as He had died'. The third stanza credits 'light and life and strength' simply and wholly 'to His grace', likewise describing the response of love to a Lord Who is Himself the personification of the 'Holy' and the 'Strong'.

The fourth verse is perhaps most characteristic of all, for here Newman stresses the rôle of Holy Church as the teaching authority of the ascended Christ. It is a stanza that embraces the wide range of the author's spiritual development and experience – the John Henry Newman who, long ago, had left the openness of the Church of England to submit himself to the defined

doctrines and discipline of Rome. Those doctrines he held, as
the hymn phrased it

> ... in veneration
> For the love of Him alone.

In short, the Christian soul about to go forth upon such a journey must not doubt but set out in confidence.

Although *The Dream of Gerontius* received many good reviews,
on 15 June 1865, the parish priest at Ryde, Isle of Wight,
Father John Telford, wrote to Newman complaining that,
although her name was mentioned,

> I should like to have seen our Dear and Blessed Lady appear
> ... [for, as Telford chose to express it] ... she must have a share
> ... in the salvation of every predestined soul, in as much as she
> had her <u>very own</u> share in our Lord's Passion.

In reply, Newman, although thanking the good priest of Ryde
for his kind letter, shrewdly observed that

> ... you do me too much honour, if you think I am to see
> in a dream every thing that *has* to be seen in the *subject*
> dreamed about. I have said what I saw. Various spiritual
> writers see various aspects of it; and under their protection
> and pattern I have set down the dream as it came before the
> sleeper. It is not my fault, if the sleeper did not dream more.
> Perhaps something woke him. Dreams are generally frag-
> mentary. I have nothing more to tell.

Conveying both humour and a modicum of irritability, the
response is important for spotlighting the simplicity of the
Gerontius vision. Newman was clearly concerned that it should
be merely a partial vision ... a vision beheld 'through a glass
darkly' so to state. Truth claims may have been crucial for one
well 'able to recognize facts as facts, and ... not afraid for the
Catholic religion' (words he addressed to the Jesuit, Father Coleridge). But if the cause was pastoral, the clarity of that vision
could be blurred; and again for the guidance of his Jesuit friend,
Newman went on record with the significant judgement that

ridicule is not the weapon for those who desire to save souls. It repels and hardens.

It was therefore *adoration*, not ridicule, that the Superior of the Birmingham Oratory used as the way to promote religion; and in the last lines of his confession Gerontius firmly placed pain and fear behind him to exchange all earthly ties for rapt adoration in the language of doxology:

> Adoration aye be given,
> With and through the angelic host,
> To the God of earth and heaven,
> Father, Son and Holy Ghost.

And a dramatic moment is reached in Newman's truly 'Dramatic poem' as Gerontius commends his soul

> ... Into Thy hands,
> O Lord, into Thy hands ...

Hitherto daunted at the very least by the mere mention of Purgatory as a place for purifying souls, the Protestant public of Victorian England was intrigued to read about the journeying of the soul described in *The Dream*. And if a recent biographer has noted that 'Newman was surprised at its enormous success', he would no doubt have been all the more encouraged to learn that a Pope would later set forth on his own journey but ten days after hearing Sir John Barbirolli conduct what Sir Edward Elgar's lively music made of that same poem. For Elgar even annotated his score with capitals more customarily found in Bach:

A. M. D. G.
(*Ad maiorem Dei gloriam*)

Just as having given the greater glory to the Almighty, the composer added in a postscript words of conviction that

This is the best of me.

Like Newman himself, Elgar held the Catholic faith of Rome; and together their vivid commentary in words and music on the mystery of death, Divine judgement and entry into purgatory has rarely been paralleled. The experience of Gerontius was set down for sharing; and this hymn, albeit now given a number of different tunes, continues to serve as a powerful homily. For above all it spells out an uncomplicated profession of faith in the Triune God; in the saving merits of Christ; and in the teachings of Holy Church. For Newman too, these were no mere heads of proposals, but a veritable trinity of credal conviction that enabled the Angel to bear home to his Creator the soul of Gerontius:

> My work is done,
> My task is o'er,
> And so I come,
> Taking it home,
> For the crown is won:
> ALLELUIA
> For evermore.

A NEWMAN DEVOTIONAL TREASURY

Better known than 'Firmly I believe and truly' are John Henry Newman's:

> Praise to the holiest in the height

and

> Lead, kindly Light, amid the encircling gloom.

But if he is best remembered for magisterial prose, there is much of spiritual worth not only in *Lyra Apostolica* but also in the latter collection of *V[erses] on V[arious] O[ccasions]*.

Dedicated to Edward Badeley 'from the Oratory, 21 Dec., 1867' and published by Burns, Oates and Company of London, the volume was prefaced by a disclaimer of 'surprise as well as ... gratification' that 'the pleasure of verse-making' has been esteemed by the public. In fact, the best of Newman's contribution to *Lyra Apostolica* (and of the 179 poems, he contributed 109 himself) was reprinted in the 1867 volume 'to bring together into one effusions I have ever considered ephemeral' (p. v).

'Solitude' well represents both, and in many ways spans the years between Newman's youth and the mature believer whose faith came to inspire *Gerontius*. A poem of praise, its lines overflow with thanksgiving for life itself; and in an acknowledgement of the sovereignty of God, the Spirit moves mere mortals to song:

> The Angels' hymn – the sovereign harmony
> That guides the rolling orbs along the sky –
> And hence perchance the tales of saints who view'd
> And heard Angelic choirs in solitude.
> By most unheard – because the earthly din
> Of toil or mirth has charms their ears to win.
> <u>Alas</u> for man! he knows not of the bliss,
> The heaven that brightens such a life as this.

A conspicuous feature of Newman's early poetry compared with the verse he wrote as an Oratorian relates to his attitude to Rome. Poems he described as 'contemporaneous, on their first appearance in 1833, with the "Tracts for the Times", and the "Church of the Fathers" ... had one object' [*Lyra Apostolica*, p. vi]. They were composed to set in focus what he considered

> to be Apostolical or Primitive Christianity, at a time when
> its principles, doctrines, discipline, usages, and spirit
> seemed, in the length and breadth of the Anglican Communion, to be well nigh forgotten.

It is an emphasis that can clearly illustrate Newman's determined attempt to recover catholic truth. But because it is critical of the Church of Rome, it must also be viewed as the meditations of a poet feeling his way towards what he later termed the 'third system' or *Via Media*. Typical of the trend is verse Newman wrote on the Eucharist and Penance, two key sacraments often sadly neglected in the parish ministry of early nineteenth-century Anglican clergy. Altogether superb in its unquestioning acceptance of Real Presence doctrine is the poem Newman composed on

'The Eucharist'. Placed under the section heading 'Life Immortal', and numbered XXXIII (p. 37), it includes the telling lines:

> I will not say with these, that bread and wine
> Have vanished at the consecration prayer;
> Far less with those deny that ought divine
>   ... is hidden there.
> Hence disputants! The din, which ye admire,
> Keeps but ill measure with the Church's choir.

Again, in the section on 'Remorse', a poem entitled 'Terror' (VIII) includes these lines in its concluding stanza (pp. 8–9):

> 'Peace cannot be, hope must be thine;
> I can but lift the Mercy-sign.
> This wouldst thou? It shall be!
> Kneel down, and take the word divine,
> ABSOLVO TE.'

As for confidence in Holy Church, it is clear that the Newman who sought to recall the 'Scattered Sheep' (cf. the section 'Dissent' and poem CIII, p. 137) with lines of welcome appropriate to the return of the prodigal:

> Wanderers! come home! when erring most
> Christ's Church aye kept the faith, nor lost
> One grain of Holy Truth:

nevertheless kept a wary eye on Rome. So much is clear from verse included in the section headed 'Disappointment', and in particular the second stanza of poem CLXXII ('Rome'):

> ... a mingled throng besets the breast
> Of bitter thoughts and sweet;
> How shall I name thee, Light of the wide West,
> Or heinous error-seat?
> O Mother erst, close tracing Jesus' feet!
> Do not thy titles glow

> In those stern judgement-fires, which shall complete
> Earth's strife with Heaven, and ope the eternal woe?

Under the same section as if to heighten the poet's 'Disappointment', is Newman's sonnet on 'The Cruel Church' (CLXXIII
p. 239). If its opening lines pose a question of searching
rhetoric:

> O MOTHER Church of Rome! why has thy heart
> Beat so untruly towards thy northern child?

the rest of the sonnet is as strangely allusive in its complexity as
its conclusion is hard-hitting:

> ... And now thou sendest foes,
> Bred from thy womb, lost Church! to mock the throes
> Of thy free child, thou cruel-natured Rome!

A fascinating mix of misgiving and the saddest memories of lost
unity, Newman's foreboding nevertheless embraced a fervent
hope expressed in the opening line of an aptly-named poem on
'The Good Samaritan' (CLXXIV, p. 240):

> O THAT thy creed were sound!

Very much a Mediterranean meditation when by himself he visited remote churches in Italy and Sicily, this was verse written
'on a foreign shore' where:

> The home-sick solitary finds a friend.

Of central significance, the credal emphasis of this early composition explains in such a simple reference Newman's whole
approach to spirituality. Opposed to extempore prayer as 'irrev-
erent' [*P.P.S.*, I, p. 260], it was Scripture that moved him to
praise in a hallowed tradition of Christian worship, particularly
in the formal context of canticles, psalms and creed. There must
be no disobedience to the heavenly vision, and faithful folk were
taught to regard psalm singing as a devotional response. In this

sense, Newman goes back beyond Isaac Watts, his love of the Psalms almost reviving Hebrew worship in a determined bid to recover catholic spirituality. If he nevertheless wrote a number of fine hymns at the Oratory, apart from compositions in praise of the Blessed Virgin, St Philip Neri and St Michael, these were largely translations of the Roman and Parisian Breviaries for use in the daily offices of Prime, Terce, Sext, None, Vespers and Compline.

After reservations about Rome in earlier days, Newman's compositions about Mary – in particular the 'Song' he wrote for Candlemas in 1849, and verse for both 'The Month of Mary' and 'The Queen of Seasons' ('Songs' penned at 'The Oratory, 1850') – more than made amends for a neglected observance. The last verse of his Candlemas 'Song' [*V. on V.O.*, CLVIII, pp. 275–6] conveys a balance to be found in Martin Luther's 'little exposition' of *Magnificat* (1521), Newman taking care to relate the rôle of Mary to the uniqueness of Christ:

> And still, though Candlemas be spent
> And Alleluias o'er,
> Mary is music in our need,
> And Jesus light in store.

But with 'The Month of Mary' (CLX, p. 280), and especially in the second stanza:

> But Mother maid, thou dost not fade;
> With stars above thy brow,
> And the pale moon beneath thy feet,
> For ever throned art thou,

there is no such caution, even if it ought to be recalled that iconography and verse praised Elizabeth I in very similar terms at the end of the sixteenth century. With his 'Queen of Seasons' too, Newman's understanding has certainly developed way beyond the reference of a Whitsuntide sermon in far-off Oxford days with its allusion to 'St Mary's hymn, which we read every evening' [*P.P.S.*, Vol. VI, No. XXII, p. 314], and which he chose to identify as a shadow or outline of that Kingdom of the Spirit, which was then coming on the earth.

At the same time, it is unlikely that he changed his view of the centrality of Psalmody to catholic spirituality when he stressed that:

> the Book of Psalms, which, if any part of the Old Testament, belongs immediately to Gospel times, and is the voice of the Christian Church ... [to remain a] ... sacred book of devotion from beginning to end.   [Ibid, p. 315]

The theme of wisdom and love that undergirds the paeon of praise with which, in *The Dream*, the Choir of Angelicals ushers the soul of Gerontius forward to a kind of Heavenly-Presence Chamber is of infinite worth for meditation. Here too words from another Oxford sermon come to mind when Newman depicted 'St Paul himself, that great Apostle ... caught up into the third heaven' where he 'heard the hymns of Angels' [*P.P.S.* III, pp. 329–330]. These verses, for example, dwell on the redeeming purpose of love in the Divine and the re-assurance it affords humanity:

> O Loving wisdom of our God!
> When all was sin and shame,
> A second Adam to the fight
> And to the rescue came.
>
> O wisest love! that flesh and blood
> Which did in Adam fail,
> Should strive afresh against the foe,
> Should strive and should prevail;
>
> O generous love! that He who smote
> In Man for man the foe,
> The double agony in Man
> For man should undergo.

Equally, the theme of 'Light' – 'kindly Light' – can prove immensely powerful as inspiration, whether the ethereal light which affords the paintings of Rembrandt such a spiritual quality; or the light of love depicted here as a kind of elusive, yet enduring, will-o'-the-wisp. At the far end of the spectrum from the precise credal conviction of 'Firmly, I believe', moreover, this hymn draws on personal recollection to move the worshipper with all the compelling force of vocational experience:

> I was not ever thus, nor prayed that thou
> Shouldst lead me on;
> I loved to choose and see my path; but now
> Lead thou me on.

And then comes that most basic *cri de coeur* as the really lasting vocational plea of all meditation and worship:

> Keep thou my feet; I do not ask to see
> The distant scene; one step enough for me.

But however effective Newman's verse, because that master of prose doubted his poetic prowess, a powerful passage from his *Parochial and Plain Sermons* on precisely this theme cannot be ignored in this context:

Let us dwell upon times and seasons, times of trouble, times of joy, times of trial, times of refreshment. How did He cherish us as children! How did He guide us in that dangerous time when the mind began to think for itself, and the heart to open to the world! How did He with His sweet discipline restrain our passions, mortify our hopes, calm our fears, enliven our heavinesses, sweeten our desolateness, and strengthen our infirmities! How did He gently guide us toward the strait gate! ... He has been all things to us.

[Ibid., Vol. V, p. 84]

Charlotte Elliott

Chapter 10

CHARLOTTE ELLIOTT

and

'Just as I am, without one plea'

1 JUST as I am, without one plea
But that Thy blood was shed for me,
And that Thou bidd'st me come to Thee,
O Lamb of God, I come!

2 Just as I am, and waiting not
To rid my soul of one dark blot,
To Thee, Whose blood can cleanse each spot,
O Lamb of God, I come!

3 Just as I am, though tossed about
With many a conflict, many a doubt,
Fighting and fears within, without,
O Lamb of God, I come!

4 Just as I am, poor, wretched, blind:
Sight, riches, healing of the mind,
Yea, all I need, in Thee to find,
O Lamb of God, I come!

5 Just as I am, Thou wilt receive,
Wilt welcome, pardon, cleanse, relieve;
Because Thy promise I believe,
O Lamb of God, I come!

6 Just as I am – Thy love unknown
Has broken every barrier down –
Now to be Thine, yea, Thine Alone,
O Lamb of God, I come!

7 Just as I am, of that free love
The breadth, length, depth, and height to prove,
Here for a season, then above,
O Lamb of God, I come!

Within a darken'd room I saw one sit,
Touching a plaintive lyre;
Upward she look'd, and then her eye seem'd lit
With transient fire:
But ever and anon I heard her sigh,
And ever and anon tears fill'd her eye.

Taken from 'The Minstrel', these lines have the authentic ring of autobiography. First published in *Hours of Sorrow* (1840), the poem was composed to comfort, and relates to those 'Seasons of Sickness, Depression and Bereavement' which made up the sad, solitary existence of a long-neglected Victorian lady. The victim of some kind of religious mania, Charlotte Elliott early succumbed to a recurrent schizophrenia that could drown her in moods of deep depression and oblige carers to confine her to the sick room. For even when acute and bright in moments of re-mission, the patient lacked companionship and was possessed, in all the asceticism of an austere faith, by an anxious yearning for her life's end and the hereafter.

Born in the year of the French Revolution, Charlotte came from a family well known for its commitment to the 'Evangeli-cal' cause. She was the third daughter of Charles Elliott of Clapham, and later Brighton where he was cabinet maker to the Prince Regent; her uncle, John Venn, was Rector of Clapham; and her mother Eling the eldest daughter of the Vicar of Huddersfield, Henry Venn. If little is known of Charlotte's early years, her sister Eleanor's brief *Memoir* makes passing reference to a literary talent and gift for humorous verse that made her 'a wel-come guest in circles where she met some of the most brilliant wits and writers of the day' (*S[elections from the] P[oems of] C[harlotte] E[lliott]*, p. 15.). With a temperament 'eminently poetical' and a 'fine and delicate ear' to foster a fondness for music, she nevertheless found herself in a world of temptation. Sister Eleanor certainly regarded such a *soirée* society as 'a perilous snare' (Ibid.), and it seems that the sensitive Charlotte, unable to avoid the blinkered religious stance of her family, suf-fered nervous breakdown. The year was 1821, and Miss Elliott thirty-two years of age when she found, in her bed of sickness, a temporary refuge from worldly lure and lust. That 'she became deeply conscious of the evil in her own heart' and 'suffered much mental distress, under the painful uncertainty whether it were possible that such an one as she felt herself to be could be saved', is evident from the *Memoir* [*S.P.C.E.*, 16]. Desperately confused by warring factions in the religious controversy of revivalism, particularly 'the disturbing influence' of various unnamed 'teachers who held inadequate notions of the efficacy of Divine grace', Charlotte eventually found solace in the counsel of a Genevan pastor, Dr Caesar Malan, the occasion of their first meeting (9 May 1822) henceforth standing sacrosanct in her calendar as

> a festal day ... the birthday of the soul to true spiritual life
> and peace.   [*S.P.C.E.*, 17]

For Malan had led Charlotte to what her sister spelled out as 'simple faith in God's own Word' [Ibid]; and in an open letter to her 'Very dear Friends' of the Venn-Elliott family circle, Charlotte held 'the cross of Jesus' as far 'better ... more efficacious than all beside'. Writing from Manchester shortly afterwards in a letter dated 18 May (1822), the good Swiss pastor instructed his convert to

> ... cut the cable, it will take too long to unloose it; cut it,
> it is a small loss; the wind blows and the ocean is before you
> – the Spirit of God, and eternity.   [*S.P.C.E.*, p. 21]

In her turn too, Eleanor noted it was at this time that her sister 'threw aside ... the authors she had found most attractive' and forsook 'discursive' reading of the kind that had drawn her to 'the noblest writers in our own language and especially the poets' who had been her 'increasing delight'. Henceforth, however much Charlotte continued to be moved by the natural beauty of the world around her – to gain inspiration as a poet when, in the summer months, various members of an extended family and friends made suitably-styled (and not so grand) tours with the sad soul otherwise confined like another Miss Havisham – she concentrated on 'the exclusive study of Holy Scripture'. 'A hidden one', her life was largely a curious kind of seclusion that offered, as the *Memoir* records, 'but few incidents and little variety.' In her despairing state of mind Charlotte thus shrank from the prospect of death, 'from unknown imagined terrors as to the circumstances of her dying hour'. Yet the disturbed, psychotic nature of her condition comprised a changeable, labile character that could disperse cloudy depression and at times afford the very assurance of salvation Malan strove to inculcate as her faithful correspondent for over forty years. At such moments Charlotte confidently rejoiced to claim with St Paul 'I know whom I have believed ...' (2 Tim. 1.12), the apostolic testimony given to Timothy. If Miss Elliott later destroyed almost all such letters in the belief that they 'might tend to self-exaltation' and 'foster vanity and pride', no more poignant *aide-mémoire* and anti-depressant can be found than the stanza Eleanor discovered inscribed in Charlotte's 'private Bible':

> Dig deep in this precious golden mine.
> Toil, and its richest ore is thine;
> Search, and the Saviour will lend his aid
> To draw its wealth from its mystic shade;
> Strive, and His Spirit will give thee light
> To work in this heavenly mine aright.
> Pray without ceasing, in Him confide,
> Into all truth His light will guide.
> [*S.P.C.E.*, p. 23. n.1.]

Such guidance resulted in an increasing commitment to the cause of Christ, and, at a time when there were few opportunities for the ministry of women, Charlotte Elliott turned to poetry. In the early 1830s, the first-fruits of her genius appeared anonymously as *Hours of Sorrow*. The title-page is particularly revealing, for not only did it carry the apostolic injunction to 'Weep with them that weep' − a text from the Letter to the Romans entirely in accord with contemporary religious revivalism and the Pauline emphasis on the fellowship of suffering endured by the working classes − but also an apt stanza from the pen of a revered High Churchman whose celebrated *Christian Year* had been published in 1827. As so often, it is the extremes of religious truth that have real appeal and validity, rarely the middle ground of liberal compromise. And Charlotte Elliott evidently felt herself to have much in common with the spirituality of John Keble who, at his best, was by no means doctrinaire, as this title-page text reflects:

> The world's a room of sickness, where each heart
> Knows its own anguish and unrest;
> The truest wisdom there, and noblest art,
> Is his who skills of comfort best.

Sub-titled *Thoughts in Verse*, Miss Elliott's preface 'To the Reader' was itself a *pièce justificative* which, penned in verse, set her apart as a sage fully aware of the loneliness and suffering many sorrowing souls had to face when laid aside in isolation and seclusion.

> Not for the gay and thoughtless do I weave
> These plaintive strains; they have not learnt to grieve:
> Their joyous days, mirth, health and gladness wing
> These are the few in such a world as this:-
> The many scarcely take the cup of bliss,
> Ere some rude stroke, e'en while its sweets they sip,
> Dashes it (oft for ever) from their lip.
> For such, for such alone, I tune my lay;
> They feel life's path a rough and thorny way.

Because it lacked the dogmatic assertiveness of the sectarian side of contemporary revivalism, Charlotte Elliott's work had a wide appeal; and although its success did not compare with that of Keble's *Christian Year*, the *Hours of Sorrow* nevertheless went through innumerable editions as the nineteenth century advanced. The unknown authoress certainly possessed genuine poetical talent, and this she consecrated to religion, determined to write 'to the glory of God, and the benefit of others' [*S.P.C.E.* p. 24]. So much further lines addressed 'To the Reader' make clear:

> To tell them where another heart found rest
> Once, like their own, disquieted, unblest;
> And where, though sought in vain on earthly ground,
> A balm of sovereign virtue may be found. [op. cit., p. 2]

Biblical imagery abounds, illustrations from Scripture effectively commending the gospel in poems like 'The Wanderer' and the gloss on Matthew 5, a sonnet on the 'Sermon on the Mount'.

But, throughout, undercurrents of depression not only continue to reflect Charlotte's troubled state of mind, but in context also bring a curiously compelling element to her verse. Typical of this tendency, and almost certainly of value as a reflection of the poet's own predicament, is a poem entitled 'On hearing a Canary-Bird sing in London'. Modest of rhyme but with brilliant imagery, the lay provides focus on an imprisoned bird of 'orient hue' whose very plumage indicates that its life should be no mere caged existence, but full and free in 'some island of splendour and light'. In autobiographical terms, the parallel is glaring and undisguised:

> Poor chorister! sadly thy lot has been changed,
> From climate and home and companions estranged!
> Immured in a city, forbid to take wing,
> Oh! what can induce thee so sweetly to sing?
>
> [op. cit., p. 102]

Despite her own confinement and renewed desolation and distress – Charlotte was, it seems, at a particularly low ebb first in 1829 when 'her health gave way entirely' and 'she became too weak to leave her room'; and again in 1836 – she had been persuaded as a 'sort of dying legacy' to edit the *Christian Remembrancer Pocket-Book* for a Miss Harriet Kiernan of Dublin, then seriously ill with 'consumption'. It was work she continued for twenty-five years from 1834, compiling a kind of period *Daily Light*, or as her sister Eleanor described it, picking 'the daily texts ... which were for so long ... chosen by herself, and carefully arranged to illustrate the particular series of spiritual subjects which in each year she thought fit to select' [*S.P.C.E.*, p. 24].

In the same year (1834), Charlotte Elliott published the *Invalid's Hymn Book*, a little pamphlet soon to be known as the sourcebook of her rightly-famed

Just as I am, without one plea.

Later to be included in successive reprints of the *Hours of Sorrow*, the hymn's initial appearance in such a source is itself significant. The first three verses thus provide a running commentary on the psychiatric state that shrouded Charlotte Elliott and prompted her to pen stanzas that convey a heartfelt cry for help. For this is

an authentic hymn which, if it re-iterates the Lord's own command that the burdened and heavy laden come unto Him for rest
(Matt. 11. 28), dramatically draws on the trials and tribulations
that had beset the writer through troublesome, tempestuous
years. She graphically describes herself as 'tossed about'

> With many a conflict, many a doubt,
> Fightings and fears within, without;

and she projects herself poetically as a figure, not of fun to be
scorned by others, but as pathetically inferior

> ... poor, wretched, blind

and in dire need of

> Sight, riches, healing of the mind.

Although the hymn has proved immensely popular in the century
and a half since it was written, no commentator has been aware of
its significance as a Communion hymn. Yet that is surely the point
of the piece, for here is a hymn that stands or falls as a personal
response to the first of the so-called 'comfortable words' in
Thomas Cranmer's incomparable liturgy *The Book of Common
Prayer*:

> ¶ *Then shall the Priest say,*
> Hear what comfortable words our Saviour Christ saith unto
> all that truly turn to him.
>   COME unto me all that travail and are heavy laden, and I
> will refresh you.   *S. Matth.* xi. 28.

If the last three verses thus reveal the lengths to which 'free love'
(verse 6) went in the crucifixion – and in so doing repeat the
opening theme

> ... that thy Blood was shed for me (verse 1, line 2)

– they also stress the only possible response of the penitent at the
Eucharist,

O Lamb of God, I come.

It was certainly this acceptance of Christ as the Lamb of God that gave Charlotte Elliott's words such a moving quality. Invariably used as a hymn of response at great gospel gatherings like the Keswick Convention, or those evangelical 'Crusades' customarily associated with evangelists like Billy Graham and John Stott, it can equally well be used Sunday by Sunday in parish churches where the Lord's Supper is celebrated and revered. Be that as it may, the emotional impact of these verses is unquestionably heightened in the context of the authoress who, in seven powerful stanzas, still preaches a powerful homily. For in 'Just as I am', almost more than in anything else Miss Elliott wrote, is to be found her determination 'to draw nearer to God as my only and all-satisfying portion' [*S.P.C.E.,* p. 30], not to mention her yearning for release and the moment when, in faith, she might claim the citizenship of heaven:

> Just as I am, of that free love,
> The breadth, length, depth, and height to prove,
> Here for a season, then above,
> *O Lamb of God, I come.*

Encouraged by this ministry, an improvement in Charlotte's health enabled her to travel in Scotland in the summer of 1835. Although her depression returned the following year, this did not prevent convalescence on the continent and a trip down the Rhine, together with a visit to Geneva, where Dr Malan helped his *protegée* enjoy a tour of the Bernese Oberland and took Charlotte on high *chaise à porteur* to view sunrise over Montanvert and the glacier. Back in England, she went to Brighton to stay with her brother Edward; and it was to help the parochial work of St Mary's Chapel that a slim volume of *Hymns for a Week* was privately printed in October, 1837. Exemplary for the personal piety and devotion to scriptural spirituality it displayed in fourteen pieces of penitence and praise, the work glossed well-known biblical texts from the Old and New Testaments. Every day was given its pastoral focus: so Sunday had mission in mind; Monday, prayer before 'The throne of Grace'; Tuesday, the need for patience and strength in the Christian life; and Wednesday, more prayer for deliverance from temptation. Expounding Matthew

26.4 for Wednesday morning, Charlotte wrote another hymn
that provided a classic homily, as

CHRISTIAN! Seek not yet repose,

for its challenging refrain, which concluded every verse with

'Watch and pray!'

has a lasting impact. On Thursday, the faithful were made to face
advice from Book of Proverbs and control their conversation
(Proverbs 13.3); Friday, commemorating the crucifixion, once
more expressed Charlotte's desire 'to depart and be with Christ,
which is far better' (Phil. 1.23.); and Saturday made much of Sabbath preparation as the 'Lord's Day' approached again.

It was very much in character that Miss Elliott chose to
publish her *Morning and Evening Hymns for a Week* privately. An
edition of fifteen thousand was printed by Charles Haselden of
Wigmore Street, London, 'to assist the funds of a Bazaar held at
Brighton, for St Mary's Hall' – and had sought anonymity on a
title-page that merely stated them to have been written 'by a
LADY'. Such modesty bemused her sister who, in the *Memoir,*
noted that:

> Surreptitious copies of these hymns were afterwards circu-
> lated and sold by an individual who claimed them as his own
> composition! This obliged the real authoress to have the
> book published with her name, and it has now reached the
> fortieth thousand. [*S.P.C.E.* p. 43]

Charlotte was not one to seek success in circulation figures.
Instead, a series of deaths in the family – first her sister-in-law
Mrs Henry Elliott in 1841, and then her mother in 1843 –
'crushed her to death'. Almost submerged in sorrow, she
channelled her sadness into composition, adding a number of
touching poems to new editions of *The Hours.* And when, in
1844, two more sisters died, Charlotte was in such a state of
shock that 'she became so alarmingly ill, from some attack in the
heart, that an immediate change of scene' was deemed
imperative by those who looked after her.

To cast Miss Elliott in a hypochondriac rôle would be to mis-understand her condition. At the same time a letter survives to indicate that, in August 1843, she believed her end to be at hand and wrote to urge both Henry and Eleanor not to weep for her. The counsel she gave her siblings was quite the reverse, for they were instructed to:

> Think of me as for ever safe, for ever pardoned, for ever holy, for ever happy through the blood of the everlasting covenant, and the unspeakable mercy of Him who 'hath loved me with an everlasting love'.

With the apostle Paul (Romans 8) she was convinced that noth-ing could separate her from such love, and convalescence at Ilfracombe revived 'her shattered frame'. The virulence of the attack on a 'poor suffering body' is suggestive of rheumatic fever – an 'acute inflammatory attack, attended with great suffering' that was later to recur – but when she returned to 'a pleasant house in Regency Square' (for the Brighton family home, No. 31, Brunswick Square, had now been sold), another twenty-five year span of life lay ahead.

These were years when, at her best, Charlotte Elliott can be pictured before an open window looking with longing at the landscape beyond, for the new house was at that time in open country. Unable to attend church, she was nevertheless regular in receiving the sacrament, clerical friends, among them a venerable archdeacon, ministering to her on Sundays. But her life remained a lonely vigil, as ascetic in its devotion as that of any regular in religious orders, for she customarily recited Scripture to herself, texts that gave her foothold on what she termed her 'morning and evening ladder' as if scaling a stairway between earth and heaven like another Jacob.

On 24 January 1865, the Reverend Henry Venn Elliott died, the brother whose ministry Charlotte had done so much to support. Such deprivation proved a double blow, not only because, now completely confined to her sick room, she was prevented from going 'even to bid him a last farewell'; but also because in all her anxiety and loneliness, she had been sustained by the fond hope that Henry, some years younger than herself, might be the one to minister to her at the last. Once again a confidence of Eleanor's

Memoir rings true when she compares the broken-hearted Charlotte's acceptance of the whole sad situation to brave words she wrote in the hymn 'Thy Will be done'. A powerful plea in prayer that appeared some years earlier to comfort the bereaved, this included several apt stanzas, in particular verses three:

> What though in lonely grief I sigh
> For friends belov'd, no longer nigh,
> Submisive still would I reply;

and 5:

> Should grief or sickness waste away
> My life in premature decay;
> My Father! still I'll strive to say,

with the refrain repeat:

> 'Thy will be done!'

In 1869, a further attack of rheumatic fever took hold of this indomitable Victorian invalid and so sapped her strength that attending physicians despaired of any rally. Eleanor was duly informed that this at last was 'the sleep of death'. But Charlotte again survived for almost two more years to spend any active moments in flower arranging, and to delight in Sussex sunsets.

> Her love for flowers was almost a passion; and to the last week of her life she would wear the nosegays sent by loving friends on her bed, and arrange them with her own peculiar and elegant taste. [*S.P.C.E.*, p. 53]

Fascinated by cloud colour like a lesser Constable too, she insisted on being roused whenever a rainbow was to be seen in the skies.

Above all, however, the ever-open Bible at the bedside was her church; and when eighty-one years of age she wrote that 'so great an age as mine requires three things – great faith, great patience, and great peace'. Such qualities were certainly in evidence when, finally taking leave of her sister, Charlotte declared with all the solemnity of an eminent Victorian:

> Our next meeting will be at the marriage-supper of the
> Lamb.

And, superbly, when a sentence from John's Gospel – 'Let not
your heart be troubled' [John 14.1] – was read to her, the evangelical death-bed scene rang with Charlotte Elliott's immediate
response:

> But my heart is *not* troubled ... My mind is full of the Bible!

MISS ELLIOTT'S DEVOTIONAL TREASURY

For one so disturbed and depressed, Charlotte Elliott's output in
both poetry and hymns is extensive, and all her verse contains a
moving quality particularly sensitive to the needs of the human
situation. From the lonely exile of her own years of isolation she
can accept physical pain and address the disabilities of the blind
and the deaf. The *Thoughts in Verse* 'chiefly adapted to seasons of
sickness, depression and bereavement' itself testifies to the rest-
less grieving and melancholy moods of what one poem in *Hours
of Sorrow* terms her 'poor widowed heart'. Any loss of family or
friends increased the invalid's loneliness to aggravate a pitiful
plight. But this state Charlotte strove bravely to parry, and in the
simplest of stanzas saw sorrow as need, a need to be 'cheered and
comforted'. So much the sixth edition of her poems recognized
with a changed title-page (1863). Highly symbolic, it was now a
recognition of mission. For Miss Elliott's appreciation of physical
pain and mental disturbance as spiritual privation enabled her to
set in clear relief what she perceived of the meaning of life itself.
And drawing on the eternal realities of 'the world unseen' in this
way, she not only came to terms with her own despair, but in
poetry and hymns as homilies actively ministered to the condition of others.

Illustrations abound, the 'Address to Sorrow', linked as it is to
the gospel theme, setting Charlotte's style:

> Then, Sorrow! thou dost guide him
> To penitence and Faith:

> These place fair Hope beside him,
> To cheer his heavenward path.
> [H[ours of] S[orrow], p. 7]

Much in evidence too, a Victorian melancholy is to be found in a poem like 'The Valley of Tears'. Invariably introspective, such subjects can depress to increase despair for those already dispirited. But this process Miss Elliott skilfully reverses with a perspective of hope. So even though it takes

> ... a period of sorrowful years,
> To mourn or toil in the valley of tears,

her last verse keeps 'that fair country in view' and

> With hope and with patience my path I pursue;
> In sadness and weariness sweet is the thought,
> That my home is not distant, my journey but
>   short;
> And that, when I have passed a few troublesome
>   years,
> I shall wander no more in the valley of tears.
> [H.S., p. 18]

For a bereaved 'Christian Friend' Charlotte sets out eternal realities with even greater clarity than before, re-using the clever poetic device of the refrain that provided such an effective response in the hymn 'Just as I am ...'. This time the pattern repeat is no longer the eucharistic allusion 'O Lamb of God, I come', but the rhetorical

> Why dost thou weep?

Peculiarly meaningful in a credal context that outlines the triumphant nature of resurrection faith in verse of real commitment, the technique is decidedly dramatic in verse 5:

> Should the ills of life distress thee?
> Grief, care, loneliness depress thee?

With thy Saviour near to bless thee,
Why dost thou weep?   [*H.S.*, p. 110]

After all, Miss Elliott was simply passing on her own experience
to indicate how Christian belief could itself transform the loneliness of the sick room – a message all too remote in these days
when concern for invalidity or social security benefits seems to
dominate both hospital patients and those visited in the wider
community far more than any propsect of comfort or reassurance
in counselling. The point is readily apparent, and the reference
all too direct, in lines

> To FAITH
> WRITTEN in ILLNESS

> Come, holy Faith! beside me stand,
> With look inspired, with eye serene;
> Unfold the bright celestial land,
> The world unseen.

And later,

> ... sounds more blest than song of bird,
> Or rills and whispering boughs impart,
> Shall in this silent room be heard,
>   And cheer my heart.
>   [*H.S.*, pp. 121–22]

This last verse duly emphasized the fact that, although nature can
parade the wonders of creation outside the sick-room window,
such imagery is provided to prompt those losing their lines as
baptized members of a holy community and household of faith.
Miss Elliott nevertheless adorned her verse with allusions that
show her to have been a genuine nature lover with acute powers of observation. Birds regularly fly through her poetry, the
symbolism of 'Noah's Dove' bringing its message from on high
just as the skylark and the nightingale blend their sweet song
'with the chorus of heaven.' [*H.S.*, pp. 32, 19 and 39.] Trees and
flowers similarly indicate how the Almighty has seen fit to cheer
the sorrowful who are thus

Nursed by fond affection [Ibid., p. 14].

With the beauty of the landscape and stunning cloud formations in mind too, Charlotte Elliott has not forgotten the affliction of deafness and was one of the first to realize the near desperation of those whose oft-forgotten disability has brought stark solitude and tragic isolation. Supremely sensitive to such deprivation, she not only wrote verse for

ONE SUFFERING FROM DEAFNESS [*H.S.*, pp. 51–2]

to make clear how the 'ear of faith' can 'whisper peace', but composed a fine sonnet on the subject which included the lines:

Let not the sigh of sorrow heave thy breast,
Since God, thy God, in communing with thee,
Asks less the listening ear than listening heart,
And there his sweetest comforts will impart.
[*H.S.*, 140]

Of her sonnets, few are better than that 'on the Scriptures'. No simple subject, she addressed the sacred page with all the skill that, setting

... heavenly truth in characters of light,

reached the triumphant conclusion and memorable judgement that:

All other volumes lose their zest and tire;
But this, the more its treasures we unfold,
Exceeding far the costliest gems or gold,
Fills to the utmost all the soul's desire:
Wisdom to guide, and balm to heal, supplies;
Enlightens, comforts, cheers, satisfies.

Such conviction certainly inspired Charlotte Elliott as a writer of hymns. For just as her selection of biblical texts in *Morning and Evening* worship provided faithful food for thought 'for a week', so the *Hours* offered hymns for both major feasts, and the unfolding year as if to please church and chapel folk alike.

'A Christmas Hymn' commends the incarnation in ten verses unknown today, to include:

> Wonderful Counsellor!
> Thee whom the Virgin bore.
>   Thee I receive;
> God e'er the world began,
> Perfect God, perfect man,
> (Mystery too deep to scan)
>   This I believe.

An imaginative 'Hymn of the Magi':

> What means that wondrous star,
> Bright streaming from afar?

was written 'for Three Voices', the last verse making good use of such a trio in the chorus

> Judea! favoured land!
> We seek thy hallowed strand;
> Our home we leave, our kindred dear,
> Without delay, regret or fear:
> GOD calls, and we obey.
> He kindled your refulgent star,
> To herald One more glorious far;
> Haste we to greet His ray!

The 'New Year' too is celebrated with:

> I take my pilgrim staff anew,

a hymn that offered every opportunity for personal dedication in the second verse:

> Throughout the year my heavenly Friend,
> On Thy blest guidance I depend;
> From its commencement to its end
>   My times are in Thy hand.

But for devotional depth, Charlotte Elliott's hymn *On the midnight preceding* Good Friday has all the power of 'Just as I am, without one plea', providing as it does rare meditative exposition. As the Christ wrestles with his destiny in Gethsemane, Miss Elliott keeps holy vigil, her use of the first person demanding all the dedication of true discipleship.

> O my Redeemer! Can I sleep
> With heart at ease, with spirits light,
> When thou for me such watch didst keep
>   On this sad night?

> Shall I not 'watch with thee one hour',
> And strive, by importuning prayer,
> Through faith and love's constraining power,
>   Thy griefs to share?

> Thence would I follow thee, in thought,
> To that lone spot so dark for thee;
> For us with light and gladness fraught,
>   Gethsemane!

And the last of nine verses:

> How can I choose but weep and wake,
> When such a night, my God! was thine?
> Thou all the penalty didst take:
>   The guilt was mine.

In many respects the theme is one Miss Elliott used in her fine commentary on Matthew 26. 41,

> CHRISTIAN! Seek not yet repose.

For the perspective is supremely Christ-centred, and as so often the writer is at her best as a really effective evangelist when commending the Saviour who gave such inspiration to her solitary existence. No wonder she counselled Eleanor to:

Place me in those arms as tender,
But more powerful far than thine:
For awhile thy charge surrender
To his guardianship divine!
Lay me on my Saviour's breast,
There to find eternal rest.

With long years of sorrow and suffering almost at an end, and
the perception conveyed in lines from a penetrating hymn for
Good Friday –

OH never can I serve Thee here,
My Saviour as I ought;
Without an unbelieving fear,
Without a wandering thought

– Charlotte Elliott nevertheless had a vision of Jesus she handed
down with a determination that ultimately defeated depression
with all the focus of her life of faith:

Oh, Jesus, make Thyself to me
A living, bright reality,
More present to Faith's vision keen
Than any outward object seen –
More dear, more intimately nigh,
Than e'en the sweetest earthly tie.

The once 'widowed heart' had at last left 'utter loneliness'
behind to approach the ecstasy of marriage as a bride of Christ.

Chapter 11

FANNY ALEXANDER

and

'There is a green hill far away'

1 There is a green hill far away,
   Without a city wall,
 Where the dear Lord was crucified
   Who died to save us all.

2 We may not know, we cannot tell,
   What pains he had to bear,
 But we believe it was for us
   He hung and suffered there.

3 He died that we might be forgiven,
   He died to make us good;
 That we might go at last to heaven,
   Saved by his precious Blood.

4 There was no other good enough
   To pay the price of sin;
 He only could unlock the gate
   Of heaven, and let us in.

5 O, dearly, dearly has he loved,
   And we must love him too,
 And trust in his redeeming Blood,
   And try his works to do.

Respectability and religious commitment ruled the world of Cecil Frances Alexander, whose hymns and poetry rarely included direct comment on the tragedy of nineteenth-century Ireland. The daughter of an army officer and land agent in 'dark Tyrone', 'Fanny' Humphreys was early acquainted with extremes of wealth and poverty, and it comes as no surprise to find that the editor of *The Oxford Dictionary of Quotations* chose to represent her considerable written output with lines that, no longer found in any hymnal, are nowadays a constant source of mirth as religion is scorned for numerous absurdities. Yet in their period setting

> The rich man in his castle,
> The poor man at his gate,
> GOD made them, high or lowly,
> And ordered their estate

– the lines Fanny penned as part of a simple children's gloss on creation in the creed – by no means deserve such ridicule and obloquy. Originally published in 1848, just over a decade before Charles Darwin brought out his *Origin of Species* (1859), they were typical of the kind of popular theology used to nurture a new generation of young people.

Of late, 'All things bright and beautiful' has suffered scathing criticism from Bishop Konstant of Leeds who, in an address to a Catholic Men's Society, referred to it as 'one of the most dreadful, even unintentionally wicked commentaries on society'. The hymn's third verse may not resonate with contemporary concepts of society or the fashionable 'relevance' required nowadays. Some hold it to mirror Victorian notions of social control, and link the libelled stanza to a mid-century clamour for political reform. But that does not make it either 'wicked' or 'dreadful'. Quite the reverse, for as a period piece it must be set in context like all the hymns considered in this book. Together with most of her religious poetry, this is a moving 'catechism-hymn' for 'little children' and represents a brave attempt on the part of Fanny Alexander to analyse and explain creation and the human situation to the very young. Bishop Konstant merely used the hymn as a damning illustration as he deplored mere acceptance of what some still term the working of 'the will of God'. He argued for a new sense of responsibility in Christian attitudes, and did so at the hymnwriter's expense. He soon had his answer too, a fine article by Mr Boris Johnson in *The Daily Telegraph* (6 September 1995) making clear that 'all of our greatest hymns contain little fossils of the age in which they were written'.

With many still in shock from a desperately disordered society rent asunder by famine and subsequent plague, it was part of her gallant attempt to train children to accept the traditional religious and social values she herself cherished. For even in a climate of doubt, Cecil Frances Alexander's convictions did not change, the poem 'Rich and Poor' she wrote and published among many *Moral Songs* in 1880, setting out the same philosophy in these two stanzas:

> But rich, or poor, one bond they know,
> Each is his neighbour's brother,
> For neither on this earth below,
> Can do without the other.

> Each has his pleasures, each his pains;
> The mean man, and the great,
> Must bow to that which GOD ordains,
> Who fixes every state. [*Moral Songs*, pp. 87–8]

Fanny early set herself the task of forwarding before friends and contemporaries ideals of God's Fatherhood and man's brotherhood. To indicate her commitment to Christian causes, she contributed pamphlets some years before her *Hymns for Little Children* first appeared in 1848. But it was of course in such seminal stanzas that she strove to forward in Ireland the ordered faith of Tractarian Oxford. That she chose what Ronnie Corbett would nowadays term 'Small Talk' for small children is also of real significance. For she made much of the medium at precisely the time her surviving neighbours and their offspring continued to reel and react from the black desert of tragedy historians now term the Irish Potato Famine. In 1845, and again in 1846, the nation's key crop failed and burdened millions in the south with bitter suffering and starvation. Almost unimaginable as a life experience, and unforgettable in consequence, 'the Wanderer' in her later poem 'The Lonely Grave', can scarcely bear to reflect on

> ... the tale of tears
> Told by a thousand hearts before,
> The anguish of those famine years,
> The useless toil, the straiten'd store.

Even then it remained a tale half told, for the flight of many victims determined to seek a New World across the Atlantic proved similarly dire. For the starvation they had faced at the time potato 'cholera' blackened their staple crop, to force the peasantry to endure a sparse diet of cabbage leaves and turnip tops, was in many cases to bring on the deadly disease itself. Within a year of their arrival in North America, cholera thus claimed almost a quarter of such emigrés.

> How, of the land we loved forsaken,
> And spurn'd from off her blighted face,
> We dared the dark deep, tempest-shaken,
> And found an exile's resting place.
> [*Moral Songs*, p. 286]

With her love of light and shade – her chosen childlike world of simple contrasts – it is no wonder Fanny Humphreys has critics. Her spatial universe made no concessions to scientific revolution, and another *Moral Song* entitled 'Looking Up' boldly re-directed the faint-hearted to glance 'heavenward':

> Because, above, a world there is,
> A higher, happier place than this;
> Where holy men who die are taken,
> Where sometimes little children go
> Who fall asleep, no more to waken
> With us upon this earth below.

Inspired by John Keble's *The Christian Year*, Fanny Humphreys wrote *Verses for Holy Seasons*. These the celebrated Vicar of Leeds, Farquhar Hook, was pleased to edit after meeting his sister's Irish

friend at Leamington Spa in 1847, just as he also took the opportunity this gave him to stress the validity of England's Reformation
divines in an attempt to counterbalance Fanny's evident zeal for
the work of Oxford's Tractarians. But although in early days she
wrote 'King Edward's Dreams' – the imaginative piece which
showed sympathy for the work of 'gentle Ridley', Hooper,
'Latimer the old' and a Cranmer whose 'martyr's fire did fiercest
shine' – her admiration for Keble was undiminished and knew few
bounds. Nor was the Vicar of Hursley slow to respond, however
much Keble made it clear that the *Hymns for Little Children* Miss
Humphreys dedicated to her godsons in 1848 had 'small need' of
either 'preface or explanation'. Nevertheless 'because the writer of
the Hymns wished for some kind of clerical *imprimatur*', as 'the
clergyman to whom she had applied', he gladly gave it, evidently
aware that 'all who know how to value true poetry and primitive
devotion' would not fail to recognize such talent.

Less than two years later, marriage to the Reverend William
Alexander, a country parson in the diocese of Derry, gave Fanny
the front-line opportunities she needed to use her hymns in the
Sunday and National School work that now became the principal focus of an increasingly active life's work among children. The
remote rural parish of Termonamongan afforded her something
of a bog- and mountain-trotting ministry as she supported her
husband not only in counselling the sick and poverty-stricken,
but supremely in the catechism of neglected children as she bat-
tled to build up the faith in distant regions where the scattered
population of fifteen hundred souls lived out their frugal existence. As William Alexander's career progressed, Fanny moved
first to the parish of Upper Fahan (1855–60), and then to her
own beloved Strabane (from 1860) before, in 1867, her husband
was consecrated Bishop of Derry.

All this time, Mrs Alexander toiled to train the young (and by
now she had given birth to some of her own) in the faith.
Although, like *The Christian Year*, her *Hymns for Little Children*
opens with a 'Morning' and an 'Evening Hymn' closely to parallel John Keble's poems for 'Morning' and 'Evening', Fanny
transposed the Kalendar and cleverly revived a focus better suited
to the young. In effect, she updated traditional *Primers*. First, the
triune name was lauded in a hymn to the Trinity. This set out
the faith to be believed by children in their baptism.

We are little Christian children
Saved by Him Who loved us most.
We believe in GOD Almighty,
FATHER, SON and HOLY GHOST.

Focus on the responsibilities of godparents followed logically as

Then we promised by our sureties,
Vowing for us solemnly,
Manfully to fight His battles,
Gentle, kind and good to be.

Patient catechism followed as, point by point, and with crystal
clarity, baptismal promises, the Creed and commandments were
set out. It takes a certain kind of genius to grasp the habits and
ways of children; and in her inimitable way Mrs Alexander used
great gifts of imagination carefully to illustrate the faith in ways
that made it most appealing. Deep doctrines she related to high
standards and a belief that behaved; and well aware that the young
rarely grasp abstract truth, she prized discipleship above all and
wrote about it in the simplest terms. Held out as 'our childhood's
pattern', she confidently upheld the life and death of Jesus as an
inspiration to good living, convinced that the Lord would lead
his children on the high road to eternity.

Do no sinful action,
Speak no angry word,
Ye belong to JESUS,
Children of the LORD.

The penultimate section of her *Hymns*, Fanny Alexander gave to
prayer. Fully persuaded of the importance of silent meditation in
the life of faith, a colourful poet's palette helped her to urge children to find time to say their prayers.

Wake, little child, the morn is gay,
The air is fresh and cool;
But pause awhile, and kneel to pray,
Before you go to merry play,
Before you go to school.

Nine hymns modelled on clauses of the Lord's Prayer followed as the poet paraded many truths from the pages of past *Primers* from late-medieval and early-modern times as aids to private devotion. In a section full of wild-life imagery –

> Who gives the ravens food?
>   ...
> Who feeds the lion's young?

– Mrs Alexander made much of 'Give us this day our daily bread'. An appealing petition, she found it of particular use as once again she pointed the young to heaven:

> Then not alone for earthly food,
> Teach us with lisping tongue to pray:-
> The heavenly meat that makes us good,
> LORD, give us day by day.

The unusual presence of a pun in the third line of the stanza suggests a theme of familiarity; and in a hymn about 'Heaven' that followed, the poet's work peaked with a glimpse of Christ in glory:

> Who shall go to that bright land?
> All who do the right;
> Holy children there shall stand
> In their robes of white;
> For that Heaven, so bright and blest,
> Is our everlasting rest.

A perfect conclusion, she devoted Hymn 40 to an explanation of the word 'Amen'. Once again her children are not patronized, but extended and given perspective. In point of fact, two verses recall not only the range and sum of church teaching offered by Mrs Alexander's *Hymns for Little Children*, but also take good care to relate such Christian education to responsible pastoral ministry:

> So be it, LORD; the prayers are prayed,
> But still we pause on bended knee,
> And lingering though the words are said,
> Look fondly up to Thee.

So down the full Church falls alone
The Pastor's voice; it sinks, and then,
Sweet echo to that solemn tone,
We breathe our soft 'Amen'.

★

Very much a devotional address or children's homily, Mrs Alexander's composition:

There is a green hill far away

was originally intended to illustrate a crucial part of her catechism in the credal clause which recorded how Jesus Christ,

... suffered under Pontius Pilate,
was crucified, dead and buried.

It is the simplest summary of the divine plan for the salvation of mankind, and has never lost its appeal to afford insight and assurance to successive generations of children and adults.

The first line offers a poet's visual imagery rather than any accurate allusion to a place of execution in Jerusalem. This at once captures the child's imagination with very much the 'Once upon a time' impact of the traditional storyteller's lyrical charm. No stranger to the walled town of Derry too, Fanny used her wit to picture for children Christ's ultimate rejection in a way they would grasp. Nor did it deter her that some small subjects later inquired why it was that the City in question lacked a wall! But the substitution of the word 'outside' (in line 2) was mercifully not to last. Instead, with the backcloth painted and in place, the drama proceeds, and in carefully-chosen words from everyday language, the poignant tale is told. Emotion is stirred, pity aroused, and faith demanded in this unique account of atonement. There's not an 'if' or 'but' in sight, but a chain-link fence of positive statements to keep out the sceptical theologian. For, its initial scene-setting apart, the scriptural basis of the hymn is never in doubt. The simple gospel of the goodness of God, paying 'the price of sin' to save 'by his precious blood', and to permit us to 'go at last to heaven', comes over with such miraculous authority that, in itself, it works a miracle in the soul. In every way compelling too, such effective but essentially straightforward stanzas have profound devotional impact, the last verse amounting to nothing less than the most basic demand for re-dedication:

> O dearly, dearly has He loved,
> And we must love Him too,
> And trust in His redeeming blood,
> And try His works to do.

That this also moved Charles François Gounod, whose small daughter loved the hymn she sang at school enough to tell her father, is a telling tribute of the time. For the distinguished. French composer at once set the words to music, describing them as 'the most perfect hymn in English' he knew.

★

A prolific poet with over four hundred compositions and a credit balance of many fine hymns, Cecil Frances Alexander has few equals in her ministry to children. When her husband succeeded to the See of Derry, Bishop William's lady could easily have enjoyed a life of leisure. But she chose quite the reverse. Early disciplines hardened, and despite family sadness and the in-built distractions that demanded constant attention for her sickly sons – at times she took them to sandy beaches along the Atlantic coast of France to soak up some of the sun that fired their mother's poetry – no one more typified the Tractarian rule of life.

If the Oxford Movement germinated as a tender plant in the Protestant part of Ireland, Mrs Alexander nurtured it with con-summate skill. Both in the privacy of her new home at the bishop's house and in public worship at the Cathedral, she personified the quiet witness of a humble piety. With the solace of Scripture, Lancelot Andrewes and John Keble to cheer early-morning vigil, she did not neglect attendance at Mattins, and made a point of weekly Communion. In the city streets and sur-rounding countryside she was also well known, walking with her dogs, talking to the children she met, and visiting the infirm. A good hostess, she was not only given to hospitality in the New Testament sense, but obliged to entertain the significant figures who came to Derry to take counsel with the bishop at a high point of crisis for the Church of Ireland.

After Catholic emancipation became law in 1829, it became all too clear that no government could continue support for an established church ministry to such a small minority of the Irish people. A Reform Act extended the franchise in the very year of William Alexander's consecration (1867), and figures as influential to the final solution as the Bishops of Lincoln and Oxford (Wordsworth and Wilberforce), not to mention Dean Stanley of Westminster, consulted together as W. E. Gladstone prepared for the inevitability of disestablishment. In the judgement of a modern historian of calibre, establishment had already become 'offensive to a majority'. And even in period context, a Tractarian like Farquhar Hook would have conceded Owen Chadwick's judgement that 'An established church could marry with democracy only if it was not a grievance to an important minority in the nation' [cf. *The Victorian Church*, II. p. 427].Taking effect from 1 January 1871, legislation from Westminster enabled the Church of Ireland to proceed, and if Bishop William lost his seat in the House of Lords, sufficient money from endowment saved his diocese, however much he deplored the fact that, by the repeal of an Ecclesiastical Titles Act, his very style was rendered illegal. For Fanny, however, there was a bonus in so far as Mr Gladstone's government shrewdly transferred resources to forward educational funding, relieve distress, assist teachers in the schools, and even ensure stores of the best seed potatoes.

Making the most of her early successes, the commercial instinct of various publishers enhanced the slim volume that was *Hymns for Little Children* to produce half- and full-plate editions of lavish illustrations and enough gold leaf on hardback bindings to raise the hymnals to Sunday School prize status. An elaborate example, produced by Joseph Masters of London, carried Chappel drawings engraved by Dalziel. A frontispiece of David praising the Lord on the harp was completed with a concluding tableau to illustrate

Therefore I say, AMEN.

This time David, crowned as King, leads from the harp, with the backing of a select Old Testament group of cymbalists and trumpeters. Replete with Holy Land vistas and Gothic revivals, these

editions added a powerful visual dimension to foster childlike
devotion. Close-ups of the Christ – his birth, baptism by John in
Jordan, childhood, his miracles, passion, death, resurrection and
ascension – provided careful images of a selected spectrum of
sacred moments to enlarge the traditional 'Stations of the Cross'.
Nevertheless the *Ecce Homo* appeal of 'Our Lord's Example of
Meekness' (1 Peter 2. 23) can best describe pastoral pressures on
the young. The pointed reference and direct method of Hymn 26:

> Do not quarrel, do not chide
> You must love each other:

with verse 3 printed alongside an engraved plate of silent suffering
in the persecuted Jesus, certainly made it impossible for impres-
sionable young readers not to 'Behold the Man'.

> Give not back the hasty blow,
> Though 'tis given wrongly;
> Let the foolish scoffer go,
> Though he tempt thee strongly:
> Keep thy gentle LORD in mind,
> Who was always meek and kind.

Another publisher to recognize the work of Mrs Alexander, the
House of Macmillan claimed her to edit a *Sunday Book of Poetry*
in 1864. If the resulting anthology provided more selection and
arrangement of material than any demonstration of the customary editorial skills, the volume nevertheless did much to help a
dedicated woman gain further funds to support the deaf. For
from the start, Fanny Humphreys had made clear that the
profits of her publications

> will be applied to the support of a School for the deaf and
> dumb children maintained altogether by voluntary offerings,
> in a small town in the north of Ireland.

In a *Preface*, 'The Compiler' set out her stall. With the determined aim 'to make Sunday a pleasant day to children' she forwarded a 'selection of sacred poetry' which she was clear could
'be placed with profit and pleasure in the hands of intelligent

children from eight to fourteen years of age'. In a subject range that starts with praise, affords focus on the incarnate and written word, provides sections on DEATH and THE HEART, the contents conclude with a long list of lyrical passages on NATURE. With extracts selected from Addison to her favourite Wordsworth, and many a hymn chosen from the work of Charlotte Elliott, Keble, Newton, Toplady, Watts and herself, the anthology deserved its success. If eminent Victorians valued the volume on their shelves, 'The Compiler' stressed its primary rôle as a teaching manual and handbook to project poetry into young minds. It was a purposeful pen that rehearsed the conviction that

A namby-pamby, childish style is most unpleasing to children, especially to boys.

Never one to patronize the young with condescension, Mrs Alexander always sought to raise their taste to a level she deemed befitting the high purpose of Christian education. Initially she found it

... surprising how soon ... [children] ... can understand and follow a high order of poetry (always supposing it is not subtle or metaphysical), especially when it assumes a narrative form, and has the aid of rhyme.

[Op. cit. *Preface*, p. vii]

But that did not prevent the prayerful prescription that her work may

... help ... to teach them to praise God the Father, Son and Spirit; to contemplate life and death and their own hearts as Christians should: to understand the spirit of the Bible; and through this fair creation to look up to Him Who is its Creator.

A kind of grand finale, her NATURE section shows the country lover in her element and, incidentally, reveals Mrs Alexander as no mean ornithologist. Here, in short, are to be found not only crows, swallows, and 'The white owl snoring from the Ivy' (the line comes from a Moral Song of her own composition), but poems from Bishop Doane (Robin Redbreast), Browning (My Doves), Longfellow (The Legend of the Crossbill), Wells (The Sea-Bird) and Wordsworth (To A Skylark). As the sun sets too, how apt that

All things bright and beautiful

concludes the book.

A regular round of writing in the 1870s, coupled as it was with charity work at a Derry 'Home for Fallen Women', and among District Nurses, widened Fanny's experience. In 1880, this gave birth to *Moral Songs*, followed the next year by *Narrative Hymns for Village Schools.*

A handsome green and gold hardback displaying a floral design, this was another lavishly illustrated work for inclusion on Sunday School prize lists. Published by Masters of New Bond Street, London, it carried the work of some twoscore artists, arranged and engraved by J. D. Cooper. Its striking land, lake and seascapes compel the reader's attention and, together with a peasant elysium of rural charm, provide a perfect setting for poetry. Written for children once again, the verse is suitably lyrical, its ease of rhythm and impressive range of tonal imagery helping to challenge emotions and calm the spirit. When in 'Wishing', a little brother in the 'let's pretend' world of childhood tells his sibling of a wish to be a lamb, a butterfly, and then a lark, the 'quiet tone' of contentment comes in her reply:

> I would be what I am.
> I'm quite content, nor wish to change,
> With bird, or fly, or lamb.
> Our happiest, fittest state, my dear,
> Be sure is that we're given here,
> And boy, or girl, we're better far
> Just where we're set, and as we are.
> [Op. cit., pp. 87–8]

In 1881, 'at the suggestion of the arranger of the Music', *Narrative Hymns for Village Schools* appeared, Cecil Frances Alexander gaining a firm foothold in the 'Infant, and the lower classes of our National Schools'. Using disestablishment to advantage, and determined not to suffer any setback in her work among children, she made the most of this invitation to supply 'in some degree a want that has been keenly felt – that of simple words, embodying the facts of our Lord's life adapted to simple airs'. With a prefatory prayer 'that these little poems may be found useful to those engaged in the work of education' she was away, hoping that children would carry home, much as Gounod's daughter had done, the simple versified homilies learned at school to make her 'the humble instrument of diffusing the love and knowledge of the LORD and SAVIOUR'. Setting the style for a full episodic focus on the life of Christ, Mrs Alexander duly attempted to practise what had been preached in the moral of 'Wishing'. Because children could not be angels, shepherds or kings, let them learn to follow Jesus:

> O teach thy children, Holy Child,
> That evermore they serve Thee thus,
> And lead us by Thy mercy mild,
> Up to the Heaven Thou left'st for us.

And using the opportunity offered by the young Christ in the Temple, these verses indicate schoolmistressly awareness of the need for disciplined devotion:

> O! Shame on any Christian child,
> Who does not love the house of prayer;
> Who goes with cold, unwilling heart,
> To serve his Father there.

> Who takes no heed when holy words
> Are spoken to his listless ears,
> Nor ever questions in his heart
> What mean the things he hears.

> And let him ask of God in heav'n,
> A spirit teachable and mild,
> A simple heart to learn and love,
> Like that sweet holy Child.

A variant on verse in an earlier collection – *The Legend of the Golden Prayers,* published in 1859 – it parallels these lines from The Angel to indicate the sublime ideals of Tractarian worship this most remarkable woman sought to set before the young.

> Not a bell is ringing now
> But the priest is praying loud,
> And the choir is answering,
> And the people murmur low,
> And the incense, like a cloud,
> Curls along the chapel proud.

Despite the aura of stained-glass sanctity that has inevitably surrounded and framed her as a Victorian figure, Cecil Frances Alexander (née Humphreys) was no mere hymnist but one who, in her use of hymns as the simplest homilies, stands tall in the history of Christendom as a notable evangelist to children.

A SPIRITUAL TREASURY OF THE WORK OF CECIL FRANCES ALEXANDER

The author of outstanding hymns on Creation, Incarnation and Crucifixion, Fanny Alexander bequeathed a casket of most costly gems to the sanctuary of Christendom. 'All things bright and beautiful', 'Once in royal David's city' and 'There is a green hill far away', all of them written in the language of children, have a timeless quality and appeal for the young in heart. If the adult world has customarily preferred her other compositions, it is not because

> The roseate hues of early dawn

is puzzling as an EVENING HYMN. And it can no more avoid the urgent summons that, on ST. ANDREW'S DAY demands discipleship, than rejoice that for THE ASCENSION

> The golden gates are lifted up!

For in a near-perfect offering in homespun verse, Cecil Frances Alexander gave of her best to afford highlights to a crowded

Church Kalendar. A hymn for <u>Advent</u> epitomizes incarnation in a single verse of simple piety:

> When Jesus came to earth of old,
> He came in weakness and in woe;
> He wore no form of angel mould,
> But took our nature poor and low.
>> [A. P. Graves (ed.), *Selected Poems of ... C. F. A.*
>> (London, 1930), p. 18]

Another made use of <u>HOLY INNOCENTS</u> to focus the rôle of children. It has a questioning start:

> We are but little children weak,
> Nor born in any high estate;
> What can we do for Jesus' sake,
> Who is so high and good and great?

At first, this seems trite catechism, but the answers afforded reveal the resolve and commitment of spiritual warfare and pilgrimage:

> We wear the cross they wore of old,
> Our lips have learned like vows to make;
> We need not die; we cannot fight;
> What may we do for Jesus' sake?

> Oh, day by day each Christian child
> Has much to do, without, within;
> A death to die for Jesus' sake,
> A weary war to wage with sin.

In short, after a rehearsal of belief radiant with 'smiles of peace and looks of love', children are recognized and encouraged in the 'good old cause':

> There's not a child so small and weak
> But has his little cross to take,
> His little work of love and praise
> That he may do for Jesus' sake.
>> [Op. cit., p. 22]

Famed for poetry that regularly refracted light, the first verse of Mrs Alexander's EPIPHANY uses such skill in an ideal context:

> STAR of the East! whose silver ray
> Was once the faithful Gentiles' guide,
> Star of our souls! Look down today,
> And lead us to Thy cradle side. [Ibid.]

Penitential devotions are especially hard to pen, yet in her hymn for LENT Mrs Alexander succeeds with compelling composition that enshrines the unique nature of healing held out by the suffering Saviour:

> When wounded sore the stricken heart
> Lies bleeding and unbound,
> One only Hand, a piercèd Hand,
> Can salve the sinner's wound.

The 'One only' refrain is especially persuasive, and presented in a wide variation of form in the hymn's five verses. And just as

> One only Heart, a broken Heart,
> Can feel the sinner's woe;

So too:

> One only Stream, a Stream of Blood,
> Can wash away the blot.

Until, with all the realism of revivalist imagery, the inescapable conclusion is reached:

> Lift up Thy bleeding Hand, O Lord,
> Unseal that cleansing tide;
> We have no shelter from our sin
> But in Thy wounded Side.   [Op. cit, p. 24]

In verse that deserves to be known more widely, a GOOD FRIDAY hymn sets a powerful spotlight on forgiveness. With careful exposition of Christ's 'Last Word' and plea for pardon from the Cross, it provides unforgettable focus on a Father's love:

> Forgive them, O My Father,
> They know not what they do!
> The Saviour spake in anguish,
> As the sharp nails went through.

Personal application in later verses heightens the emotional force of the composition to ensure real devotional impact:

> For me was that compassion,
> For me that tender care:
> I need His wide forgiveness
> As much as any there.
>
> It was my pride and hardness
> That hung [*] Him on the Tree;
> Those cruel nails, O Saviour,
> Were driven in by me.
>
> And often have I slighted
> Thy gentle voice that chid;
> Forgive me, too, Lord Jesus:
> I knew not what I did.
> [*for *hanged!*]

The triumphant EASTER hymn

> He is risen! He is risen!
> Tell it out with joyful voice

is also neglected nowadays despite superb economy of words in a powerful gospel proclamation the apostle particularly prized. Four times the trumpet sounds:

> Death is conquered, man is free,
> Christ hath won the victory.

...

These glad tidings to them tell:
Christ hath conquered death and hell.

...

Jesus all our sorrows bore,
Sin and pain can vex no more.

...

Death's dominion now is o'er,
Praise to Thee for evermore.

And the echo endures.

For the rest, it is appropriate to make brief reference first to the skilful way Mrs Alexander makes both antithesis and alliteration serve themes of denial and repentance on ST PETER'S DAY

Saint Peter, when the cock crew clear
Went out and wept his broken faith;
Strong as a rock through strife and fear,
He served his Lord till death.

Secondly, the last verse she provided for a COMMUNION HYMN has evident merit to make it a contribution of distinction to a difficult genre:

Come, bread of Heaven, to feed our souls,
And with thee, Jesus, enter in;
Come, wine of God, and as we drink
His precious Blood, wash out our sin.

[Op. cit., p. 36]

Finally, no sanctuary unadorned with flowers can symbolize the spiritual treasury of a nature lover whose work lost no opportunity to share her wonder of creation with the young. The joy of walks along 'the highways and the hedges' never left an observant woman well aware of the

Daisies white with crimson edges
That the children love to hold.

But such fascination always had a wider appeal and in a H<small>YMN</small> <small>FOR</small> F<small>LOWER</small> S<small>UNDAY</small>, the Christian context of the poet's true mission is to be found:

> In the highways Thou hast sought them,
> From the hedges plucked Thy flowers;
> Precious souls! Thy blood has bought them,
> Souls of theirs and souls of ours.
>
> [Op. cit., p. 37]

Chapter 12

JOHN ELLERTON

and

'The day Thou gavest, Lord, is ended'

1 The day Thou gavest, Lord, is ended,
    The darkness falls at Thy behest;
  To Thee our morning hymns ascended,
    Thy praise shall sanctify our rest.

2 We thank Thee that Thy Church unsleeping,
    While earth rolls onward into light,
  Through all the world her watch is keeping,
    And rests not now by day or night.

3 As o'er each continent and island
    The dawn leads on another day,
  The voice of prayer is never silent,
    Nor dies the strain of praise away.

4 The sun that bids us rest is waking
    Our brethren 'neath the western sky,
  And hour by hour fresh lips are making
    Thy wondrous doings heard on high.

5 So be it, Lord; Thy throne shall never,
    Like earth's proud empires, pass away;
  Thy Kingdom stands, and grows for ever,
    Till all Thy creatures own Thy sway.

Every feeling ... which enters into any act of true worship may fitly find expression in a hymn.

Although not directly involved in the original publication of *Hymns, Ancient & Modern* (1861), John Ellerton's command of hymnology was well known and widely respected at the time, and his own compositions were to ensure him a place on the Committee appointed to revise that *magnum opus* and bring out the *Supplement*. They also endeared him to many because it was rare to find marvellous inspiration for worship which came not from the cloistered seclusion of close or cathedral precinct, university college or rural parish calm, but from a committed and active urban ministry of no mean popular appeal. This brief extract can therefore spotlight the conscientious professionalism of a priest of dutiful genius. Taken from an article in the *Churchman's Family Magazine* (1864), the words not only provide precise focus on Ellerton as a gifted editor and sensitive compiler, but serve to set him apart from most of his predecessors and contemporaries.

A purist who deeply respected the Western tradition, John Ellerton treasured St Augustine's definition of a hymn. Renowned for authoritative scholarship in a normative writing such as *On Christian Doctrine*, the saintly style of the Bishop of Hippo's *Commentary* on Psalm 72 included a classic judgement in a brief paragraph of profound impact:

Hymns are praises to GOD sung; hymns are songs containing praise to GOD. If, therefore, there be praise but not to GOD, it is no hymn. If it be praise, and even praise to GOD, yet not sung, it is no hymn. A hymn, therefore, if it is to be a hymn, must have these three characteristics – praise, praise to GOD, and praise to GOD sung.

In his essay on 'Principles of Hymn-Book construction', Ellerton neatly summarized such Augustinian complexity as

Praise, the praise of God, and song.

To him it was 'sufficiently clear and precise', but he wondered if it might be 'too narrow' a definition. In an attempt to 'fix our limit' too, he offered his reader a mature survey of the whole subject, a survey that after many an acute observation reached its climax with these words of masterly appraisal:

> Hymns may express adoration, thanksgiving, commemoration of God's mercies; they may be prayers, penitential, supplicatory, intercessory; they may be devout aspirations after God; but in any case they must be forms of worship. It is not enough that they <u>suggest</u> devotion, they must be capable of <u>expressing</u> it. The observance of this rule would clear the ground at once of much irrelevant matter with which the Hymn-books of every Church and sect are at present encumbered. The whole multitude of didactic and hortatory verses, the addresses to sinners and saints, the paraphrases of Scripture prophecies, promises, and warnings, the descriptions of heaven and hell, the elaborate elucidations of the anatomy and pathology of the soul; all these, whatever their value in the chamber, the study, or the pulpit, ought utterly and for ever to be banished from the choir. [Quoted in Henry Housman, *J[ohn] E[llerton, being a] C[ollection of his] W[ritings on] H[ymnology]* (London, 1896), pp. 228–9]

It is fascinating to recall that Matthew Arnold, for whom 'The true meaning of religion' was 'not simply morality, but morality touched by emotion', held John Ellerton to be 'the greatest of living hymnologists'. Educated at Cambridge, where he read theology, Ellerton was early in debt to the textual criticism and social concerns of F. J. A. Hort who remained his life-long friend. But if scholarship remained a vital *raison d'être*, visions of ministry soon gained priority as the scholar felt his true vocation to be that of 'a country parson'. This aim was initially realized when, after ordination in Chichester Cathedral, Ellerton served a first curacy at Easebourne, West Sussex. But such Keble-like expectations were not to last. Instead, apart from four years (1872–1876) in the village of Hinstock on the Shropshire-Staffordshire border, he was claimed in turn by Brighton, Crewe and Barnes before, weary of well-doing and almost sixty, he spent seven years as Rector of White Roding near Dunmow, Essex, to

combine country ministry with editorial work. It was almost as
if busy pastoral pressure nourished Ellerton's compositions; and
just as work among the children of St Nicholas, Brighton,
prompted his *Hymns for Schools and Bible Classes* in the mid-fifties,
so a parish at Crewe Green with a congregation made up of railway mechanics and 'rustics' generated hymns for Cheshire choir
festivals ten years later.

Written in 1856, his <u>Morning</u> and <u>Evening</u> hymns were sub-
titled 'Before' and 'After School'. They stand in a long tradition
hallowed, among others, by Thomas Ken. The first line of the
<u>Morning</u> <u>Hymn</u>

> Day by day we magnify Thee –

Ellerton derived from the Te Deum, before, in the rest of the
verse, he projected praise to God from classroom routines:

> When our hymns in School we raise;
> Daily work begun and ended
> With the daily voice of praise.

It was a theme he re-echoed in the afternoon, for Ellerton gave
children an office of their own in his 'After School' hymn:

> The hours of School are over,
> The evening calls us home;
> Once more to Thee, O Father,
> With thankful hearts we come:
> For all Thy countless blessings
> We praise Thy Holy Name,
> And own Thy love unchanging,
> Through days and years the same.

Eventide recollection at Crewe continued to inspire Ellerton's best
compositions, and one hymn in particular, revised in 1868, gained
widespread recognition as a doxology he designed to be sung on
'Sunday Evening, After Service', especially 'After Festivals':

> Saviour, again to Thy dear Name we raise
> With one accord our parting hymn of praise:

We stand to bless Thee 'ere our worship cease;
Then lowly kneeling wait Thy word of peace.

The last verse proved particularly successful, and was widely
acclaimed for the way it cherished the kindred sentiments of
dedication and ultimate valediction.

Grant us Thy peace throughout our earthly life,
Our balm in sorrow, and our stay in strife.
Then, when Thy voice shall bid our conflict cease,
Call us, O Lord, to Thine eternal peace.

But of all John Ellerton's work, and a particularly appropriate
focus for the last chapter of this little book about the 'Pops'
among traditional hymns,

The day Thou gavest, Lord, is ended

deserves careful attention. Another fine Evening Hymn it was
written in 1870 and originally appeared in *A Liturgy for Missionary Meetings*. Thereafter, its five first-rate verses, with their wide
appeal, soon guaranteed his composition a secure place in a
growing number of Victorian hymnals. According to Henry
Housman, who served as Ellerton's curate for a time, the first line
was borrowed from an anonymous hymn published in a book of
Church Poetry (1855). That acknowledgement made, the original
way the author opens out daily offices to afford the Almighty a
full panoply of praise is truly inspirational. In simple but
effective style, verse 1 sets out the idea of day and night, light
and darkness, to stress that there are no off-peak periods for
divine praise. In short, even when the day is past, morning hymns
have already ascended to ensure that

Thy praise shall sanctify our rest.

In verse 2, a combination of simple observation and elementary
astronomy prompts grateful recognition of vigilance:

We thank Thee that Thy Church unsleeping
While earth rolls onward into light,
Through all the world her watch is keeping,
And rests not now by day or night.

The missionary context enhances this theme in verse 3, to make a ceaseless clamour of prayer and praise both at home and abroad. For

As o'er each continent and island,
The dawn leads on another day,
The voice of prayer is never silent,
Nor dies the strain of praise away.

In verse 4, dramatic symbolism of the rising sun is used to magnify and heighten an ever-increasing crescendo of praise when

... hour by hour fresh lips are making
Thy wondrous doings heard on high.

And in a conclusion of infinite power, John Ellerton's fifth and final verse proves the epitome of praise. Human transience is cleverly contrasted with eternal values, the memory still recalling fading themes of night and day, darkness and light, to reach a final climax and magnificent affirmation in two renowned lines of acceptance and hope:

Thy Kingdom stands, and grows for ever,
Till all Thy creatures own Thy sway.

It was, no doubt, with such a couplet in mind that Queen Victoria chose Ellerton's hymn to conclude the great Service of Thanksgiving that marked her Diamond Jubilee in 1897.

★

In the 'Principles of Hymn-Book Construction', John Ellerton, in a criticism of Christopher Wordsworth's insistence that hymns must have a teaching rôle, undoubtedly had real reservations about the idea of hymns as homilies. The Bishop of Lincoln's judgement that

> A Church which forgoes the use of hymns in her office of teaching, neglects one of the most efficacious instruments for correcting error, and for disseminating truth, as well as for ministering comfort and edification, especially to the poor ...,

he confronted head on. His priorities preferred devotion to definition; and it was this principled conviction which conditioned both his own compositions and his choice of other work in the endless editorial rôle of hymnal selection that preoccupied his last years. For in Ellerton's opinion, no amount of meditation on matters theological could produce a hymn, if only for the good reason that mental and philosophical gymnastics never attain devotional heights. It was an issue he viewed as yet another round in the age-old rivalry between faith and reason. Just as reading tracts in church provided no substitute for the liturgy, so too

> those doctrinal hymns are always the best which, if not addressed to GOD, pass, 'ere they close, into a direct utterance of prayer or praise.

Rarely had a hymn-writer been so specific about his art, and in the praise of stanza after stanza John Ellerton reflected the reality of what for him became a single-eyed quest for true hymns. When he joined the 'Compilers' with an invitation to help revise *Hymns, Ancient and Modern*, Ellerton's work with the *Supplement* published in 1889 (in which, out of 165 new entries, 13 hymns were his own composition) proved very much a treasure-trove experience. That his services were highly valued too, is evident from some gracious words of the Committee Chairman, Cosby White, in the introduction:

> It would scarcely be possible to exaggerate the value of the assistance which was rendered by Mr Ellerton in the production of the complete edition.

An accolade and no polite protocol, it was a credit that recognized genuine expertise, and this was his due for three main reasons. First, Ellerton had proved himself to be a hymn-writer of no mean achievement. Secondly, long years of front-line ministry had given him the sensitivity needed to understand and instruct others in the service of the sanctuary. And thirdly, concentrated specialist studies had made him a master of hymnology. Some twenty years earlier, his letter to Beardmore Compton of SPCK effectively provided a gratuitious review of the first edition of *Hymns, Ancient and Modern*. Here, although he admitted that 'The existing Hymnal has the advantage of representing more than one School of English devotional theology' to contain 'many hymns of sterling worth and beauty', Ellerton was quite emphatic about its 'great defects'. These he proceeded to list in reasoning altogether fascinating for its maturity of judgement.

At the outset, he argued that only the widest scrutiny of sources could guarantee the best selection of hymns. A translator of some skill himself, Ellerton had worked with Hort on *Beata nobis gaudia* and deplored the absence of Latin and Greek compositions. He felt sure that

> an examination of the best mediaeval hymns will convince you that there is no real reason for their exclusion, any more than for that of the contemporary collects which fill so large a space in our Prayer-Book.

If unwilling to support work 'which is unsuitable for the use of a Reformed Church', he was nevertheless well aware that 'there are many ... older hymns full of true congregational spirit, of simplicity, devotion and depth, which would adorn any collection'. In his view it certainly followed that 'the great position of the SPCK' gave that Society 'a matchless opportunity for investigating foreign hymnody'. With a surprisingly open world-view for the period too, he urged the Committee to consider Germany as 'a very wide field'; to remember Denmark, and the *Chants Chrétiens* of Protestant France 'quite unknown to us here'; and to take notice of the 'new Hymnal for the Protestant Episcopal Church' at that time being compiled in the United States of America. Constructive criticism followed as Ellerton deplored 'too many of the hymns in the Society's present book' for a mediocrity he found altogether 'dull and colourless'. This fault he attributed to the kind of clerical compromise which preferred 'to steer a safe course by omitting what will offend one or other school in the Church'. With the firm reminder that the SPCK represented the whole Church and no 'sectarian' viewpoint, he thus drew a parallel with the *Book of Common Prayer* to argue for the representation of 'each side (within due limits)'. Nor did he leave his meaning obscure, and in the context of a consideration of communion hymns offered precise illustration of his wish to

> retain the old evangelical hymns of Watts and Doddridge which are justly dear to thousands; [to] ... insert such hymns as 'Thee we adore, O blessed Saviour, Thee', and one or two more which give that side of the doctrine which the Catechism and Communion service express; and [to] ... exclude such hymns as ... are simply vague.

Likewise loath to recommend private hymns for public worship, he took good care to avoid compositions 'which are nothing more than religious meditations or paraphrases of texts'.

This letter of 1868 set out sentiments similar to those John Ellerton had expressed in the article written in 1864. It was an approach he used again at Barnes where the simple scriptural sermons he preached as Rector encouraged a 'questioning spirit' and 'the scientific inquiry' he valued as 'so remarkable a feature of our time'. Published by Macmillan in 1882, the Lenten course he entitled *Holiest Manhood and its Lessons for busy lives*, was carefully prepared as an antidote for the highly-pressurized lives of upwardly mobile parishioners. 'We all feel,' he urged, 'especially in and around London, the pace at which we live. Energy in work, absorption in business, excitement in pleasure, activity in our very amusements; these are the conditions of our time' [op. cit. p. 31]. A priest whose daily work personified private devotion to his people, Ellerton did all he could to cultivate personal religion for those in his care. Such were entreated 'never to use a religious phrase' they had 'not thought out' [ibid, p. 151], just as in one penitential address he urged his congregation to seek 'self-recollection, meditation' and the 'devotion' he held to be 'nourishment ... for the inner life' [ibid, p. 32]. Sunday worship he particularly prized as a principal focus of the Christian community spirit, and another sermon from the Barnes' collection referred to

the unspeakable value of Sunday, not merely as a day of rest,
but as a day ... of meditation and spiritual refreshment.

[op. cit., p. 41]

Barely two years later, poor health and exhaustion brought on by
the unrelenting routines he demanded of himself, obliged John
Ellerton to resign his 'populous suburban parish'. After a brief
spell of recuperation – during which he served a chaplaincy in a
Lake Genevan retreat of near-paradise for the poet – Ellerton was
presented to the living of White Roding (May, 1885). It proved
a hallowed haven where he enjoyed writing in the 17th-century
Rectory 'with a cat on the chair beside me'. If it was also his
hope to get a neglected house and garden 'in a tidy state', these
were largely years of devoted committee work. For not only did
he continue to offer careful counsel on compositions selected for
various hymnals, but in 1888 accepted an invitation from SPCK
to edit a *Manual of Parochial Work* which embraced articles 'by
writers who have special knowledge or experience in the subjects of which they treat'. Sharing his skills 'for the use of the
younger clergy', Ellerton concerned himself with 'The Parish
Church', and as well as writing about the place of 'The Sacraments' and 'Occasional Offices' in ministry, concluded a chapter
on 'Choir Work' by a Tutor at Chichester Theological College
(Henry Housman, BD, formerly his curate at Barnes) with a
four-page summary on the choice of a hymn-book. His carefully-chosen words forward the shrewdest counsel as he advised
'the new comer ... not to change' an unsatisfactory hymnal
without careful consultation of the kind that has 'accustomed his
people to care for better hymns than he has found in use' [*Manual*, pp. 108–109]. Even then, he was convinced

that it would be well to consult not only the churchwardens, but the great body of parishioners, before making a
change.   [Ibid.]

As to the choice of hymnal, autobiographical indulgence
indicated that the 'days are past when a clergyman thought it
needful to compile his own hymn-book'. Even so, he did not
recommend *Hymns, Ancient and Modern*, but argued that 'from
time to time' it was necessary to supplement the book the pas-

tor 'likes best'. For

> Every hymn-book has its deficiencies as well as its
> redundancies.   [Ibid.]

Resort to 'cheap collections' (and he named among others the
London Mission Hymn-book, 1884, the *Durham Mission
Hymn-book*, and *Church Militant Hymns*, 1884), most of them
'published at a penny', can provide an ideal source of hymns for
special occasions and seasons, but a cautionary note drew
attention to 'the law of copyright' if such supplements are 'to be
sold'. Generosity itself in this respect, Ellerton indicated that

> the great majority of living hymn-writers will be always
> found ready to waive their copyright on being asked.
>   [op. cit., p. 110]

This same year witnessed Ellerton's transformation of what he
once termed his 'two bantlings' in the publication of some
seventy-six hymns and a number of particularly fine translations
as *H[ymns] O[riginal and] T[ranslated]* (Skeffington, Piccadilly).
The substance of a dedicated life's work, the book was dedicated

TO
THE RIGHT HONOURABLE
LORD CREWE
in remembrance of nearly thirty years
of unbroken friendship and
continual kindness
White Roding   April, 1888

It included neither introduction nor preface, but dated every
entry and carefully recorded later revisions. The following year
the 'Complete Edition' of *Hymns, Ancient and Modern* appeared,
and with it John Ellerton's last compositions; but in 1891, and
again in 1892, when away at Torquay for convalescence, a series
of strokes paralysed his frail frame. He died on 15 June 1893, and
few hymn-writers can have received such a send-off, the funeral
service being quite literally shrouded with much of his finest

work. For at the parish church of St John on 20 June 1893, after the customary sentences, psalm and scripture reading, a large congregation sang

> GOD of the living in Whose eyes.

A choral eucharist followed, with

> When the day of toil is done,
> When the race of life is run,
> Father grant Thy wearied one
> Rest for evermore!

added to the introit. During the administration, choir and communicants sang

> Grant us Thy peace throughout our earthly life
> Our balm in sorrow, and our stay in strife

(a hymn more readily recognised as the last verse of Ellerton's much loved 'Saviour, again to Thy dear Name we raise'); and concluding prayers then introduced

> Now the labourer's task is o'er;
> Now the battle-day is past;

and, as the procession left the sanctuary for the churchyard, the mourners sang

> O shining city of our God.

More was to come even then, and after the body was lowered into the grave, and the officiating priest concluded the Burial Service with the celebrated resurrection collect, the choir burst forth again to render what many regarded as the most moving of all John Ellerton's translations – *Rerum Deus tenax vigor* – the hymn attributed to St Ambrose which he had translated with Hort:

> O Strength and Stay, upholding all creation
> Who ever dost thyself unmoved abide.

Including as it did his own third verse:

> Hear us, O Father, gracious and forgiving,
> Through Jesus Christ thy co-eternal Word,
> Who with the Holy Ghost by all things living
> Now and to endless ages art adored

this provided the perfect doxology.

AN ELLERTON SPIRITUAL TREASURY

> A Church hymn-book is not a statue gallery erected that
> men may pass through it and admire the skill of each artist;
> it is a temple for the worship of the Most High, in which
> every stone, rough-hewn or cunningly carved, is fitted to its
> place and subordinated to the one Spirit which informs and
> consecrates the whole.   [*J.E.C.W.H.*, p. 271]

Taken from the paper he read to a Church Congress at Stoke-on-
Trent in 1875, these words clearly indicate John Ellerton's
disciplined approach to worship. Convinced of the inspiration
hymns afford spiritual life, he stressed the importance of
selection, and went on to argue that 'self-restraint in our choice of
hymns' can alone preserve the Church from 'mere fashion and
caprice'. It will therefore come as no surprise to find his own compositions conceived with a care intended to bring congregations
'certainty of faith'. With few exceptions, there is a
consistency about Ellerton's hymns, this same paper on 'Hymns
and Hymn-Singing' spelling out a dedicated priest's determination
to uplift his people in a worship

> calm with the consciousness of God's presence, lowly with
> the reality of penitence, [and] joyful with the sincerity of
> thankfulness.   [Ibid., p. 275]

Readily discernible in his own work as a hymn-writer, such
attributes stem from the principles that guided Ellerton's composition. An earlier paper had listed the 'few particulars' he was
clear afforded 'excellence' to a hymn; and some examination of

these can be both informative and relevant to a selection of his writing in a brief spiritual treasury.

First, Ellerton rated sincerity most highly of all, and illustrated his point with reference to the *Book of Common Prayer* where he found

> no overstrained expressions either of sorrow or of joy; no invitation to one another to weep, or prayers for 'a fount of tears'.

A pertinent observation, it is well reflected in the frank recognition of a hymn composed for <u>Wednesday</u>, the mid-week sandbank when, particularly among rural communities, worship itself seems becalmed.

> THOU in Whose name the two or three
> Art met to-day to meet with Thee,
> Fulfil to us Thine own sure word,
> And be Thou here Thyself, O Lord!
> > [*H.O.T.*, p. 11]

In the last verse of his powerful <u>GOOD FRIDAY</u> (Midday) hymn too, a deep sincerity confronts the facts of the human situation:

> LORD, should fear and anguish roll
> Darkly o'er my sinful soul,
> Thou, Who once was thus bereft
> That Thine own might ne'er be left,
> Teach me by that bitter cry
> In the gloom to know Thee nigh.

And frustrated by the heedless majority who, unmoved by Christ's crucifixion, regarded Good Friday as just another day, Ellerton's 'Evening' hymn faced reality with a simple vocational candour in the second verse:

> The busy world that knows Thee not,
> And daily crucified Thee still

> Has passed unmarked the sacred spot,
> In thoughtless mirth or proud self-will.

The same emotional restraint is at once evident in Ellerton's baptismal hymn. With children – often tiny infants – involved, a subject that offers condescension full scope nevertheless sustains sincerity.

> O FATHER, bless the children
> Brought hither to Thy gate;
> Lift up their fallen nature,
> Restore their lost estate;
> Renew Thine image in them,
> And own them, by this sign,
> Thy very sons and daughters,
> New-born of birth divine.
>   [*H.O.T.*, p. 30]

A work of serious purpose, the hymn deals with difficult doctrines without a hint of compromise and explains why, in its author's pastoral experience 'many have been awakened to spiritual life by the Prayer-Book'. [*J.E.C.W.G.*, p. 239]

Secondly, John Ellerton emphasized that

> A hymn must be vigorous! [Ibid.]

Once again, his compositions indicate a practice capable of arresting Church congregations at every season of the Kalendar. No simple task in itself, the fourth verse of

> King Messiah, long expected,

a hymn for 'The Circumcision of Christ' (1 January), is especially assertive:

> Father of the new creation!
> Prophet of the latter time!
> Leader of the ransomed nation
> To the better Canaan's clime!
> Though from Gentile stock arising

Alien branches once were we,
Thou hast said, in our baptizing
We are circumcised in Thee.

[*H.O.T.*, p. 12]

For the 'Conversion of St Paul', Ellerton's

We sing the glorious conquest
Before Damascus' gate

has a similarly powerful fourth verse:

Lord, teach Thy Church the lesson,
Still in her darkest hour
Of weakness and of danger
To trust Thy hidden power.
Thy grace by ways mysterious
The wrath of man can find,
And in Thy boldest foeman
Thy chosen Saint can find.

But it is in hymns he composed as processionals, and for choir festivals and occasions of national thanksgiving that this aspect of Ellerton's strength can best be appreciated. The London Mission of 1884 secured his

ONWARD, brothers, onward! march with one accord;
Jesus goes before us, all-victorious Lord!

[*H.O.T.*, p. 54]

A glorious example of vigour in action, these first two lines provided a singularly effective refrain repeated after all five verses. For the Chester Choir Festival of 1870 too, these lines had a very similar impact:

Come forth, O Christian brothers,
In ordered, fair array;
Come forth with strains of gladness
To greet your festal day!
Rejoice in God your Saviour;

> Your hearts and voices raise,
> His gates with songs to enter
> And tread His courts with praise.
>   [*H.O.T.*, p. 55]

But in terms of <u>National</u> <u>Thanksgiving</u> for the avoidance of war in 1871, a certain jingoism coloured Ellerton's

> PRAISE to our God, whose bounteous hand
> Prepared of old our glorious land;
> A garden fenced with silver sea;
> A people prosperous, strong and free.
>   [*H.O.T.*, p. 57]

The 'Children's Hymn' he wrote for Queen Victoria's Jubilee, with the refrain repeat

> GOD, save the Queen!

was also forcible. But its second verse:

> Dusky Indian, strong Australian,
> Western forest, Southern Sea,
> None are wanting, none are alien,
> All in one great prayer agree

clearly qualified colonialism in Christ. And to indicate that establishment must take its toll of any principle, verse 5 reflected a concern for Albert, Prince Consort, to inculcate a long tradition hallowed by the *Book of Common Prayer* in emulation of 'The Prayer for the Royal Family':

> Then He sent the years of sorrow,
> Took the one she loved the best,
> Left her lonely, till the Morrow
> Brings her His eternal Rest,
>   God save the Queen!

Despite such qualifications, it would be hard to deny the resolute character of such writing. For in recognition of symbolic periods in Church history, Ellerton sets such work in relief with the memorable judgement that

> The whole faith of the Primitive Church shines out from the *Te Deum*; the whole piety of the Middle Ages is in *Dies Irae* and *Stabat Mater*; the whole power of the Reformation rings through *Ein feste Burg*.   [*J.E.C.W.H.*, p. 240]

Thirdly, Ellerton pleaded for simplicity, and deplored the complexity of compositions which, by metaphor and imagery, confused their true intent. It was a point he expressed succinctly in the purposeful statement that

> Hymns are not for the few, but for the many, not chiefly to be read and pondered over, but chiefly to be sung.

Written for children and adults, an unusual hymn of 1871 entitled <u>Catechizing</u>, indicates this skill particularly well in verses one and three:

> MARY at the Master's feet
> Sat to hear His gracious word;
> So before Thy face we meet:
> Still be Thou our Teacher, LORD!
>
> Word by word, and line by line,
> Infant lips their faith profess;
> Creed and Law, and Prayer Divine –
> Mystery of godliness!   [*H.O.T.*, p. 31]

Nothing is allowed to frustrate the purpose of the hymn <u>In Time of Pestilence</u>, its message of dependence on the divine, seeking both forgiveness for social ills and unquestioning faith to understand the devastation of cholera in the light of God's will

> O LORD of life and death, we come
> In sorrow to Thy throne;
> Yet not bewildered, blind and dumb,
> Before some Power unknown.

The scourge is in our Father's hand;
The plague comes forth from Thee:
Oh give us hearts to understand,
And faith Thy ways to see!

Forgive the foul neglect that brought
Thy chastening to our door;
The homes uncleansed, the souls untaught,
The unregarded poor.

The slothful ease, the greed of gain,
The wasted years, forgive;
Purge out our sins by needful pain,
Then turn, and bid us live.

So shall the lives for which we plead
Be spared to praise Thee still;
And we, from fear and danger freed,
Be strong to do Thy will. [*H.O.T.*, p. 62]

And on a less controversial, if equally profound subject – the out-pouring of the Holy Spirit – the first and last verses of a hymn Ellerton revised for <u>Whit-Sunday</u> in 1877 used the simplest language to bring home the biblical record:

THIS day the Lord's disciples met
According to His Word,
And waited for the promised Gift
Of their ascended Lord.

O greatest Teacher, surest Guide,
True Comforter, be here;
Make all Thy children feel and know
That Thou indeed art near.

Finally, Ellerton noted the value of brevity as a 'boundary line' in his prayerful quest for true hymns. But although he suggested that

Eight four-line stanzas or thirty-two lines may be taken as a limit which it is not desirable a hymn should exceed,

[*J.E.C.W.H.*, p. 242]

few of his compositions actually ran to more than five verses.

Modest enough to appreciate that such 'hints by no means exhaust the subject', Ellerton made further deference to St Augustine and reminded his reader that the *cum cantico* principle demanded writing 'adapted to music' [Ibid.]. To achieve this he upheld simplicity as the handmaid of sincerity, virtues readily apparent in the examples chosen to illustrate this little treasury of his work.

It was John Ellerton's plea that

The Hymnody of our land ought to be criticized in a spirit of reverence, of humility, and of brotherly kindness.

Such qualities are certainly evident in the many gifted compositions he hoped would challenge, succour and sustain the devotional life of the Church and nation he sought to serve.

APPENDIX 1

A Note on TEXT and TUNE

Of all the hymn writers featured in these pages, only Martin Luther possessed musical genius. The rest wrote in an accent and metre chosen either to match known tunes, or to be married to music in the divine worship of congregational praise. Altogether fascinating, the subject is one of immense complexity. It has received admirable discussion in Maurice Frost's historical introduction to *Hymns, Ancient & Modern*, and in the dense factual thickets of Erik Routley's *Music of Christian Hymnody* (1957).

Dr Routley has aptly described hymn tunes as 'the folk songs of the Christian faith' (op. cit., p. 5), and there has never been a time in the long history of Christendom when the faithful have not communed in psalms and hymns and spiritual songs. From New Testament to contemporary times, the triune God has been praised. During the Middle Age plainsong interspersed with 'office' hymns predominated; and at the time of the Reformation of the 16th century many variations found their way into the worship of the Church established by Henry VIII and Edward VI, and re-established under Elizabeth I. But John Calvin's conviction that the Almighty was best praised in the hallowed inspirational setting of the Psalms handed down a long tradition of metrical psalmody. In consequence, Martin Luther's attempt to express in rhythms beyond plainsong the enthusiams of his 're-discovered' gospel was kept at bay in an England where Swiss theology gained the advantage as a more acceptable form of 'protestantism' than the conservatism of Wittenberg. Calvin founded Genevan worship on his understanding of an Early Church which he was clear held the Old Testament praise of the psalms in the highest esteem. Any compositions attempted by man alone had to be inferior and inappropriate. By contrast, once free of the restrictions of Rome, Luther used his considerable acquaintance with Saxon folk songs to popularize the New Testament message in melodies which later achieved wide fame in the great chorales.

In England and Scotland metrical psalms, with the 'office' hymns and canticles retained in the liturgy, were to dominate worship for two centuries. But the time came when popular disapproval of a drear dimension in services of worship both prompted and promoted change. Those of near 'puritan' conviction found the Psalter insufficiently literal, whilst more traditional church folk sought inspiration from work possessed of greater literary quality. If the Restoration of Charles II weakened the Puritan cause, Prayer-Book revision nevertheless kept psalm singing alive. But it was invariably singing of the kind that proceeded by a primitive means of dictation, the cantor, precentor or minister 'lining out' phrases his people then repeated in dull unison. Tunes were anonymous, for Holy Scripture provided the key principle to be observed. With Isaac Watts, however, the New Testament began to be used in public praise; and in their turn, the Wesleys used simple melodic music to convey the gospel message of revival that contributed so much to English religion in the eighteenth century. The kinship with German Pietism proved an important cross-current; and Luther's legacy at last enlivened English worship to give new meaning to the sixteenth-century adage of Thomas de Vio, Cardinal Cajetan, that 'he has conquered us by his songs'. John Wesley certainly translated many German hymns, and his brother Charles added to his already ample range by imitating German metres in a number of compositions.

Above all, metres were married to striking new melodies, and for both chapel and parish church an important period of revivalism enriched worship in consequence. Hymn books were shortly to be linked to 'tune books', not printed separately; and

the old localism of what was often merely parochial use was gradually abandoned in favour of the widest horizons of praise that
made both old and new hymns familiar to thousands.

'Methodism was born in song', and it was the great merit of
John Wesley's tune book, *Sacred Melody*, to afford 149 'select
hymns' no fewer than 76 tunes. For congregations the appeal was
heightened because of the book's *melody only* emphasis; and the
valuable way tunes were arranged in order of the 23 different
metres supplied. At last all metres in Charles Wesley's own long
list of compositions could find a tune, John having failed his
brother in 1742 when a smaller *Collection of Tunes, set to Music as
... commonly sung at the Foundery* had offered only twelve
variations of metre. The code had been cracked, and henceforth
the best of chants uplifted psalmody, reinforced the noble
chorales derived from Luther, and provided music for the prolific
period of 18th- and 19th-century hymn composition. A fascinating future, in small degree symbolized and sampled in these
few chapters, lay ahead for assiduous compilers of church and
chapel hymnals, for in turn each and every denomination
mirrored Wesley's achievement. Many a critic also enjoyed his
field day, and the conscientious reader will recall the qualified
praise John Ellerton gave the first edition of *Hymns, Ancient and
Modern* (1861).

Almost inevitably, and from every sectarian source, legions of
frowns faced any misalliance of text and tune. It is a grievance
still felt today when hymns chosen for weddings or funerals confront irregular churchgoers with tunes different from those of
their childhood memory. For melody matters to both migrant
birds of passage and regular worshippers; and in days when a fine
range of tunes is at hand to fit any metre, a moment's dilemma
need be cause for dismay no more. Instead let those who plan
ahead ponder full well the need to provide tunes that appeal. For
then, as many a televised 'Songs of Praise' has demonstrated to
the nation at large, genuine acts of Christian worship uniquely
display the spiritual unity of the people of God.

APPENDIX 2

A Chronological chart:
Hymns in Context
1600–1900

Hymns & Hymn Writers 1600–1900	Contemporary Events Political	Social	Some Cultural & Ecclesiastical Landmarks	Parallel Events in Europe	North America
	1660 Restoration of Charles II			1660 Diego Velasquez d.	1660 Navigation Acts
1662 *Book of Common Prayer* revised and restored				1663 Thomas Wilson b.	1663 Navigation Acts
				1665 Nicolas Poussin d.	
				1669 Rembrandt van Rijn d.	
				1670 Wm. Congreve b.	
1672 Thos. Ken teaching at Winchester College			1672 Newton's Law of gravitation	1672 Heinrich Schütz d.	
1674 Isaac Watts b.			1674 John Milton d.	1673 Molière d.	
1675 Thos. Ken's *Manual*				1675 Jan Vermeer d.	
				1678 Antonio Vivaldi b.	
			1678 Andrew Marvell d.		
			1679 Thos. Hobbes d.		
1683 Thos. Ken Chaplain to Charles I				1681 Georg Philipp Telemann b.	1681 Penn founds Pennsylvania
				1684 Leibnitz *Calculus*	
				1684 Antoine Watteau b.	
				1684 Turks besiege Vienna	
1685 Thos. Ken consecrated Bishop of Bath & Wells	Charles II d. James II King		1685 G. F. Handel b.		
1685 Ken's *Catechism*					
			1686 Thos. Wilson ordained		
			1687 Isaac Newton's *Principia*		
	1688 James II flees				
	1689 William & Mary succeed				

1679 Peter Tsar of Russia

1689 The Non-juring schism

1691 Thos. Ken deprived

1695 Henry Purcell d.
1697 Thos. Wilson, Bishop of Sodar & Man.
1700 John Dryden d.

1701–17 War of the Spanish Succession
1702 William III d. Anne Queen

1702 Philip Doddridge b.

1703 John Wesley b.

1704 John Locke d.

1706 Isaac Watts *Horae Lyricae*
1707 Watts, *Hymns & Spiritual Songs*

1709 Samuel Johnson b.

1709 Peter the Great defeats Sweden at Poltava

1709 Darby at Coalbrookdale

1711 Thos. Ken d.

1714 Anne d. George I King
Jacobite Rising

1715 Louis XVI d.

1715 Watts, *Divine Songs*

1717 David Garrick b.

1718 Charles XII of Sweden d.
1718 Sweden's Baltic dominance ends

1719 Watts, *Psalms of David Imitated*

1721 Antoine Watteau d.
1723 Joshua Reynolds b.
1725 Henry, Venn b.
Oxford's Holy Club
1727 Thos. Gainsborough d.

1725 John Newton b.

1727 George I d. George II King

Hymns & Hymn – Writers 1600–1900	Contemporary Events Political	Contemporary Events Social	Some Cultural & Ecclesiastical Landmarks	Parallel Events in Europe	North America
			1728 Oliver Goldsmith b.		
			1728 John Gay's *Beggar's Opera*		
			1732 Franz Joseph Haydn b.		
			1733 Joseph Priestley b.		
			1734 George Romney b.		
			1737 Michael Haydn b.		
1738 Conversion of John Wesley					
1739 Charles Wesley's *Hymns & Sacred Poems*					
1740 John Wesley's Sermon *On Free Grace*; A.M. Toplady b.				1740 Maria Theresa, Empress of Austria	
				1740 Frederick the Great, King of Prussia	
		1741/2 G.F. Handel's *Messiah*			
		1741 Antonio Vivaldi d.		British & French struggles in India 1740–1763	
1745 Doddridge *On the Rise and Progress of Religion in the Soul*	The '45: Jacobite Rising				
1747 Charles Wesley's *Redemption Hymns*					
1748 Isaac Watts d.		1748 Jeremy Bentham b.		1748 Montesquieu *L'esprit des Lois*	
			1749 Henry Venn, Fellow of Queen's, Cambridge		
1751 Philip Doddridge d.			1751 Richard Brinsley Sheridan b.		
		1752 Coke of Holkham b.			
			1755 Bishop Wilson d.		
	1756 Start of Seven Years' War			1756 W.A. Mozart b.	
			1757 William Blake b.		

1759 Wolfe takes Quebec

1765 Stamp Act for Britain's
American Colonies

1762 Catherine Empress
of Russia
1762 Rousseau, Du
Contrat Social
1763 Peace of Paris

1759 Charles Simeon b.
1759 **Wm. Wilberforce b.**
1759 Henry Venn, Vicar
of Huddersfield
1759 John Venn b.
1759 Robert Burns b.
1759 G.F. Handel d.

1763 Cobbett 'Champion   1763 Henry Venn's
of the Poor' b.   *Complete Duty of Man*

1767 George Philipp
Telemann d.
1768 Royal Academy
established: Sir Joshua
Reynolds first president

Joseph Priestley's
History of Electricity
1767 Hargreaves
'Spinning Jenny'
1768 Arkwright's
water frame

1769 Josiah **Wedgwood**'s
'Etruria' works
nr. Hanley

1760 George II d.
George III King

1763 Seven Years' War
ends

1762 A.M. Toplady
ordained

1764 John Newton
ordained/Newton's
Authentic Narrative
1764 Toplady's *Church
of England vindicated*

Hymns & Hymn – Writers 1600–1900	Contemporary Events		Some Cultural & Ecclesiastical Landmarks	Parallel Events in	
	Political	Social		Europe	North America
1770 Newton's *Review of Ecclesiastical History*			1770 Beethoven b.	1770 Captain Cook completes circumnavigation	
		1771 Robert Owen b. Watts and Boulton improve steam engines			
			1772 S.T. Coleridge b.	1772 First Partition of Poland	
			1774 Oliver Goldsmith d.		
		1775 Crompton's mule	1775 J.M.W. Turner b.		1775 Battle of Lexington
1776 Toplady's *Psalms and Hymns*			1776 John Constable b.		1776 Declaration of American Independence
1778 Toplady d.					
1779 John Newton's *Olney Hymns*			1779 David Garrick d.		
1780 Newton begins his ministry at London's St. Mary Woolnoth	1780 Wm. Wilberforce MP for Hull				
					1781 Yorktown surrender
			1782 Simeon Fellow of King's, Cambridge		
			1783 Simeon ordained, vicar of Holy Trinity, Cambridge		
		1784 Cort's puddling process and industrial advance	1784 Dr S. Johnson d.		1784 Thomas Coke, Superintendent American Methodism
		1786 Cartwright's power loom			
1788 Newton's *Thoughts on the African Slave Trade*	1788–95 Impeachment of Warren Hastings		1788 Byron b. 1788 Thos. Gainsborough d. 1788 Hannah Moore's *Thoughts on Society manners*		

1789 Charlotte Elliot b.

1792 John Keble b.

1801 J.H. Newman b.

Canal 'mania'

Robert Owen's New Lanark Community

1789 Gilbert White's *Natural History of Selbourne*
1790 Bruke's *Reflections on the French Revolution*
1791 Boswell's *Life of Johnson*
1791 W.A. Mozart d.
1792 John Venn, Rector of Clapham
1792 Joshua Reynolds d.
1795 Thos. Carlyle b.
1795 John Keats b.
1796 Robert Burns d.
1797 Henry Venn d.
1797 Wilberforce at Clapham
1797 Franz Schubert b.
1798 Wordsworth and Coleridge *Lyrical Ballads*
1798 CMS founded
1798 Eugène Delacroix b.
1801 Hon. A.A. Cooper (to become the Earl of Shaftesbury) b.
1802 George Romney d.
1803 Bible Society founded.
1803 Hector Berlioz b.

1789 Outbreak of French Revolution

1792 Louis XVI executed. First French Republic
1793 Second Partition of Poland

1797 George Washington d.

American Constitution framed: George Washington U.S. President

1801 Thos. Jefferson U.S. President

Hymns & Hymn – Writers 1600–1900	Contemporary Events Political	Contemporary Events Social	Some Cultural & Ecclesiastical Landmarks	Parallel Events in Europe	Parallel Events in North America
		1804 Richard Cobden 'Apostle of Free Trade' b.	1804 Joseph Priestley d.	1804 Napoleon Emperor of France	
		1804 Slavery Abolition bill passed			
				1805 Nelson defeats French fleet at Trafalgar	
				1806 Michael Haydn d.	
1807 John Newton d.					
			1809 Tennyson b.	1809 Mendelssohn b.	1809 Thos. Jefferson d.
				1809 Franz Joseph Haydn d.	
				1810 Chopin b.	
				1810 Robert Schumann b.	
	1811 George III declared insane: REGENCY		1811 *Sense and Sensibility*	1811 Liszt b.	
		1813 Owen and Bentham's New Lanark		1813 Wagner b.	
				1814 Jean Millet b.	
				1814 Louis XIV restored in France	
1815 John Keble ordained			1815 Thos. Arnold Fellow of Oriel, Oxford	1815 Battle of Waterloo	
			1816 Jane Austen, *Emma*		
			1816 Sheridan d.		
			1819 Charles Kingsley b.		
	1820 REGENCY ends: George IV King				
			1821 John Keats d.		
1822 J.H. Newman, Fellow of Oriel					
1824 J.H. Newman ordained deacon	Hon A.A. Cooper MP		1824 Byron d.	1824 Anton Bruckner b.	
					1825 Opening of Erie Canal

1826 John Ellerton b.
1827 Keble's *Christian Year*
1828 Newman, Vicar of St. Mary's Oxford

1831 Keble, Professor of Poetry at Oxford

1833 Keble's Assize Sermon

1834 Miss Elliott's *Invalid's Hymn Book*

1829 Catholic Emancipation
1829 Robert Peel Home Secretary: 'Peelers' or 'Bobbies' for London Police
1830 George IV d. William IV King
1832 Great Reform Act
1833 Abolition of Slavery in British Colonies
1833 Factory Act limiting child employment

1829 Stephenson's 'Rocket'

1833 Tolpuddle 'martyrs' deported for Union activity
1833 Brunel, Engineer to GWR

1827 Wm. Holman Hunt b.
1827 Wm. Blake d.
1828 Thomas Arnold Headmaster of Rugby School
1828 George Meredith d.
1829 William Booth b.

1830 Frederic Leighton b.

1832 Manning, Fellow of Merton

1833 Hannah More d.

1836 The Oxford *Library of the Fathers*
1836 Christopher Wordsworth Headmaster of Harrow

1827 Beethoven d.
1828 Franz Schubert d.

1830 Louis Philippe King of France

1832 Edouard Manet b.

1833 Brahms b.

1834 Edgar Degas b.

Hymns & Hymn – Writers 1600-1900	Contemporary Events Political	Contemporary Events Social	Some Cultural & Ecclesiastical Landmarks	Parallel Events in Europe	Parallel Events in North America
1837 Miss Elliott's *Hymns for a week*	1837 William IV died. Victoria Queen		1837 John Constable d.		
		1839 Chartists' Six Demands		1839 Alfred Sisley b. 1839 Paul Cézanne b.	
1840 Miss Elliott's *Hours of Sorrow*	1840 Penny Post		1840 The Cambridge Parker Society founded 1840 Samuel Wilberforce, Chaplain to Prince Albert	1840 Tchaikovsky b. 1840 Claude Monet b.	
1841 Newman's *Tract XC*		1841 Railway 'mania'	1841 *The Library of Anglo-Catholic Theology* 1841 Manning Archdeacon of Chichester	1841 Pierre August Renoir b.	
1843 Newman resigns living of St. Mary's Oxford					
1845 Newman 'received' into Roman Church		1845 Irish Potato Famine	1845 Samuel Wilberforce Bishop of Oxford		
		1846 Repeal of Corn Laws		1846 Pius IX Pope	
		1847 Ten Hours Bill	1847 The Gorham Judgement	1847 Mendelssohn d.	
1848 Fanny Humphreys, *Hymns for Little Children*			1848 Paul Gauguin b. 1848 Marx & Engels Communist Manifesto	1848 Abolition of slavery in French Colonies 1848 Second French Republic. Revolution in Germany	

1850 J. Ellerton ordained	1851 Great Exhibition proclaims British Industrial ascendancy	1851 Manning 'received' into Roman Church	1848–9 Italian War of Independence
1852 Newman's *Idea of a University*	1852 Duke of Wellington d.	1852 Convocation of Canterbury revived	1848 Paul Gauguin d.
1853 Ellerton curate in Brighton		1854 Wilberforce founds Cuddesden	1849 Chopin d.
		1854 Dogma of the Immaculate Conception of the BVM	1850 Guy de Maupassant b.
1856 Ellerton's *Morning and Evening Hymns*		1857 Elgar b.	1852 Harriet Beecher Stowe's *Uncle Tom's Cabin*
		1859 Darwin's *Origin of Species*	1852 Napoleon III Emperor of the French
1860 Ellerton, Vicar of Crewe	1860 London Underground under construction	1861 Convocation of York revived	1853 Vincent van Gogh b.
1861 *Hymns, Ancient & Modern*	1861 Albert, Prince Consort, d.		1856 Robert Schumaun d.
			1858 Bernadette's visions at Lourdes
			1859 Georges Seurat b.
			1860 Mahler b.
			1861 Abraham Lincoln 16th US President
			1861–65 American Civil War
			1861 Pasteur and the pasteurization of milk and beer
1864 Mrs Alexander's *Book of Sunday Poetry*		1864 *Syllabus of Errors* Pius IX claims control of all culture and science for church.	1863 Edouard Munch b.
			1863 Eugène Delacroix d.
			1863 *Credit Lyonnais*
			1864 Société Générale

Hymns & Hymn – Writers 1600–1900	Contemporary Events		Some Cultural & Ecclesiastical Landmarks	Parallel Events in	
	Political	Social		Europe	North America
1865 Newman's *Dream of Gerontius*			1865 Manning, Archbishop of Westminster	1865 Sibelius b.	1865 Lincoln assassinated
			1865 Wm Booth's East End 'Christian Missions'	Kipling b. in Bombay	
1866 John Keble d.			1865 Henry Venn Elliott d.	1866 Transatlantic cable laid	1867 Mark Twain's *Tom Sawyer*
1867 Wm. Alexander, Bishop of Derry	1867 Second Reform Act				1867 Dominion of Canada
			1869 Vatican Council	1869 Henry Matisse b.	
				1869 Berlioz d.	
				1869 Opening of the Suez Canal	
				1869 Christopher Wordsworth, Bishop of Lincoln	
				1869 J.T. Coleridge *Memoir of Keble*	
	1870 Forster's Education Act		1870 Pius XI claims Papal Infallibility	1870 Franco-Prussian War	
	Irish Land Act		1870 British Red Cross Society founded		
1871 Charlotte Elliott d.	1871 Church of Ireland disestablished				
1872 Ellerton, Vicar of Hinstock		1872 F.M. Maurice d.	1872 Piet Mondrian b.		
			1873 Charles Kingsley Chaplain to Queen Victoria		
	1874 Disraeli P.M.				1874 Typewriter invented

1876 A.G. Bell patents
    telephone
1877 Bell Telephone Co.

1879 Edison patents
    Electric light bulb

1881 Charter of Canadian
    Pacific Railway

1885 Canadian Pacific
    Railway completed

1875 Jean Millet d.
1875 Thos. Mann b.

1878 William Booth founds
    Salvation Army
1878 John Masefield b.
1879 Paul Klee b.

1881 Picasso b.

1881 Thos. Carlyle d.

1882 Edward Hopper b.

1883 Edouard Manet d.
1883 Richard Wagner d.

1884 Gore, Principal of
    Pusey House

1885 François Mauriac b.
1885 Liszt d.

1889 Robert Browning d.

1889 Gore edits *Lux Mundi*
1890 Booth's *Darkest
    England*

1889 Eiffel Tower
    completed
1890 Bismarck dismissed

1875 Charles Kingsley d.

1874 Factory Act
1875 Public Health Act
1876 Victoria Empress
    of India

Agricultural Depression

1883 John Maynard
    Keynes b.
1883 Karl Marx d.
1884 Third Reform Act

1887 Victoria's Jubilee

1876 Ellerton, Rector
    of Barnes

1879 J.H. Newman
    Cardinal
1880 Mrs Alexander's
    Moral Songs
1881 Book of Narrative
    Hymns for Village
    Schools
1882 Ellerton's *Lenten
    sermons* at Barnes
    published

1885 Ellerton Rector of
    White Roding

1888 Ellerton's *Hymns
    Original and Translated*

1890 John Henry,
    Cardinal Newman, d.

Hymns & Hymn – Writers 1600–1900	Contemporary Events Political	Social	Some Cultural & Ecclesiastical Landmarks	Parallel Events in Europe	North America
			1891 Leo XIII *Rerum novarum*: 'workers' Pope' on relations between capital and labour	1891 Georges Seurat d. Max Ernst b.	
1893 Ellerton d.	1893 Indepdent Labour Party founded		1893 Guy de Maupassent d.		1893 Henry Ford's first petrol-driven car
	1894 W.E. Gladstone resigns		1894 Marx, *On Capital*		
	1897 Queen Victoria's Diamond Jubilee			1896 Anton Bruckner d.	
				1897 Brahms d.	
				1898 Paris *Métro* under construction	
				1899 Alfred Sisley d. Commonwealth of Australia	
1900 Elgar sets *Gerontius* to music					1900 New York 'subway' construction
	1901 Queen Victoria d.				1901 Theodore Roosevelt, 26th U.S. President

SELECT
BIBLIOGRAPHY

For the most part, the sources on which this book is based are well enough known, and notes have been kept to the minimum to protect the pleasures of a good read. In the text, necessary references appear in square [brackets], and this booklist will feed the appetites of those readers who, having enjoyed something of a starter, now seek the sustenance of a main course.

The place of publication is London unless stated otherwise.

PRIMARY PRINTED SOURCES

Alexander, C.F., *The Legend of the Golden Prayers and other Poems,* 1859.

—*The Sunday Book of Poetry,* 1864.

—*Moral Songs,* 1880.

—*Narrative Hymns for Village Schools,* 1881.

—*Poems,* 1896.

(*See also* under Humphreys, C.F., below)

Alexander, W. and C.F. (edited by Graves, A.P.), *Selected Poems,* 1930.

Children's Hymn-Book for use in Children's Services, Sunday Schools and Families. Arranged in Order of the Church's Year (edited by Mrs Carey Brock, with a *Preface* by J. Ellerton), 1881.

Church Hymns (ed. Compton, B., How, W., and Ellerton, J.), 1871.

Church of England Hymn-Book, adapted to the Daily Services of the Church throughout the Year (ed. Thring, G.), 1882.

Doddridge, P., *Hymns founded on Various Texts in the Holy Scriptures,* 1755.

Ellerton, J., *The Holiest Manhood and its Lessons for busy lives. Sermons preached in Barnes Church,* 1882.

—*Hymns Original and Translated,* 1888.

Ellerton, J. (editor), *Manual of Parochial Work,* 1888.

Elliott, Charlotte, *Hours of Sorrow Cheered,* 1823.

—*Hours of Sorrow Cheered and Comforted* (revised title first appearing on sixth edition, 1863).

—*The Invalid's Hymn Book,* 1834.

—*Morning and Evening Hymns for a Week,* 1837.

—*Hymns,* 1869.

Elliott, Charlotte (editor), *The Christian Remembrancer Pocket-Book* (from 1834 to 1859).

Humphreys, C.F., *Verses for Holy Seasons,* 1846.

—*Hymns for Little Children,* 1848.

Hymns, Ancient and Modern, 1861.

Keble, John, *The Christian Year,* 1827.

—*Tract IV,* 1833.

—*The Works of that learned and judicious divine Mr Richard Hooker, with a Preface by J.K.,* 3 vols. 1841.

—*On Eucharistical Adoration,* 1859.

—*Life of Bishop Wilson,* 1863.

Ken, Thomas, *Manual of Prayer for Winchester Scholars*, 1675.
—*Practice of Divine Love*, 1685.
Luther, Martin, *see* Leupold, U.S. (editor), *Liturgy and Hymns*, Vol. 53 of *Luther's Works*, American Edition (Lehmann, H.T. and Pelikan, J., General Editors), Philadelphia, 1965.
Mace, T., *Musick's Monument*, 1676.
Newman, John Henry, *Apologia Pro Vita Sua*, 1864.
—*An Essay on the Development of Christian Doctrine*, 1845.
—*Lectures on Certain Difficulties felt by Anglicans in submitting to the Church Catholic, 1850*.
—*Lectures on Justification*, 1838.
—*Lectures on the Prophetical Office of the Church viewed relatively to Romanism and Popular Protestantism*, 1837.
—*Lyra Apostolica*, 1836.
—*Parochial and Plain Sermons*, 8 volumes, 1834–1843.
—*Verses on Various Occasions*, 1868.
Newton, John, *Authentic Narrative of some ... Particulars in the Life of J.N.*, 1764.
—*A Review of Ecclesiastical History*, 1770.
—*Thoughts on the African Slave Trade*, 1788.
—*Olney Hymns in Three Books*, 1779.
—*The Subject and Temper of Gospel Ministry*, 1779.
Toplady, Augustus Montague, *The Church of England vindicated from the charge of Arminianism*, 1769.
—*Absolute Predestination Asserted*, 1769.
—*Historic Proof of the doctrinal Calvinism of the Church of England*, 1774.
—*Free-Will and Merit fairly Examined*, 1774.
—*Good News from Heaven*, 1774.
—*The Existence and Creed of Devils*, 1776.
—*Psalms and Hymns for Public and Private Worship*, 1776.
—*Toplady's Dying Avowal*, 1778.
—*Course of Prayer* (posthumous work, n.d.).
Watts, Isaac, *Horae Lyricae*, 1705; 1706; 1709; and 1736 etc.
—*Hymns and Spiritual Songs*, 1707.
—*Guide to Prayer*, 1715.
—*Divine Songs Attempted in Easy Language for the use of Children*, 1715.
—*The Psalms of David imitated in the Language of the New Testament*, 1719–20.

—*Prayers composed for the Use and Imitation of Children*, 1728.
—*Logick*, 1733.
—*Miscellaneous Thoughts*, 1734.
—*The Improvement of the Mind*, 1741.
Wesley, Charles, *Redemption Hymns*, 1737.
Wesley, John (editor), *Morning Hymn-Book*, 1741.
—*Hymns and Spiritual Songs, intended for ... real Christians of all Denominations*, 1753.
—*Hymns with Tunes Annext*, 1761.
—*A Collection of Hymns for the use of the People called Methodists*, 1779.
—*Large Hymn-Book*, 1780.
—*The Journal of John Wesley* (edited in 8 vols. by Nehemiah Curnock), 1909.
Wilson, Thomas, *Sacra Privata*, n.d.
Wither, George, *The Hymnes and Songs of the Church, Divided into two Parts*, 1623.

SECONDARY SOURCES

Battiscombe, Georgina, *John Keble: A Study in Limitations*, 1963.
Benson, L.F., *Studies of Familiar Hymns* (Philadelphia), 1923.
Bishop, Selma L., *Isaac Watts: Hymns and Spiritual Songs, 1707–1748: A Study in Early Eighteenth-Century Language Changes*, 1962.
Bouyer, L., *Newman and his Life and Spirituality*, 1958.
Chadwick, Owen, *The Victorian Church* (3rd edition), 2 vols, 1971.
Chandler, M., *The Life and Work of John Mason Neale, 1818–1866*, Leominster, 1995.
Church, R.W., *The Oxford Movement, 1833–1845*, 1891.
Davis, A.P., *Isaac Watts*, 1948.
Dessain, C.S., *John Henry Newman*, 1966.
Escott, H., *Isaac Watts Hymnographer*, 1962.
Gill, F.C., *The Romantic Movement and Methodism*, 1954.
Gilley, Sheridan, *Newman and his Age*, 1991.
Green, V.H.H., *John Wesley*, 1964.
Hildebrandt, F., *From Luther to Wesley*, 1951.
Horder, W.G., *The Hymn Lover*, n.d.

Housman, H., *John Ellerton: His Life and Writings on Hymnology*, 1896.

Julian, J., *A Dictionary of Hymnology setting forth the Origin and History of Christian Hymns of All Ages and Nations*, 1892 (revised 1907).

Ker, I., *The Achievement of John Henry Newman*, 1990.

Leask, G.A., *Nineteenth-Century Hymn Writers*, 1902.

Liddon, H.P., *Life of E.B. Pusey*, 4 vols., 1893–97.

Manning, B.L., *The Hymns of Wesley and Watts*, 1942.

Nuttall, G.F., *The Holy Spirit in Puritan Faith and Experience*, 1946.

Pollard, A., *English Hymns*, 1960.

Rattenbury, J.E., *The Evangelical Doctrines of Charles Wesley's Hymns*, 1941.

Robinson, C.S., *Annotations upon Popular Hymns* (Ohio), 1893.

Routley, Erik, *I'll Praise my Maker*, 1951.

—*Hymns and the Faith*, 1954.

—*The Music of Christian Hymnody*, 1957.

—*English Religious Dissent*, 1960.

—*Words, Music and the Church*, 1968.

Rupp, E.G., *Six Makers of English Religion*, 1957 (reprinted 1964).

Shairp, J.C., *John Keble: An Essay on the Author of 'The Christian Year'*, 1866.

Sheppard, W.J.L., *Great Hymns and their Stories*, n.d.

Southey, Robert, *The Life of Wesley*, 2 vols., 1925.

Telford, J., *England's Book of Praise*, 1929.

Trevor, M., *Newman, the Pillar of the Cloud*, 1962.

—*Newman, Light in Winter*, 1962.

Walker, D., *The Songs of Zion, or Famous Hymns, and who wrote them*, 1906.

Ward, W., *The Life of John Henry, Cardinal Newman*, 2 vols., 1912.

Welch, E., *Spiritual Pilgrim: A reassessment of the life of the Countess of Huntingdon* (Cardiff), 1995.

Whitely, W.T., *Congregational Hymn-Singing in England*, 1933.

Wiseman, F.L., *Charles Wesley, Evangelist & Poet* (Abingdon), 1932.

Wright, T., *Augustus M. Toplady and contemporary Hymn-Writers*, 1911.

ARTICLES

Payne, E.A., 'The Theology of Isaac Watts as Illustrated in his Hymns' in *The Hymn Society of Great Britain and Ireland Bulletin*, Vol. 2, No. 4 (Oct. 1948).

Routley, Erik, 'Isaac Watts: An Appreciation' in *The Christian World*, No. 4778 (11 Nov. 1948).

Routley, Erik, 'The Bi-centenary of Isaac Watts' in *The Hymn Society of Great Britain and Ireland Bulletin*, Vol. 2, No. 5 (Jan. 1949).

Sampson, G., 'Isaac Watts' in *The Spectator* (19 Nov. 1948).

Unsigned Article on Watts entitled 'An Educational Divine', *T.E.S.* (27 Nov. 1948).

INDEX

ABRAHAM, 87
Absolution, 27, 163, 173
Abstract truth, 205
Absurdities, 201
Accent, 243
Acceptance, 227
Actions in worship (*see* Ceremonial)
Adam, 119, 176
Adam, Thomas (of Lincolnshire),
    113
Addison, Joseph, 211
Adey, Lionel, xv
Admonition, 92
Adoption (in Christ), 71
Adoration, 47, 52, 58, 76, 152, 153,
    158, 170, 224
Advent, 39, 74, 75, 144, 146, 215
Affirmation, 227
Africa, 115
Africans, 102, 116
Ages, Rock of, 82
Albert, Prince Consort to Queen
    Victoria (1819–61), 238
ALEXANDER, Cecil Frances, *née*
    Humphreys (1818–1895), xi,
    xiv, 198–219, 256, 257, 259;
    inspired by Keble's *Christian
    Year*, 203; married to William
    Alexander (1849), 204; parish
    work in Upper Fahan
    (1855–60), 204, and in Strabane
    (1860), 204; sympathy for the
    English Reformation divines,
    204; trained the young, 212–13;
    visited the sick, 204;
    commitment to Christian
    education, 205, 206, 211, 213;
    her 'All things bright and
    beautiful', 212, 214; her charity

work, 212; her *Hymns for Little
    Children* (1848), 202, 204, 206,
    209, 256; her *Moral Songs*
    (1880), 202, 212, 259; her
    *Narrative Hymns for Village
    Schools* (1881), 212, 259; her
    'Once in Royal David's City',
    214; her spatial universe, 203;
    her 'There is a green hill…'viii,
    199–200, 207–208, 214; her
    Verses for Holy Seasons, 203;
    notable child evangelist, 204,
    208, 214; and her support of a
    School for deaf and dumb
    children, 210.
Alexander, William Bp of Derry
    (1867), 204, 208, 209, 258
Alice, 56
Almighty God, 66, 70, 170, 193,
    205, 243
Alleluia, 171, 175
Alliteration, 218
Alpha, 14, 70
Altar, 153
Ambiguity, 164
America, United States of, 105, 134
American visitors, 127
Ampleforth, xii
Amusements, 230
Ancient & Modern (*see* Hymnals)
Ancient sights, 161
Andrewes, Bp Lancelot (1555–1626),
    141, 165, 208
Angelicals, 167
Angels, 23, 63, 75, 94, 96, 131,
    145, 153, 158, 168, 171, 172,
    176, 213
Anger, 71, 108
Anglicanism, 165

Anglicans, 84, 85, 165, 172
Anglo-Catholicism (*see* High Church and Tractarians)
Anguish, 217
Anna, 133
Anne, Queen of Great Britain and Ireland (1702–14), 55, 249
Antigua, 105
Anti-litany, 165
Antiquarians, 165
Antiquity, Christian, 136
Anthems, vii, 10, 14, 45
Antithesis (*see also* Law and Gospel), 218
Anxiety, 104, 111, 150, 189
Apartheid, 115
Apathy, 60
Apocalyptic, 62
Apostasy, 129, 162
Appointments, Church, 28
Apostles (the Twelve), 23, 92, 104, 135, 136, 150, 163, 164, 168
Apostolical succession, 136, 137, 138, 162, 164, 172
'Arminianism' (so-called), 83, 85, 87, 88, 90
Arminius, Jacobus (Jakob Hermandszoon), 84
Arnold, Matthew, 224
Arnold, Thomas, 139, 255
Art, 184
Articles, XXXIX, 85, 113, 115, 166
Ascension (of Christ), 15, 150, 214
Asceticism, 189
Assembly, 52
Assurance (of salvation), 27, 71, 107, 183, 207
Astronomy, 226
Atheism, 89
Atlantic ocean, 102, 203, 208
Atonement, 82, 207
Attributes (*see also* under fountainhead, rock, shelter, shield, etc. for scriptural attributes of Christ), 111
Augsburg, 13
Augsburg, Confession of (1530), 11
Augustine, Saint, of Hippo

(354–430), 223, 241
his definition of a hymn, xiii, 223
Augustinians, 6
Austen, Jane, 101, 161, 254
her *Persuasion*, 101, 161
Authority, Church, 136, 164, 168
scriptural, 119, 207
Autobiographical insights, vii, 71, 105, 111, 120, 122, 159, 181, 185
Autumn, 147

BACH, J. S., 8, 170
Badeley, Edward, 171
Bainton, Roland, 13
Ballads, 7, 15
Balm, 145, 194, 226, 233
Banality, 164
Baptism, vii, 27, 105, 114, 204, 237
of infants, 114
Baptismal vows, 27
Baptists, 113
Barbirolli, Sir John, 170
Baring-Gould, S. (1834–1924), Author of 'Onward, Christian soldiers', 95
Barnes, 224, 230
Barrier, 180
Bath, Somerset, 85, 91
Battiscombe, Georgina, 129
Battles, 205
Baxter, Richard (1615–91), 42
Bedford, Duchess of, 43
Bees, 118, 119
Behaviour, 68
Belief, Christian, xv, 24, 85
Believers, 68, 100, 110
Bells, 14, 214
Bereavement, 130, 181, 190, 191
Bernese Oberland, 187
Berridge, John (of Everton), 113
Bible (*see also* Holy Scripture, Scriptures and Word of God), xiv, 6, 73, 75, 78, 190, 191
Books of (by name and order), Old Testament, Genesis, 119, 120; Leviticus, 43, 53; Deuteronomy, 72; Job, 44;

Psalms, 44, 54, 55, 223;
Proverbs, 44, 188; Song of
Solomon, 111; Isaiah, 39, 41,
89, 91; Malachi, 45
New Testament, Gospels:
Matthew, 46, 132, 144, 185,
187, 196; Luke, 39, 40, 44,
149; John, 47, 162, 191; Acts of
the Apostles, 44; Epistles:
Romans, 107, 183, 189; II
Corinthians, 122; Galatians, 58;
Ephesians, 84, 92, 114;
Philippians, 188; Colossians, 92;
II Timothy, 183; James, 163; I
John, 71; the Book of the
Revelation, 44, 61.
Biblical imagery (*see* imagery)
language, 146
Bible, the English, 73, 211
Authorized (King James) version
(1611), xiv
Bible-reading, 68
Bibles, 131, 152
Bible studies, 117
Bibury, 127
Bigotry, 113
Birds (*see also* ornithology), 56, 118,
146, 148, 185, 193
Birdsong, 118
Birmingham, 60, 170
Birth, the new, 67, 71
Biscay, Bay of, 160
Bishops, 29, 108
Blasphemy, 73, 101
Blessing, 17, 71, 126, 132, 134, 225
Blind, 38, 42, 180, 186, 191, 239
Blindness, 167
Blood (of Christ), 82, 84, 96, 110,
120, 121, 146, 152, 180, 189,
200, 207, 216, 218
Book of Common Prayer, xiv, 26, 27,
28, 29, 67, 73, 85, 92, 95, 108,
114, 131, 132, 138, 140, 142,
144, 145, 146, 149, 152, 162,
186, 230, 235, 236, 244, 248;
Prayer-Book Catechism, 109;
Collects, 133, 149;
Confirmation service, 140;

'Comfortable Words', 67;
Epistles, 132; Evening Prayer,
92, 133; Gospels, 132; Holy
Communion, 140, 152, 186,
208; Morning Prayer, 95, 208;
Order for the Ministration of
Baptism, 108–9, 114, 140;
Order for the Burial of the
Dead, 109, 233; *Preface* (1662),
29; Psalter, 73; rubrics, 27–8,
114
Boswell, James, 107
Bournemouth, 150
Bourton-on-the-Water, 127
Bouyer, Louis, 159, 163
Bowden, J.W., 160, 162
Boys, 211, 212
Bread, 151, 206, 218
Breviaries:
Parisian, 175
Roman, 175
Bride of Christ, 197
Brighton, 160, 181, 187, 188, 189,
224, 225
Bristol, 83
Britain, 129, 134, 140
Victorian, 129
BBC, viii
British Isles, 53, 55, 127
British Magazine, 137, 160
Broadsheets, 8
Brooks, Grace, ii
Brotherhood of man, 202
Browning, Robert, 212
Brussels, 6
Buckinghamshire, 108
Bunyan, John (1628–88), 95, 133
Pilgrim's Progress, xiii, 28
Burford, 127
Burns, Oates, publishers, 171
Business 230
Butterflies, 212

CAIN, 120
Cajetan, Cardinal Thomas de Vio
(1469–1534), 244
Calvary, 58, 59, 72, 121
Calvin, John (1509–64), 42, 83, 88,

93, 118, 243, 244
Institutio christianae religionis (1536), 88
Calvinism, 51, 56, 73, 83, 84, 85, 87, 88, 90, 92, 93, 94, 105, 116, 117, 118, 120, 121
the 'Five Points', 93, 117
moderate Calvinism, 85, 116
Cambridge, vii, viii, 39, 43, 113, 141
Colleges, Downing, vii, viii; King's, 39; Queens', 113; Robinson, viii, ix; St. John's, vii; Trinity, 39; Theological Colleges, Wesley House, x; Westminster, ix, x, xi
University Library, x–xi; University Press, 141
Cambridgeshire, x, xi, 74
Campaigning, 70
Canaan, 147, 236
Candlemas, 175
Canons, 166
Canterbury, vii
Archbishops of, 29; Cranmer, Thomas (1533–1556), xiv, 149, 164, 165, 186, 204; Laud, William (1633–45), 137, 141; Ramsey, Michael (1961–74), 134; Sancroft, William (1678–89), 27, 28; Whitgift, John (1583–1604), 136
St Augustine's College, 139
Canticles, 174
Cantor, 244
Cardwell, Edward, 135
Care, 70, 150, 192
Carlisle, 113
Carlyle, Thomas, 10, 253, 259
Caroline divines, 165
Carols, 39
Carroll, Lewis (Charles Dodgson), 56
Cats, 231
Catechism, 24, 56, 68, 93, 105, 128, 134, 144, 205, 207, 215
Catechism-hymn, 201, 239
Catechisms, xii
Catechism, The, 230

Catechumens, 141
Cathedrals, 127, 128, 223, 224
Catholic truth, 54, 121, 133, 166, 172
Men's Society, 201
Catholic Emancipation (1829), 209, 255
Catholicism, 121, 137, 164, 169
Catholicity, 32
Luther's (1529), 77
Catlett, Jack, 105
Cecil, Lord David, 57
Celibacy, 17
Cerberus, 139
Ceremonial, 137
bowing at the name of Jesus, 137
crossing, 137
observing holy days, 137
turning to the East, 137
Certainty, 234
Chadwick, Dr John, ix
Chadwick, Dr W. O., 209
Chalcedon, Council of (451), 165
Fathers of, 165
Chandler, Michael, 153
Chants, 245
liturgical xii, 51
Chants Chrétiens, 229
Chapel, 31, 39, 52, 74, 85, 86, 194, 214, 244
Charismatic movement, 42
Charity, 148
Charles II, King of England and Scotland (1660–85), 26, 28
Charles V (1500–1558), Holy Roman Emperor (1519–56), 11
Charlestown, 105
Chatham, 102, 106
Chelsea, 130
Chester, 237
Chichester cathedral, 224
Theological college, 231
Child, of God, 100
Children, 45, 56, 68, 77, 92, 134, 140, 201, 202, 204, 205, 210, 211, 213, 214, 215, 218, 236, 239
Chipping Campden, 127

Choirs, 39, 214, 233
All Saints', Chevy Chase, viii;
Bethesda-by-the-Sea, Florida,
viii; Downing College, viii;
Indian Hill, Cincinnati, viii; St
John's College, Cambridge, vii;
St John's Logan, Utah, viii; St
Peter's, Saint Louis, Missouri,
viii; Trinity College, ix
Choir Festivals, 237
Cholera, 203, 239
Chorales, 244, 245
Christ (*see* Jesus Christ)
Christendom, xv, 5, 11, 14, 23, 58,
61, 76, 83, 136, 144, 150, 214,
243
Christian, 52, 53, 55, 67, 68, 188
Christian faith, 60, 67, 68, 168
Christianity, 143, 172
Christian life, 187
Christians, 7, 16, 24, 43, 105, 211
Christian Year (*see* Keble, John)
Christlikeness, 71
Christocentric, 61
Christmas, 15, 75, 145, 195
'Christ's poor', 41
Church, 31, 32, 44, 53, 60, 62, 150,
222, 226, 228, 230, 237, 241
'Branch', 166
Catholic, 165
Christian, 176
Congress (at Stoke, 1875), 234
of England, vii, 26, 29, 85, 101,
107, 112, 113, 115, 135, 136,
137, 139, 162, 164, 166, 168
of the Fathers, 135, 172
pilgrim, 53
primitive, 104, 164
Protestant Episcopal (of America),
229
Roman, 135, 136, 138, 150, 164,
169, 172, 174
year (*see* under Advent, Christmas,
Lent, Easter, Whitsun; and *also*
under Saints and Saints' Days),
74, 75, 76, 144
Church, R.W., 138
Churches, parish, 39, 88

Churchill, Sir Winston (1874–1965),
English statesman, 87
Churchmanship, 136
Churchmen, 86, 91, 117, 194
Churchwardens, 231
Circumcision (of Christ), 236, 237
Cirencester, 127
Citizenship (of heaven), 187
City, of God, 4
City wall, 200
Civil War, the English, 23
Clarendon, Edward Hyde, 1st Earl of
(1609–74), 26, 28
Clarendon Press, Oxford, 135
Clarity, 59, 62, 122
Cleanse, 180
Clergy, xv, 40, 172, 204, 231
Climax, 227
Clouds, 190, 194
Clunie, Alexander, 106, 107
Colenso crisis (1864), 139
Coleridge, Father Henry, S.J., 169
Coleridge, S. T. (1772–1834), 129,
135, 140, 150, 151, 252, 253
his *Memoir of John Keble*, 117f.
Collects (*see also Book of Common
Prayer*), 30, 33
College politics, 160
Coln, river, 127
Coln St Aldwyns, 127
Colonialism, 238
Colossae, 15, 92
Colour, 118, 145, 190
Comfort, 33, 184, 193, 228, 240
'Comfortable words', 67, 186
Commandments, the Ten (*see also*
Law), 25, 27, 205, 239
Commentaries, 111, 120
Commerce, 102
Commitment (*see also* Service), xiv,
59, 63, 68, 70, 106, 115, 150,
192, 201, 202
Commons, House of, 115
Commonsense, 68
Commonwealth, 115
Communication (of the gospel), 88,
92
Communion, Holy (*see also*

Eucharist, Lord's Supper and Mass), vii, 17, 28, 45, 54, 58, 151, 208, 218, 230
Hymns, 17, 45, 58, 186, 218, 230
of Saints, 122, 140, 148
Communism, 166
Companionship, 181
Compassion, 70, 217
Composition, 34, 55, 63, 67, 69, 72, 73, 74, 77, 89, 91, 92, 93, 94, 95, 96, 111, 112, 117, 118, 119, 122, 133, 146, 153, 159, 188, 223, 228, 241, 244
Compromise, 164, 229
Compton Beardmore, 229
Compton, Henry (1632–1713), Bp of Oxford and London, 28
Confession, 27, 28, 143, 162
Confessors, 167, 168
Confidence, 106, 169, 189
Confirmation, 141
Conflict, 186
Congregationalism, 108
Congregationalists, 52
Congregation(s), 24, 41, 42, 43, 51, 58, 59, 60, 63, 70, 72, 88, 91, 113, 114, 132, 133, 136, 145, 167, 225, 234, 236, 243, 245
Consecration, 173
Conscience, 110
Consolation, 10, 78
Constable, John (1776–1837), 190, 256
Consumption, 185
Contempt, 58
Context, 60
Controversy, 73, 83, 86, 87, 90, 92, 96, 136, 151, 182
Conventicles, 26, 85
Conversation, 24, 188
Conversion, 67, 69, 70, 74, 84, 101, 104, 105, 109, 112, 115, 121, 166
of St Paul, 237
Converts, 83
Conviction, 42, 43, 62, 63, 73, 76, 88, 108, 114, 129, 163, 170, 171, 194, 202, 228

Cooper, Bp Thomas (1520–94), 136
Cooper, J.D., engraver, 212
Corbett, Ronnie, comedian, 202
Corfu, 160
Corinth, 15, 109
Cornucopia, 71, 93
Corpus Christi, 17
Correspondence, 105
Cosin, John, Bp of Durham (1660–72), 141
Cotswolds, 127, 130
Councils of the Church, xii
Counsel, 134
Counselling, 193, 204
Counsellor, 195
Countryside, 117, 127, 130, 147, 189, 208, 218
Country walks, 118, 218
Court of the Arches, 139
Covenant theology, 62, 84, 91, 94, 189
Cowper, William (1731–1800) poet and friend of Newton, 109, 115, 116, 117, 118
Cradle, 126, 216
Cranach, Lucas, the Elder (1472–1553), x
Cranmer, Thomas (1489–1566), Abp of Canterbury, xiv, 149, 164, 165, 186, 204
Creation, 71, 93, 118, 146, 148, 158, 193, 201, 211, 214, 218, 233, 236
Creator, 151, 171, 211
Creatures, 222, 227
Creed:
the Apostles, 138, 201, 205, 239
the Athanasian, 163
Creeds, 68, 140, 163, 167, 174, 207, 239
Crescendo, 227
Crete, 104
Crewe, 224
Crewe, Lord, 232
Criticism, 134, 164, 229
textual, 224
Crito, 114
Crocodile, 56

Cromwell, Oliver (1599–1658), soldier, statesman and Lord Protector of England, 23
Crosiers, 161
Cross (of Christ), 50, 58, 59, 60, 72, 82, 89, 118, 120, 121, 145, 152, 182, 217
Last words from, 152, 217
Crowds, 107
Crown, 50, 58, 59, 66, 68, 71
Crucifix, 58, 121
Crucifixion (of Christ), 7, 58, 74, 91, 121, 145, 168, 186, 188, 200, 214, 235
Cruelty, 102
'Crusades', 187
Cupid, 70
Cure, 82
Curnock, Nehemiah, 92
Cymbalists, 209

DAILY LIGHT, 185
Daily Telegraph, 202
Daisies, 218
Dale, R. W., 52
Dalziel, 209
Damascus, 237
Damnation, 73
Darkness, 95, 222, 226
Dartmouth, Lord, 108, 117
Darwin, Charles (1809–82), 201
his Origin of Species (1859), 201
David, King, 6, 8, 14, 18, 24, 52, 54, 55, 209
Dawn, 222, 227
Day, 222, 227
Deacon, in Holy Orders, 84, 128
Deaf, 191
Deafness, 194
Death, 58, 61, 82, 92, 100, 112, 120, 121, 158, 167, 190, 211, 217, 218, 239
Dedication, 26, 46, 130, 135, 195, 196, 226
Definition, 228
Delft, blue and white tiles, 43
Delight, 120
Deliverance (from sin), 104, 109, 187

Democracy, 209
Demons, 168
Denial, 218
Denmark, 229
Denominationalism, 113, 114
Depression, 181, 183, 185, 191, 192, 197
Depth, 97
Derry, 204, 207, 208
Desolation, 185
Despair, xiv, 70, 71, 72, 104, 108, 191, 192
Desperation, 194
Dessain, C. S., 166
Devil, 69
Devils, 4
Devon, 83, 85, 88, 89
Devotion(s), xiv, 31, 40, 51, 52, 68, 109, 138, 151, 153, 174, 187, 189, 204, 206, 210, 213, 216, 228, 230, 241
Dévots, 84
Dictation, 244
Dies Irae, 239
Dilemma, 129
'Disappointment', a poem, 173, 174
Discipleship, xiv, 24, 59, 71, 72, 118, 120, 205, 214
Disciples, 168
Discipline, 72, 128, 142, 151, 169, 172, 177, 196, 213
Disease, 34
Disestablishment, 209, 212, 258
Dissent, 55, 58, 106, 108
Dissenters, 42, 113, 114, 117
Dissenting Academies, 113
'Dissenting meetings', 51
Distress, 118
District nurses, 212
Divine sovereignty, 84
Divines, 83, 141, 165
Divine service (see also under Book of Common Prayer, Hours and the Liturgy), 107
Divinity, 42, 67, 87
Divisions, 150
Doane, Bp, 212
Doctrine, xiv, 53, 83, 84, 85, 86, 89,

92, 93, 101, 105, 110, 118, 119, 133, 136, 145, 150, 168, 169, 172, 205

DODDRIDGE, Philip (1702–51), x, xiv, 36–47, 106, 230, 249–50; as Pastor, 41, 42; at Castle Hill Chapel, Northampton, 39; at the Kibworth Academy, 43; his 'catechism-hymns', 40; his *Hymns founded on Various Texts in the Holy Scriptures* (1755), 44, 45, 47; his 'Jacob's *Vow*', 44; his love of the countryside, 47; his loyalty to Scripture, 39, 40, 41, 47; his piety, 42, 46; his remarkable output, 39; his '*The Active Christian*', 44; 'no ear for Musick', 41

Doggerel, 68

Dogma, 73

Dogs, 56, 105, 208

Dons, xii, 129, 131, 134

Doubt, 95, 180, 186, 202

Doxology, 23, 54, 93, 110, 122, 170, 225, 234

Drake (Independent Minister at Olney), 113

Drama, 59, 122, 207

Dreams, 169

Dryden, John, 69, 70, 249

Dublin, 84, 89, 185

Dumb, 239

Dunmow, Essex, 224   .

Duty, 25, 28, 163

Dyson, Charles, 127, 131

EARTH, 96, 122, 133, 148, 158, 170, 222, 227

East, 137, 216

Easter, 76, 144, 146, 217

Ecce Homo appeal, 210

Ecclesiastical History, 104, 239

Ecclesiastical Titles Act, 209

Ecstasy, 197

Ecumenical outlook, 117

Eden, 47, 84, 148

Edification, 228

Education, xiv, 41, 209, 213

Edward VI, King of England and Ireland (1547–53), 204, 243

Election (*see also* predestination), 86, 93, 94

Elgar, Sir Edward, 134, 167, 170, 260

Elias, Edward Alfred, his Library of Hymnology, ix, x, xi

Elizabeth I, Queen of England and Ireland (1558–1603), 175, 243

Elizabethan Church, 136

ELLERTON, John (1826–93), xi, xiv, 220–241, 245, 255, 257, 258, 259, 260; educated at Cambridge, and read Theology, 224; Easebourne curacy, 224; friend of F.J.A. Hort, 229, 233; his committee work, 228, 231; active urban ministry, 223; work at Crewe Green, 224, 225, 257; translator, 229; defines the hymn, 224, 228, 234; his 'The day Thou gavest ...', 221–2, 226–7; his 'Principles of Hymn-Book construction', xiv, 223, 227; his *Hymns for Schools and Bible Classes*, 225; his *Liturgy for Missionary Meetings* (1870), 226; his *Holiest Manhood* (1882), 230; recuperation by Lake Geneva (1884–5), 231; vocation as 'country parson', 225; Rector of White Roding, Essex (1885), 224, 231, 259; his *Hymns Original and Translated* (1884), 232, 259; work on *A & M Supplement* (1889), 228, 231; his funeral service (20 June, 1893), 232–3

Elliot, Sir Walter, 101

Elliott, Charles, of Clapham, 181

Edward, 187

Eleanor, 181, 182, 185, 188, 189

Henry Venn, 189

ELLIOTT, Charlotte (1789–1871), xi, xiv, 7, 178–197, 211, 253, 256, 258; breakdown (1821), 181, 188; continuing depression, 182; counselled by Dr Malan

(1822), 182, 183, 187; effective evangelist, 191, 196; Eleanor Elliott's brief *Memoir*, 181, 182, 183, 187, 188, 189, 190, 196–7; inspired by her 'private Bible', 183; *Invalid's Hymn Book* (1834), 185; love of Scripture, 191; edited *Remembrancer Pocket-Book* (1834–59), 185; rheumatic fever and suffering, 188–9, 190; visits Switzerland (1836), 187; her *Hours of Sorrow* (1840), 181, 183, 184, 185, 188, 191, 192, 193, 194, 256; its many editions and success, 184; her *Hymns for a Week* (1837), 187, 188, 256; her 'Just as I am …', 180, 185–7, 192, 196; her 'lonely vigil', 190, 191, 193; her support for St Mary's Chapel, Brighton, 187, 188; her sensitivity to sufferers from deafness, 191, 194; her *Thoughts in Verse*, 184, 191f.
Eloquence, 135
Emancipation, Roman Catholic, 159
Emotion, 42, 77, 145, 207, 212, 217
Empires, 222
Encouragement, 133
England, 105, 144, 161, 170, 244
English Christianity, 164
English language, 68, 73, 78, 83, 89, 92, 116, 159
Englishmen, 102
Envy, 18, 70
Epiphany, 144, 216
Erasmus (c. 1466–1536), 6, 84
Erastianism, 162
Erfurt, 6
Error, 228
'Error-seat' (Rome), 173
Escott, Harry, 54, 59
Esschen, Johannes van den, 6
Essex, 224
Establishment, the English Ecclesiastical, 84, 95, 106, 108, 114, 129, 137, 159, 161, 162, 164
Eternal rest, 197
Eternity, 18, 63, 168, 182, 205

Eucharist (*see also* Communion, Lord's Supper and Mass), 27, 45, 143, 151, 152, 172–3, 186, 192, 233
celebration of, 23
choral, 233
consecration of, 173
Real Presence in, 17, 152, 172
sacrifice of, 152
Europe, 10, 130, 160
Eutychians, 165
Evangelical cause, 73, 101, 106, 108, 113, 181
Evangelicalism, 77, 113
Evangelical revival 67, 83, 109, 112, 120, 182, 183
Evangelicals, xiv, 113, 128
Evangelical theology, 71, 113
Evangelical tradition, 41, 54, 230
Evangelism, 5, 7, 51, 59, 70
Evangelist(s), 83, 187, 196
Evening, 153, 189, 194, 204
hymns, 29, 30, 194, 214, 225, 226–7, 235
Prayer ('Evensong'), according to the *Book of Common Prayer*, 92, 133
Evil, 86, 102, 119, 120, 182
Example, 210
Excommunication, 142
Exhortation (*see also* Preaching), 92, 107
Exhortations, Prayer-Book, 28
Exile, 203
Experience, religious, 70
Exposition, 56, 85, 110

FAIRFORD, 127, 128, 130
Faith, 40, 43, 57, 60, 61, 67, 68, 70, 71, 86, 89, 91, 92, 101, 104, 109, 121, 128, 145, 149, 152, 187, 190, 191, 193, 196, 197, 205, 207, 228 (*see also* 'catholic' faith, justification by faith, 'protestant faith')
Faithful people, 76, 89, 110, 112, 119, 150
Fall, 84

Famine, the Irish Potato (1845–6), 202, 203, 256
Farmers, 5, 166
'Farm lads', 140
Fatalism, 83
Fatherhood (of God), 93, 104, 158, 170, 190, 202, 205, 211, 217, 240
Fathers, Early Church, 135, 138, 141, 160, 164
    Tridentine, 136, 165
Fauna, 146, 147
Fear, 76, 100, 111, 119, 121, 170, 186
Feeding (the five thousand), 145
Fellowship (of suffering), xiv, 183
Festivals, 74, 131, 138, 225
Fever, 159
Fiction, 51
Fightings, 186
Fire, 42, 46, 76, 97
Fish (the miraculous draught), 149
Flood, 122
Flora, 146, 147
Flower arranging, 190
Flowers, 118, 145, 146, 151, 190, 193, 218, 219
    cowslip, 118
    primrose, 147
    roses, 148
Folk songs, 7, 243, 244
Forgiveness, 106, 217
Formularies, 165
'Forty-five', the rebellion of 1745, 106
Fossils, 202
'Foundery', the London, 84, 245
Fountain, 82, 111
Fox, Charles James (1749–1806), 115
Foxe, John (1516–87), the martyrologist, 88
France, 208, 229
Freedom, 107
Free-grace, 89
Free-thinkers, 101, 106
Free will, 74, 83, 88
Friday (*see also* Good Friday), 188
Frost, Maurice, 243

Froude, Richard Hurrell (1803–36), 128, 132, 135, 143, 160, 161
Froude, Robert, Archdeacon of Totnes, 160, 161
Fruit, 47
Fruitfulness, 47
Fundamentals, 68
Funerals, vii, 116

GALATIANS, 58
Garden, 231
Gardiner, Colonel, 106
Gay, 184, 205
Gems, 194, 214
Geneva, 83, 88, 137, 182, 231, 244
Genius, 58, 69
Gennesaret, 145
Gentiles, 216, 236
George I, King of Great Britain and Ireland (1714–27), 249
George II, King of Great Britain and Ireland (1727–60), 56, 249, 251
George, Prince Regent (1811), 181
Georgia, 83
Germany, 15, 229, 244
Gerontius, the Dream of, 167–170, 171, 172, 176, 258
Gethsemane, 196
Ghost, the Holy (*see* Holy Ghost and Holy Spirit)
Gibbet, 59
Girls, 212
Gladness, 184, 196
Gladstone, William Ewart (1809–98), 90, 139, 209
Glad tidings, 218
Glory, 8, 26, 59, 61, 66, 71, 72, 93, 96, 112, 148, 152, 184
Gloucestershire, 127
God, 24, 28, 56, 62, 63, 68, 72, 73, 75, 77, 84, 85, 86, 93, 94, 96, 104, 114, 115, 118, 121, 126, 130, 133, 136, 139, 145, 148, 150, 158, 167, 168, 195
Godhead, 70
Godliness, 239
Godparents, 205
Gold, 57, 194

Golgotha, 59
Gomarus, Franciscus (1563–1641), 84
'Good Book' (*see also* Bible, Scripture and Word of God), 131, 132
Good Friday, 145, 196, 197, 216, 217, 235
Good news, 67
Good Samaritan, 174
Gorham Judgement (1847), 139, 256
Gospel (the Christian), xiii, xiv, 8, 14, 15, 17, 43, 44, 46, 52, 53, 60, 61, 62, 67, 68, 69, 71, 83, 85, 88, 91, 92, 95, 101, 106, 109, 110, 111, 114, 117, 119, 122, 163, 187, 191, 207
Gospel ministry, 69, 76, 187
Gospel proclamation (*kerygma*), 15, 44, 61, 83, 85, 88, 92, 95, 110, 111, 150, 217
Gospels, the Four, 29, 145
Gospel times, 176
Gothic revival, 209
Gounod, Charles François, 208, 213
Grace, 16, 17, 24, 66, 67, 70, 73, 82, 84, 88, 89, 91, 93, 96, 100, 104, 107, 111, 120, 133, 137, 158
Graham, Dr Billy, 187
Great Britain, 55
Greed, 18
Greek, 9, 108, 229
Green, Dr V.H.H., 67
Gregorian chant, xii
Grief, 190, 192, 196
Grimshaw, William (1708–63), of Haworth, 113
Guardianship, 197
Guest, Dr George, vii–viii
Guidance, on entering a Church, 152
Guilt, 82, 196
'Gunpowder, Treason and Plot', 55, 150

HALIFAX, George Savile, 1st Marquis (1633–95), 28

Hallelujah, 30
Hampden, R.D., 139
Handel, George Frederick (1685–1759), 116, 248, 250, 251
his *Messiah* (1741–2), 116, 250
Hanoverian succession, 55, 249
Happiness, 33, 89
Harps, 93, 94, 209
Haselden, Charles, London printer, 188
Hate, 18
Havisham, Miss, 182
Haweis, Thomas, Rector of Aldwinckle, 108
Hawkins, William, 26, 29, 33, 159, 160
Hayward, Gareth and Jenny, Thomas, William and Richard Peter, viii
Healing, 111, 180, 186
Health, 33, 105, 184
Heathcote, Sir William, 127
Heart(s), 40, 46, 70, 75, 77, 100, 110, 117, 126, 133, 134, 184, 196, 211, 216
Heaven(s), 10, 16, 25, 38, 43, 57, 62, 66, 69, 71, 74, 83, 96, 107, 126, 146, 147, 148, 149, 151, 158, 163, 167, 170, 172, 174, 182, 187, 192, 193, 200, 203, 206, 207, 213
Hebrew, 44, 53, 175
Hell, 4, 12, 25, 56, 83, 218
Henery, C.R., 134
Henry VIII, King of England (1509–47), 243
Heresy, 5, 165
Heritage, 38, 133
Hermits, 168
Hierarchy, Church, xii
'High Church', 91, 132, 137, 141, 143, 150, 183, 256
Hill, Richard, 85
Hill, Rowland, 69
Hinstock, 224
Historians, 128, 135, 202
History, 76, 92, 165

Church, 104, 239
English, 29, 55
Holborn, 113
Holiness (*see also* Sanctity), 68, 77,
    89, 96, 134, 189
Holy Child, 213
Holy Church, 158, 168, 171, 173
'Holy Club' (the Oxford), 83
Holy Ghost, 76, 106, 158, 170, 205,
    234
Holy Innocents, 215
Holy Land, 145, 209
Holy Orders, 108
Holy Spirit, 31, 122, 168, 240
Holy Writ (*see also* Bible, Scripture),
    xiv, 244
Homage, 46
Homily (homilies), xiv, 5, 8, 23, 31,
    40, 53, 58, 59, 78, 90, 91, 111,
    119, 134, 153, 168, 171, 187,
    191, 207, 213, 227
Homilies, Book of the, 85, 113
Honey, 89, 147
Hook, Farquar (Vicar of Leeds from
    1837), 203, 209
Hooker, Richard (c. 1554–1600),
    135, 136, 137, 138, 142
    his *Laws of Ecclesiastical Polity*, 135
Hooper, John, Bp of Gloucester and
    Worcester (1550–1555), 27, 204
Hope, 60, 68, 71, 73, 150, 158, 168,
    173, 177, 192, 227
Hort, F.J.A. (1828–92), 224, 229, 233
Hosanna, 38, 43, 44
Hospital patients, 193
Hosts, 66, 71
House of Lords, 209
Housman, A. E., 57
Housman, Henry, 226, 231
Humanity, 68, 72, 74, 86, 109, 168,
    176, 191, 201
Humility, 111, 131, 141, 241
Humour, 169, 181
Huntingdon, 116
Hursley Park, 127, 134, 139, 141
Huss, Jan (c. 1369–1415), 11
Hyde, Edward (*see* Clarendon)
Hymn melodies:

Croft's Hanover, 41
Croft's St Anne, 41
Webbe's Rockingham, 41
Hymnals, 42, 76, 110, 167, 245
    Ancient & Modern (1861), 223,
        228–229, 231–232, 243, 245,
        257
    Ancient & Modern Revised, viii
    Ancient & Modern Supplement
        (1889), 228, 231
    Church Militant Hymns (1884), 232
    Durham Mission Hymn-Book
        (1884), 232
    London Mission Hymn-Book (1884),
        232, 237
    The Methodist Hymn Book, 90
    The New Catholic Hymnal, 110
    Wittenberg Hymn Book (1524), 8
    Wittenberg Hymnal (1528), 9
Hymnody, 8, 15, 41, 133
Hymnology, 223, 229
Hymns (*passim* but *see also* under
        hymnwriters named by chapter
        and theme):
    Baptismal, 236
    Communion, 230
    creation, 118
    evangelical, 10, 133
    German, 229
    'Gospel', 40
    medieval, 229
    missionary, 226
    'office', 243, 244
    processional, 237
Hymnsinging, 62, 92, 234
Hymnwriters, vii, xiii, 5, 51, 88, 97,
    243
Hypochondriac, 189

ICONOGRAPHY, 175
Idealism, 10, 68
Idolatry, 164
Iffley, 166
Ignorance, 26
Ilfracombe, 189
Illness, 193
Illusions, 165
Imagery, 23, 47, 67, 90, 91, 111,

133, 161, 184, 185, 193, 206, 207, 212, 216, 239
Images, 164, 210
Imagination, 205, 207
Imitatio Christi (of Thomas à Kempis), 103
Impiety, 101, 138
Incarnation (of Christ), 40, 132, 133, 145, 168, 195, 214, 215
Incense, xv, 46, 214
Independent congregations and ministers, 113, 114
Indifference, 52, 83
Inner life, 131
Innocents, the Holy, 168, 215
Insight, 68, 72, 105, 207
Inspiration, xiv, 68, 117, 150, 159, 176, 182, 205, 223, 234, 244
Instruction, 153
Intellectualism, 43
Intercession, 31, 163
Interpreter, 75
Introspection, 72, 192
Invalids, 191
Ireland, 160, 201, 202, 208
Irenaeus, St (c. 130– c. 200), 141
Irish Church disestablishment, 137
Irreligion, 26
Isaiah (*see also* under Bible, Old Testament), 39, 41, 89, 91
Isle of Man, 142
Israel, 6, 44, 87, 133
Israel, children of, 111
Israelites, 43, 111, 159
Italy, 26, 104, 161, 174
Ivy, 211

JACKSON, Carl, viii
Jackson, Bp William, 136
Jacob, 44, 73, 120
James, Duke of York, 28
James, Lord Strange, of Knowsley, 142
James, P.D., Baroness, 51
Jealousy, 70
Jehova, The Lord, 63, 91
Jenkins, Claude, 128
Jennings, 106

Jerusalem, 55, 207
Jesuits, 5
Jesus Christ, 4, 5, 6, 9, 12, 15, 33, 40, 42, 44, 45, 50, 52, 53, 54, 58, 59, 60, 62, 67, 68, 70, 72, 74, 75, 76, 77, 78, 82, 83, 84, 88, 89, 91, 93, 99, 100, 104, 106, 107, 109, 110, 111, 112, 114, 115, 120, 121, 122, 126, 133, 137, 139, 145, 149, 152, 168, 171, 173, 175, 177, 182, 183, 186, 188, 197, 205, 207, 210, 213, 215, 218, 234
  baptism, 210
  birth, 68, 75, 168, 210
  blood (*see also* Blood, of Christ), 184
  childhood, 210
  circumcision (*see also* Circumcision of Christ), 148
  crucifixion (*see also* Crucifixion of Christ), 67, 74, 82, 91, 120, 133, 158, 182, 207
  death, 76, 207, 210
  gospel (*see also* Gospel, Christian), xiii, 67
  love, 93
  mediator, 91
  passion, 58, 210
  Prince of Peace, 43
  resurrection and ascension, 15, 76, 210, 214
  saviour, 15, 46, 59, 68, 74, 82, 94, 109
  second coming, 40, 75
  uniqueness, 175
Jewel, John, Bp of Salisbury (1559–71), 136, 165
Jews, 24
Jingoism, 238
John the Baptist (*see also*, Saints), 144
Johnson, Boris, Journalist, 202
Johnson, Dr Samuel (1709–84), 60, 107, 249
Jordan, river, 145
Joseph, 133
Joy, 42, 61, 63, 111, 177, 218, 235
Joys, 122

Jubilee:
  the Lord's, 38, 43
  papal, 26
  royal, 227, 259
Judaea, 55, 195
Judaism, 52
Judge (Christ as), 152
Judgement, 24, 82, 163, 168, 171
  'the Great Day of', 24
Justification by faith *alone*, 67, 71,
  85, 164

KALENDAR (the Church's
  liturgical) 131, 132, 133, 144,
  204, 215, 236
Katherine von Bora, 17
KEBLE, John (1792–1866), xi, xiv,
  124–154, 160, 183–4, 203, 204,
  208, 211, 253, 254, 255, 258;
  'double first', 128; his family,
  130–1, 135, 149; caring College
  Tutor, 129, 142; ordained
  (1815), 127, 129, 254; Curate
  of Eastleach and Southrop
  (1823), 127; his sister Elizabeth,
  128, 135; *The Christian Year*
  (1827), 126, 127, 130, 131–135,
  144–150, 151, 153–4, 183, 184,
  203, 204, 255; elected Professor
  of Poetry at Oxford (1831),
  129, 133, 135, 255; his 'Assize
  Sermon' (1833), 128, 129, 137,
  162, 255; married to Charlotte
  Clarke (1835), 127, 135, 140,
  150, 151; Vicar of Hursley with
  Otterbourne, Hants, 127, 128,
  134, 139, 140, 154, 204; helped
  to revive Convocation (1852),
  140; his hymns, and 'Bless'd are
  the pure in heart', 125–6,
  132–3, 144; tone deaf, 144; his
  love of the *Book of Common
  Prayer*, 133, 136, 145; *On
  Eucharistical Adoration* (1859),
  143, 151; opposition to
  secularization, 138; his pastoral
  priorities, 131, 141, 143, 149,
  153; poetry for the *British

  Magazine*, 137; regarded
  Catechism crucial in teaching
  ministry, 140; work on *The
  Library of Anglo-Catholic
  Theology*, 141, 256; and on
  Library of the Fathers (1836),
  141, 255; concern for
  University reform, 138; deeply
  moved by natural phenomena,
  127, 146, 147–8, 149; love of
  flora and fauna, 127, 146,
  147–8, 149;
KEN, Thomas (1631–1711), x, xiv,
  20, 23–33, 225, 248–9; Bp of
  Bath and Wells (1685–91), 23,
  27, 248; his *Catechism*, 23, 25,
  28, 32, 248; his 'Collect for
  Health', 33; his conflict with
  the State, 25, 29; his disciplined
  piety, 31, 33; his doxology, 22,
  23, 26; his 'Ejaculations' (brief
  Collects), 30; his 'Evening
  Hymn', 29, 30; his *Exposition of
  the Church Catechism*, 27; his
  ideal priest, 33–4; his *Manual of
  Prayer*, 23, 24, 27, 31; his
  Meditations, 32–3; his 'Midnight
  Hymn', 29, 31, 33; his
  'Morning Hymn' 22, 23, 25,
  30; his pastoral commitment,
  23, 27; his *Practice of Divine
  Love*, 24, 27; his shroud, 30; his
  Winchester scholars, 23; Ken at
  Longleat, 31; his Last Will and
  Testament, 32
Kennedy, Studdert ('Woodbine
  Willie'), 59–60
Kent, 101
Keswick convention, 187
Keys, 149
Kiernan, Harriet, of Dublin, 185
King, Christ as, 100, 112, 126, 236
Kingdom:
  of God, 7, 62, 222, 227
  of the Spirit, 176
Kings, 23, 62, 133, 137, 213
Kneller, Godfrey, x
Knox, John (c. 1505–72), 88

Konstant, Roman Catholic Bp of
Leeds, 201
Köstlin, Julius, 11

LABOUR(s), 72, 82
Laity, 162, 166
Lamb, of God, 61, 96, 118, 120,
180, 187, 191, 192
Lambs, 212
Landbeach, viii
All Saints' Church, viii
Landscapes, 189, 194, 212
Language, 54, 61, 62, 67, 68, 83, 92,
168
Latimer, Hugh, Bp of Worcester
(1535–45), 165, 204
Latin, xii, 90, 135, 229
Laud, William, Abp of Canterbury
(1633–45), 137, 141
Law-Gospel antithesis, 107
Law, Mosaic (*see also* Ten
Commandments), 27, 53, 82,
91, 94, 239
Leadership, 84
Learning, 34, 138
Leamington Spa, 204
Leaves, 146
Leeds, 203
Leicestershire, 43
Lent, 75, 140, 144, 216, 230
Leviticus, 53
Lewis, C.S., 27
Liberalism, 139, 160
Liberty, 53, 70
Liddon, H.P., 129, 136
Life, in Christ, 100, 112, 120, 126,
158, 191
Life eternal, 43, 67, 96
Light, 118, 139, 158, 176, 185, 194,
216, 222, 226, 227
'Lining out', 244
Lions, 206
Litany, 95, 168
Liturgy, 95, 108, 114, 136, 144, 228,
244
Liverpool, 96, 105
London, 83, 84, 85, 86, 88, 105, 107,
113, 114, 116, 166, 185, 237

Loneliness, 184, 189, 191, 192, 194,
197
Longfellow, H.W., 212
Lord, Christ as, 100
Lord God, 56, 63, 73, 76, 100, 105,
112, 120, 126
'Lord's Board', 58
Lord's Day, 31, 188
Lord's Prayer, 27, 206
Lord's Supper (*see also* Communion,
Eucharist and Mass), 45, 46, 54,
187
Love, of God (in Christ), 9, 38, 42,
45, 47, 50, 53, 58, 59, 62, 63,
66, 68, 69, 70, 71, 72, 74, 75,
76, 93, 94, 100, 111, 112, 114,
115, 122, 147, 150, 169, 176,
180, 186, 189, 196, 217
Lowliness, 126
Lübeck, 16
Luke, St (*see also* under Saints and
Scripture), 39
Lust, 181
LUTHER, Martin (1483–1546), x,
xiii, 2–18, 41, 52, 72, 77, 175,
243, 244, 245; novice, 6;
postulant, 6; Prior, 6; and the
'pure', 'rediscovered' gospel,
xiii, 8, 12, 16, 244; and the
Word of God, 8, 13, 16, 18;
and St Paul, 8; and
Anfechtungen, 9; and the 'noble
army of martyrs', 6; and the
'psalm-hymn', 6, 8, 15; his
commitment to hymns as
homilies, 10, 14; his 'catechism
hymns', 15; the 'Wittenberg
nightingale', 8–9; his 'From
Trouble deep ...' (1523), 15,
16; '*Ein feste Burg* ...', vii, 9,
10, 11, 12, 14, 239; his pastoral
concern, xiii, 5, 10, 41; and the
Peasants' Revolt (1525), 9; his
marriage (1525), 17; his
'children's' *Catechism* (1529), 77;
and the Mass, 10; at Schloss
Coburg (1530), 11; his *Treatise
on the Last Words of David*

(1543), 6; trials and tribulations, 9; *Table Talk* 5; and 'Dame Music', 17; his idealism, 10; and legacy, 17
Lutherans, vii, 11
Lyra apostolica (1836), 137, 138, 160, 161, 171–2
Lyre, 18, 181
Lyrical charm, 207
Lyricism, 68, 112, 133, 212
Lyrics, 10

MACE, Thomas, 52
Macmillan, publishers, 210, 230
Magi, 195
Magnificat, 175
Malan, Dr Caesar, 182, 183, 187
Majesty, 68
Malta, 160
Manchester, 182
Manesty, 105
Manhood, 158
Mania, 181
Mankind, 94, 207
Manna, 100, 111
Manning, B.L., 55
Manx language, 143
Marriage-Supper (of the Lamb), 191
Marlow, Dr Richard, viii
Marriage, 197
Marseillaise, 10
Marseilles, 159
Martin, B., 102, 106, 107
Martyrs, 6, 168, 204
Mary, the Blessed Virgin, 133, 168, 169, 175, 195, 239
    'Queen of Seasons', 175
Mary II, Queen of Great Britain and Ireland (1689–94), 28, 248
Mass, 10, 59
    Agnus Dei, 10
    Gradual, 10
    Sanctus, 10
Masters, Joseph, London publisher, 209, 212
Mattins, 208
Mayle, Peter, 134
Meditation, 24, 25, 71, 72, 91, 94,

108, 127, 130, 131, 133, 144, 167, 174, 176, 177, 205, 228, 230, 231
Mediterranean, 159, 160, 174
Meekness, 210
Meetings, Dissenting, 52, 108, 113
Meeting House, 86
Melancholy, 127, 191, 192
Melanchthon, Philipp (1497–1560), 9, 11, 13
Melody, xiii, 18, 41, 244, 245
Memorial, vii
Memory, 40, 154, 227
Men, 68, 72, 92, 126
Mendips, 89
Mental distress, 182
Mercy, 53, 74, 94, 103, 109, 120, 121, 130, 150, 189, 213, 224
Mercy-Seat, 117, 120
Messiah, 6, 54, 236
Messina, 160
Metaphors, 89, 239
Methodism, 68, 70, 87, 245
Methodists, 117, 128
Methodist Societies, 84
Metre(s), 41, 54, 149, 243, 244
Middle Ages, 239, 243
Middle Temple, 116
Milk, 147
Milner, Isaac (of Queens' College, Cambridge), 113
Ministers (of religion), xv, 88
Ministry, 52, 61, 62, 68, 69, 83, 84, 85, 90, 108, 109, 112, 114, 117, 129, 134, 135, 150, 153, 162, 172, 187, 204, 206, 224, 229
Miracle(s), 53, 59, 103, 133, 207
Mirth, 172, 184, 201, 236
Mischief, 56, 102
Missionary, 226–7
Mission, 16, 67, 68, 73, 83, 117, 121, 133, 140, 145, 149, 187, 191, 219, 238
Moberly, George, 139
Moderation, 115
Modesty, 96, 105, 131
Monday, 187

Monophysites, 165
Moods, 191
Moon, 148, 175
Montanvert, 187
Month, literary magazine, 167
Morality, 224
Moralizing, 85
Moral standards, 143
Moravians, 117
More, Hannah (1745–1833), 115
More, Sir Thomas (1478–1535), 130
Morning, 153, 189, 194, 204
  hymns, 74, 194, 222, 225
  Prayer (*see also* under *Book of
  Common Prayer*), 95
Morris, James, Methodist lay
  preacher, 84
Moses, 52, 55, 159
Mourning, 33
Music, xv, 5, 7, 8, 9, 14, 17, 31, 33,
  41, 51, 68, 100, 112, 116, 134,
  144, 167, 170, 171, 175, 181,
  208, 212, 241, 243, 245
Mystery:
  of the Eucharist, 151
  of the Godhead, 68, 70, 121, 145,
  195
Mystics, 117

NAKEDNESS, 82
Name (of Jesus), 100, 110
Naples, 159, 160
Nails, 59, 217
Nash, Miss J.P., viii
Nation, 70, 237, 241
National Schools, 204, 212
Nature, 59, 120, 146, 148, 182, 193,
  211
Navy, 101
Nazareth, 41
Neale, John Mason (1818–66), 153
Negro slave trade, 102
Neighbour, 202
Neo-scholasticism, 84
New birth, 67, 71, 120, 236
Newfoundland, 102
New life, 121
NEWMAN, John Henry

(1801–1890), xi, xiv, 128, 129,
  134, 135, 138, 139, 140, 141,
  156–177, 253, 254, 255, 256,
  259; Oxford career as Tutor of
  Oriel, 159, 160, 166, 254, and
  Vicar of St Mary the Virgin
  (1828), 159, 162, 163, 164,
  255; his *Parochial and Plain
  Sermons*, 128, 162, 163, 164,
  174, 175, 177; his 'Lead, kindly
  Light...', 159, 161, 162, 166,
  176; his library, 166; mother
  and sisters, 160, 166; search for
  a *Via Media*, 164, 165; his
  *Lectures on the Prophetical Office
  of the Church* (1837), 164; *Tract
  XC* (1841), 165, 256; received
  into the Roman Church (1845),
  166, 256; Superior of the
  Birmingham Oratory, 166, 172,
  175; his '... *certain Difficulties felt
  by Anglicans* (1850), 166; his
  Apologia Pro Vita Sua (1864),
  129, 159, 162; *Dream of
  Gerontius* (1865), 167–170, 171,
  172, 176; 'Firmly I believe and
  truly', 157–158, 167, 177;
  'Praise to the Holiest...', 167,
  168, 171; created Cardinal
  (1879), 167, 259; his humour,
  169; his irritability, 135, 169;
  his spiritual stature, 164, 174–5,
  177; his *Verses on Various
  Occasions*, 171, 172–3
Newport Pagnell, 113
New Testament (*see also* Bible for
  Books cited), 43, 44, 45, 52,
  62, 106, 244
NEWTON, John (1725–1807), xi,
  xiv, 7, 98–122, 249, 251, 252,
  254; early life, 101; Mary
  Catlett of Chatham, 102, 105,
  115, 116; their marriage, 105,
  115; a self-proclaimed 'Free-
  thinker', 101, 106; on board the
  Greyhound, 102; Mate of the
  Brownlow, 105; Captain of the
  Duke of Argyle, 106; his epilepsy,

106; Tide Surveyor at Liverpool, 108; his *Authentic Narrative*, 101, 102, 103, 106, 112, 251; his recollections, 101–102; evangelical conversion, 106, 112; studies New Testament Greek, 108; ordained deacon (1764), 109; made priest (1764), 109; Curate of Olney, 108, 109, 111, 112, 116, 117; the *Olney Hymns*, 111, 117, 252; 'How sweet the Name of Jesus sounds', 99–100, 111–112; supported by John Thornton, 112–113; his *Review of Ecclesiastical history* (1770), 104, 107–8, 113, 252; his attempt to vindicate 'Reformation doctrines', 113; his mission, 112, 113, 117, 121, 122; his *Journal*, 102; Rector of St Mary Woolnoth, 113, 114, 252; significant preacher, 122; his *Thoughts upon the African Slave Trade* (1788), 102, 115

New World, 203
New Year, 195
Night, 222, 226, 227
Noah, 122, 193
    his Ark, 122
    his 'Dove', 193
Non-Conformity, 55
North, 83
Northampton, 39, 40
Nosegays, 190
Notoriety, 128
Nunc dimittis, canticle, 133
Nürnberg, 8

OATHS, 101
Obedience, 149
Objectivity, 133
Obligations, 24, 163
Obloquy, 201
Observance, ritual and general:
    pilgrimage, xiii, 23, 24, 45, 72, 95, 105, 134, 215
    stations of the Cross, 210

Observation, 132f., 178, 181f.
Odium theologicum, xiii
Offerings, 153
Offices, daily:
    Prime, 175
    Terce, 175
    Sext, 175
    None, 175
    Vespers, 175
    Compline, 175
Old Masters, 58
Old Testament (*see also* under Bible), 43, 44, 45, 53, 54, 62, 159, 179, 209
Olivers, Thomas, Methodist publisher, 87
Olney, 108, 109, 112, 113, 122
    Hymns, 109, 111, 112, 116, 122
    the 'Great House', 117, 118, 119
Omega, 14, 70
Oranges, 159
Orders, Religious, 24
Ordination, 108, 136, 149
Organs, 14
Ornithology, 211; species mentioned:
    Blackbird, 148
    Canary, 185
    Crossbill, 212
    Crow, 211
    Dove, 148, 193, 212
    Kite, 148
    Lark, 212
    Nightingale, 193
    Owl, 211
    Raven, 206
    Robin, 212
    'Sea-bird', 212
    Skylark, 193
    Swallow, 211
    Thrush, 118
Orthodoxy, 84, 95
Orton, Job, 39, 40, 43, 46
Oxford, viii, 43, 83, 85, 108, 127, 128, 129, 131, 133, 135, 138, 141, 142, 159, 161, 162, 166, 175, 176, 202, 204
    Colleges of the University: Christ

Church, viii, 128, 136; Corpus
Christi, 129, 130; Keble, xi,
129; Oriel, 127, 128, 129, 135,
159, 160, 166; St Edmund Hall,
85; St Mary Hall, 85
Oxfordshire, 127
Oxford University: its motto, 138;
Church of St Mary the Virgin,
128, 159, 162, 163; Press
(Clarendon), 135; Proctorial
authority, 85; Oxford
Publications mentioned, *Book of
Christian Verse*, 57; *Dictionary of
Quotations*, 201; Theological
Society, 138; Vice-Chancellor
Durrell, 85
Owen, David, Lord, 84
Oysters, 159

PAIN, 60, 170, 191, 200, 202, 218
Paintings, 177
Palermo, 159
Palestine, 55, 147
Pamphlets, 202
'Papists', 117
Paraphrases, 40
Pardon, 67, 180
Parents, 56
Parishes, 107, 127, 128, 133, 140,
172, 187, 223
Parishioners, 118, 141, 154, 230,
231
Parker, James (of Oxford), 131, 141
Parker Society, 141, 256
Parliament, 160
Parochial system, 107, 113
Parodies, 55–6, 86
Parry, Sir Hubert, 77
Passion, 70
Passion (of Christ), 91, 169
Pastoral appeal, 95, 112
    care, 116, 129
    duties, 166
    idealism, 122
    ministry, 112, 138, 140, 143, 153,
    206, 236
    practice, 165
    priorities, 117, 130, 149

Pastors, 73, 113, 118, 150, 207
Patience, 187, 190, 192
Patriotism, 134
Patristics, 165
Pattern, 126, 205
Paul, Apostle, Martyr and Saint, 8,
10, 15, 58, 84, 104, 109, 115,
122, 163, 176, 183, 189, 237
Payne, Ernest, 44, 57
Peace, 38, 43, 111, 126, 173, 190,
215, 226
Peasants, 203, 212
Peccadilloes, 71
Pedants, 128, 165
Pedantry, 128
Peel, Sir Robert (1788–1850), English
statesman, 128, 159, 255
People, 214
Penalty, 196
Penance, 167, 172
Penitence, 59, 112, 187, 191
Penitents, 142
Penitential devotions, 216, 230
Pentateuch, 44
Penzance, 141
Perfection, 71
Persecution, 55
Perseverance, 93
Perspective, 62, 134, 206
Pestilence, 239
Peter, Apostle, Martyr and Saint, 23,
104, 136, 149, 218
    his 'successors', 136, 149
Petrine devices, 149
Philosophy, 57, 202
Pietism, 244
Piety, 24, 28, 29, 42, 59, 60, 68, 77,
84, 95, 112, 132, 134, 135,
144, 187, 215
    Caroline, 28, 29
    medieval, 153, 243
    popular, 132
Pilate, Pontius, 207
Pilgrimage, xiii, 23, 24, 45, 72, 95,
105, 134
Pitt, William, the Younger
(1759–1806), English statesman,
115

Pity, 60, 207
Plainsong, 243
Plague, 202, 240
Play, 205
Pleasure, 202, 230
Poems, 56, 111, 133, 170, 172, 181,
    185
Poetry, xv, 15, 29, 42, 45, 61, 68,
    76, 77, 97, 119, 127, 130, 131,
    132, 134, 144, 148, 149, 150,
    151, 153, 160, 161, 171, 172,
    183, 184, 191, 201, 204, 205,
    211, 212, 216
  metaphysical, 211
Poets, 10, 40, 54, 57, 60, 68, 70, 73,
    77, 78, 85, 116, 118, 119, 148,
    182, 208, 231
Polemicism, 55
Political reform, 201
Politicians, 161
Politics, 84
Poor (the deprived and
    impoverished), 38, 41, 42, 83,
    186, 201, 202, 204,, 240
Pope(s), 10, 26, 149, 164, 165, 170
  Clement X (1670–76), 26
'Popery', 164
Portugal, 160
Potato 'cholera', 203
Potatoes, 209
Pottery, 132
Poverty, 201
Power, 42, 53, 61, 82, 88, 91, 112,
    121, 239
Praise, vii, 5, 23, 25, 26, 39, 52, 53,
    54, 55, 59, 61, 62, 63, 66, 70,
    71, 74, 75, 77, 87, 90, 92, 93,
    95, 100, 110, 111, 112, 114,
    116, 133, 163, 172, 176, 187,
    211, 222, 223, 227, 243
Prayer(s), xiv, xv, 23, 24, 25, 46, 54,
    68, 69, 71, 74, 86, 92, 100,
    104, 107, 108, 110, 111, 114,
    117, 134, 138, 146, 152, 153,
    168, 187, 188, 190, 196, 205,
    206, 222, 224, 227
  extempore, 174
  for the dead, 164

  for the Royal Family, 238
  intercessory, 224
  Lord's, 27, 151, 206
  penitential, 224
  private, 144
Prayer meetings, 113, 117
Praying, 85, 214
Preacher(s), 5, 40, 42, 43, 44, 51,
    73, 83, 85, 112, 122
Preaching (*see also* Exhortation), 40,
    61, 62, 83, 85, 86, 92, 93, 101,
    105, 114, 116, 117, 122, 165
  Lay, 85
Precentor, 244
Predestination (*see also* Election), 73,
    83, 85, 86, 89
Presence (of Christ), 126, 134, 152
Pride, 71, 167, 183, 217
Priest, 29, 33, 34, 100, 135, 138,
    143, 214, 230
  Christ as Great High Priest, 112,
    133
Priesthood, xii, 129, 149
Priest's Orders, 128
Primers, 132, 204, 206
Prince, of Glory, 50
  of Peace, 38
Prince Consort, 238
Prince Regent, 181, 254
Principles, Christian, 128, 139, 172
Priorities, 129, 228
Privy Council, 115, 139
  Judicial Committee of, 139
Prizes (Sunday School), 209
Processions, 128
'Profaneness', 161
Promise, 132, 180
Promised Land, 111
Prophecy, 112, 129
Prophet (Christ as), 100, 112
Prophets, Old Testament, 15, 44,
    150
Prose, 54, 68, 114, 151, 153, 171,
    177
Protestants, 55, 136, 165, 170, 208,
    229
Protestant Episcopal Church of USA,
    229

Protestantism, 16, 138, 139, 164, 244
Provence, 134
Providence, 29, 33, 86, 102, 104, 105, 106, 108, 114, 118, 120, 121
Psalm-hymns, 15
Psalmist, 26
Psalmody, 52, 62, 163, 176
metrical, 51, 62, 243, 244
Psalms, viii, xii, xiii, 5, 6, 7, 8, 15, 24, 30, 44, 51, 52, 53, 73, 92, 94, 162, 163, 174, 176, 223, 243
of 'Consolation and Hope', viii; specific references: Psalm XII, 8, 16; Psalm XIV, 8; Psalm LXVII, 16; Psalm LXXII, 223; Psalm XCVI, 6; Psalm CXIX, 30–31; Psalm CXXXVII, 94
Psalm-singing, 60, 174
Psalter, the Hebrew, 6, 51, 163, 244
Psaltery, 15
Psycho-assertion (see Subjectivism)
Pulpit, xiv, 40, 88, 105, 107, 116
Purcell, Henry, 69, 249
Purgatory, 167, 168, 170, 171
Purification, of the Virgin Mary, 126, 132
Puritan, 32, 136
Puritanism, 34
'Puritans', 41, 136, 244
Purity, 68, 133
Purpose, 106
Pusey, Edward Bouverie (1800–82), 128, 135, 138, 141, 143
his tomb, in Christ Church Cathedral, Oxford, 128–9

RAILWAY MECHANICS, 225
Rainbows, 148, 190
Ramsey, Michael, Abp of Canterbury (1961–74), 134
Rationalism, 138, 139
Rattenbury, F. E., 78
Reason, 57, 69, 83, 84, 228
Reassurance, 120, 193
Recollection, 152, 230

Redeemer, 46, 74, 196
Redemption, 70, 93, 133, 200
Rededication, 208
Reformation, 62, 86, 113, 135, 164, 239, 243
doctrine, 164
sixteenth-century, xii–xiii, 5, 7, 11, 86
Reform Bill (1832), 160, 255
Refrains, 73, 188, 192, 216
Regeneration, 85
Rejoicing, 73
Religion(s), 39, 51, 52, 67, 68, 69, 72, 83, 106, 107, 118, 132, 134, 136, 141, 144, 164, 170, 184, 201, 244
biblical, 72
Christian, 106
practical, 132
Protestant, 26, 164
Roman Catholic, 28, 164
Religiosity, 24
Religious education, xiv
Religious observance, 101
Religious Orders, 189
Religious verse, 131
Rembrandt van Rijn (1606–69), 248
Remembrance, 117
Remission, 181
Remorse, 91, 173
Repentance, 28, 67, 83, 106, 218
Respectability, xiv, 201
Responses, xii, 192
Responsibility, 202
Repose, 188
Repression, 102
Rest, 70, 100, 184, 186, 222
Restoration (of Charles II, 1660), 26, 244
Resurrection, 7, 15, 130, 192, 233
of Christ, 121
Return, of the Prodigal, 173
Revelation, 68
Reverence, 24
Revival, 52, 83, 91, 101, 120, 182, 183, 184, 244
Revivalists, 84, 122, 216
Revolutionary movements, 160

Revolution:
  the French (1789), 181, 253
  the 'Glorious' (1688–9), 28
  the scientific, 203
Rhetoric, 53, 86
Rhine, river, 187
Rhyme, 68, 114, 185, 211
Rhythm, 68, 212, 243
Rich, 201, 202
Riches, 73, 107, 180, 186
Richmond, George, xi, 143
Ridicule, 201
Ridley, Nicholas, Bp of Rochester
  and London (1547–55), 165,
  204
Righteousness, 68, 92
Ritual, 164, 166
Ritualism, 128
Rivalry, 84, 105
  between Faith and Reason, 228
Robes, 206
Rochester, 105
Rock (Christ as), 91, 100, 111, 218
'Rock of Ages', 82, 89, 90, 91
Rocks, 103–4
Romaine, William (1714–95), 85
Romanticism, 47, 69, 130, 131, 146
Rome, 5, 26, 55, 139, 141, 150,
  160, 164, 166
  Church of, 55, 169, 172, 173,
  174, 175, 244
Routley, Erik, 60, 95, 96, 109, 243
Rowell,Geoffrey, 134
Rubrics (*see* under *Book of Common
  Prayer*)
Ruddigore, 136
Rupp, E. G., xv, 55
Rustics, 225
Ryle, J. C., 1st Bp of Liverpool
  (1880–1900), 96–7

SABBATH, 39, 188
Sachs, Hans, 8
Sacraments, 131, 144, 166, 172, 231
Sacred, 61, 210
Sacrifice(s), 50, 53, 138, 151
Sacrilege, 137
Sadness, 111

Saint(s), 9, 23, 60, 61, 67, 93, 94,
  128, 131, 148, 163, 168, 172,
  175. References to individual
  Saints:
Ambrose, 233
Andrew, 162, 214
Augustine of Canterbury, 143
Augustine of Hippo, 9, 223, 241
Jerome, 9
John the Baptist, 149
Joseph, 133
Mary, the Blessed Virgin, 133
Michael, 175
Peter, 23, 149, 166, 218
Paul, 8, 10, 15, 23, 183, 237
Philip Neri, 166, 167, 175
Swithun, 23
Saints' Days, 131, 144, 214, 218
Salvation, 7, 27, 45, 54, 66, 70, 71,
  73, 89, 93, 104, 109, 114, 133,
  166, 169, 207
Salve Regina, 16
Salzburg, 39
Sancroft, William Abp of Canterbury
  (1678–89), 27, 28
Sanctification, 67, 71, 73
Sanctity (*see also* Holiness), 71, 151,
  214
Sanctuary, 110, 218, 229, 233
Sandon, Henry, viii
Satan, 9, 12, 38, 56, 87, 100, 110
Saturday, 188
Saul, 18
Saviour (Christ as), 38, 42, 43, 57,
  59, 61, 74, 75, 82, 90, 94, 183,
  192, 194, 196, 213, 216, 217,
  225, 230
Saxony, Ernestine, xiii, 9, 11, 244
Scandinavia, 15
Scepticism, 207
Schism, 165, 166
  the East/West (1054), 141
  the Non-Juring (1688), 28–9, 249
Schizophrenia, 181
Scholars, 131
Scholarship, 129
Schools, 205, 209, 225
Schütz, Heinrich, 8, 248

Scotland, 187, 244

Scourge, 240

Scripture, Holy (*see also* Bible and Word of God), xii, xiv, 30, 39, 41, 42, 46, 47, 53, 54, 73, 76, 86, 91, 95, 106, 110, 111, 112, 116, 122, 133, 140, 143, 144, 153, 163, 164, 165, 174, 182, 184, 187, 194, 208

Sea, 101, 102, 104, 212

Seafaring, 102

Seasons, 161

Secret, 126

Sect(s), 162, 184

Secularism, 138

Secularization, 137

Self-discipline, 46

Selfishness, 71

Self-will, 236

Selina, Countess of Huntingdon (1707–91), 108

Sellars and Yeatman, 11, 55, 56

Sellon, Walter, 87

Senses, 25

Sensitivity, 51, 67, 117, 229

Sentimentality, 91

Septuagesima, 148

Seraphs, 94

Sermon(s), xiv, 7, 16, 40, 51, 84, 87, 88, 91, 103, 107, 112, 116, 129, 137, 146, 162, 164, 176, 230

   'branching', 51

   on the Mount, 132, 184

Servants, of God, 77

Service (*see also* Commitment), 60, 70, 149

Services, Church, 26

Settlement, of Religion, 136

Shame, 106, 119, 121

Sheep, 149, 173

Shepherd, the Good, 100, 112, 117

Shepherds, 213

Shock, 188, 202

Shrines, 127, 161

   medieval, 58

Shropshire, 224

Sicily, 159, 161, 174

Sick (suffering), 204

Sickness, 33, 181, 184, 190, 191

Sick room, 181, 184, 189, 193

Sierra Leone, 105

Sight, 180

Silver, 16

Simeon, 133

Simeon, Charles (1759–1836), Fellow of King's College, Cambridge, 113, 251, 252

Simplicity, 40, 44, 58, 62, 68, 111, 119, 131, 207, 213, 215, 239, 240, 241

Sin, 33, 72, 75, 82, 91, 93, 100, 106, 109, 110, 200, 207, 218

Sincerity, 44, 63, 153, 235, 236, 241

Singing, hymns, xiii, 18, 74, 85

Sinners, 67, 72, 73, 96, 120, 121, 122, 146, 150

Sins, seven deadly, 27

Sion, 113, 150

'Six', the Oxford (Kay, Jones, Grove, Matthews, Middleton and Shipman), 85

Sky, 77, 146, 190

Slaves, 105

Slavery, 105

   Abolition Bill (1804), 115, 254

Slave Trade, 102, 105

Social concerns, 224, 239

   conscience, 41, 115

   Security, 193

Society, 101, 181, 201, 202

SPCK, 229, 230, 231

Soldiers, of Christ, 77

Solemnity, 97

Soliloquy, 149

Solitude, 172

Somerset, 84, 89, 101

Son, of God, 96, 158, 170, 205, 211

Song(s), 6, 8, 11, 15, 17, 38, 40, 51, 52, 53, 95, 111, 167, 175, 223

'Songs of Praise' (BBC), viii, 92, 245

Song of Solomon, 111

Sonnets, 174, 184, 194

Sorrow(s), 18, 50, 58, 95, 100, 188, 191, 193, 197, 218, 226, 233, 235, 239

Soul(s), 5, 24, 25, 27, 28, 38, 41, 45,
    47, 50, 51, 59, 74, 95, 100,
    104, 109, 111, 112, 114, 115,
    117, 121, 126, 131, 132, 139,
    145, 149, 153, 167, 168, 169
    170, 180, 194, 218, 219, 235
South Africa, 140
Southampton, 51
Southey, Robert (1774–1843), 83
Sovereignty (Divine), 84, 172
Splendour, 185
Spiders, 118, 119
Spirit, The Holy (*see also* Holy
    Ghost), 7, 31, 38, 39, 42, 57,
    63, 70, 76, 85, 88, 89, 93, 106,
    110, 122, 158, 162, 172, 182,
    183, 211, 240
Spirituality, xii, 24, 28, 58, 89, 134,
    174, 175, 176, 183, 187
    'Puritan', 58
Spiritual life, 131, 182, 234
Spring, 118, 146
Spurgeon, C. H (1834–92), 44
Stabat Mater, 239
Stable, 57
Staffordshire, 224
Stanley, Arthur, Dean of Canterbury,
    209
Stanzas, 39, 44, 58, 63, 71, 91, 93,
    95, 132, 133. 134, 144, 145,
    146, 151, 1⁻ 167, 173, 185,
    187, 191, 2ₒ2, 206, 208, 241
Stars, 145, 175, 195, 216
Starvation, 202, 203
State, 138, 142
Stations of the Cross, 210
Steel, Sir David, 84
Stewardship, 33
Stoke-on-Trent, 234
Stott, J. R. W., 187
Stow-on-the-Wold, 127
Strength, 89, 158, 187
Strife, 226, 233
Stuart, Royal House of, 28
Style, 53, 59
Subjectivism, 24
Subtleties (J. H. N. s' 'Subtilties'),
    165

Succession, episcopal, 136
    Hanoverian (1714), 55
Suffering, 183, 184, 197, 202, 216
Summer, 182
Sun, 23, 62, 88, 147, 212, 222, 227
Sunshine, 148
Sunday(s), 51, 75, 84, 88, 92, 130,
    131, 140, 154, 187, 189, 210,
    230, 231
Sunday School, 204, 209
Sunsets, 190
Sureties, 205
Sussex, 190
Symbolism, 122, 159, 227
Synagogue, 6, 39, 41
Synods, 166

TABERNACLE, 44, 84
Talent, 184
Teachers, 209, 239
Teaching(s), 7, 8, 61, 68, 72, 76, 78,
    92, 101, 134, 140, 158, 167,
    227, 228, 240
Tears, 82, 192, 203, 235
Te Deum, canticle, 95, 163, 225, 239
Telegraph, Daily, 202
Telford, Father John, Priest of Ryde,
    169
Temple(s), 66, 71, 126, 133, 134,
    213
Temptation, 75, 105, 181, 187
'Terror' (a poem), 173
Texts, of Scripture, 116, 185, 230,
    245
Thames, the South Bank, 113
Thankfulness, 93
Thanksgiving, vii, 111, 153, 163,
    172, 224, 238
    National (1871), 237, 238
Theology, 5, 14, 83, 84, 92, 93, 95,
    109, 143, 201, 207, 224, 229
    devotional , 229
    popular, 201
    Swiss, 244
Thief, on the Cross, 152–3
'Third system', 165, 172
Thomas à Kempis (c. 1380–1471),
    102

Thorns, 50, 58, 59
Thornton, John, 112
Throne (of God), 63, 94, 222
Thursday, 188
Times, The, xiv
Tithes, 138
TOPLADY, Augustus Montague
    (1740–1778), x–xi, xiv, 80–97,
    211, 250, 251, 252; Curate of
    Blagdon, Somerset (1762), 84,
    91; Curate of Farley
    Hungerford (1764), 85; his
    Farewell Sermon (Blagdon,
    1764), 91; Vicar of Fen Ottery
    (1766), 85; Vicar of Broad
    Hembury (1774), 85; deacon
    (1762), 84; remarkable preacher
    and poet, 85, 93; ruthless
    controversialist, xiv, 86, 87, 88,
    92; his 'Chamber hymn', 93; his
    Church of England vindicated
    …(1769), 85, 251; *Letter* to
    John Wesley, 87–8; *Psalms and
    Hymns* (1776), 88, 89; his
    'Rock of ages', 81, 82, 89, 90;
    his translation of Zanchy, 86; his
    uncompromising Calvinism, 85,
    86, 87, 88, 93; his work for the
    Gospel Magazine, 88, 89, 94, 96;
    his verse, 88, 91, 96, and its
    penitential character, 91; his
    poor health, 85, 96
Tories, 55
Torquay, 232
Tourists, 127
Tractarians, 128, 134, 136, 143, 202,
    204, 208, 209, 214
Tracts, 103, 136, 228
Tracts for the Times (1833–45), 129,
    138, 143, 153, 164, 172
    Tract IV, 138
    Tract XC, 138, 165
Tradition (and Traditionalism), 95,
    131, 133, 138, 151, 153
    the English Religious, 95, 131
    the 'High Church' (or catholic),
    153, 163, 164
Tragedy, 202

Translations, 68, 95
Treasury, 100, 111
Treasury, Devotional and Spiritual,
    xiii, 15–18 (Luther); 29–34
    (Ken); 44–47 (Doddridge);
    60–63 (Watts); 74–78 (Wesley);
    92–97 (Toplady); 116–122
    (Newton); 131; 144–154
    (Keble); 171–7 (Newman);
    191–7 (Elliott); 214–19
    (Alexander); 234–41 (Ellerton)
Tress, 147, 193
    cedars, 147
    figs, 147
    oaks, 147
    willows, 94
Trials, 186
Triangular trade (*see also* Slave
    Trade), 102
Tribulations, 186
Trinity College (Cambridge), 39
Trinity College (Dublin), 84
Trinity, Season of Church's Year,
    147, 149, 151
    Sunday, 84, 109, 144
    The Holy, 54, 76, 158, 163, 168,
    204
Triumph, 61
Troubles, 111
Trumpets, 38, 43, 73, 209, 217
Trust, 40
Truth(s), 53, 59, 63, 73, 74, 91, 97,
    112, 115, 139, 153, 172, 173,
    183, 228
Truth claims, 169
Tuesday, 187
Tucker, William, 88–9
Tuition, as pastoral care, 129
Tune(s), 54, 69, 243, 245
Tune books, 224, 245
Typhoid, 159
Tyranny, 72
Tyrone, 201

UNBELIEF, 197
Unction, 97
Unfaithful, 119
Unison, 244

United Kingdom, 15, 84
   Provinces, 84
   Societies, 84
   States of America (see America,
      United States of)
Unity, Christian, 42, 245
Universalism, 73
University, 42, 223
Unwin, Mrs, of Olney Green, 116

VALEDICTION, 226
Valley, of the Shadow, 118
Values, 202
   Christian, 161
Vanity, 183
Veneration, 158, 169
Venn-Elliott family, 182
Venn, Henry (1725–97), Vicar of
   Huddersfield, 113, 181, 249,
   250, 251, 253
Venn, John (1759–1813), Rector of
   Clapham, 113, 181, 251, 253
Venus, 69
Verse, 31, 44, 57, 63, 68, 74, 77, 88,
   91, 96, 109, 114, 131, 132,
   133, 134, 144, 149, 159, 171,
   181, 184, 185, 215
Via Media, 164, 172
Victoria, Queen of Great Britain and
   Ireland (1837–1901), 129, 227,
   228, 256, 259, 260 (her
   Diamond Jubilee, 1897), 227,
   238, 260
Victorians, 131, 144, 145, 153, 170,
   181, 190, 191, 201, 211, 214,
   226
Victory, 61, 217
Vigil, 189, 196, 208
Vigilance, 24, 226
Vine (Christ as the True), 47
Vineyard, 47, 161
Vio, Thomas de, Cardinal Cajetan,
   244
Virgin (*see* Mary, the Blessed Virgin)
Virgins, 168
Virtues, 184
Vision, 24, 62, 67, 71, 133, 164,
   169, 174, 197, 224

Vocation, 85, 93, 108, 129, 149,
   177, 235
Voices, 195, 222
Vos, Henricus, 6
Vows, 46, 137, 215
Voyage, 103

WALKER, Samuel (of Truro), 113
Walks, 218
'Wanderer' (a poem), 184
War-cry, 139
Warfare, 215
Warwick, 180
Watch 188, 196, 222, 227
WATTS, Isaac (1674–1748), x, xiv,
   48–63, 175, 211, 230, 244,
   248–49, 250; small in stature,
   56; his brother Enoch, 51;
   Minister of Mark Lane Chapel,
   London, 51; his *Divine Songs*
   (1715), 56, 249; his evangelism
   by hymn singing, 53, 59, 60,
   61; his 'laboratory notebooks',
   57; his love of children, 56, 57;
   his love of 'fine language', 53,
   54; his New-Testament
   emphasis, 53, 54; his pastoral
   care, 52, 53, 62; his *Preface to
   Psalms of David Imitated* (1719),
   52, 62, 249; his *Revelation*-based
   praise, 61; his *Short Essay toward
   the Improvement of Psalmody*, 51;
   his 'When I survey the
   wondrous Cross', 58–60
War, 134
Water, 82, 117
Watson, Dr Sydney, viii
Waves, 102, 104
Way, Christ as the Way, 112
   the Christian, 100
Weakness, 215
Wealth, 161, 201
Wedding(s), vii
Wednesday, 187–8, 235
Wellington, Arthur Wellesley, 1st
   Duke of, 128
Wells, C. J., 212
WESLEY, Charles (1707–88), x, xiv,

7, 64–78, 101, 105, 113, 244, 245, 250; his conversion, 67, 70, 74; his mother Susanna, 77; his sister Kezia, 69; his poetry the handmaid to piety, 68; his *Journal*, 69; his *Redemption Hymns* (1747), 70; his 'Love divine …', 66, 69, 70, 71; his seven thousand hymns, 67; his longing for sanctity, 71; his 'universalism', xiv, 73; his 'Wrestling Jacob', 73

Wesley, John (1703–91), 7, 67, 71, 74, 83, 84, 86, 87, 92, 101, 104, 105, 113, 130, 244, 245, 250; his Aldersgate Street Meeting experience (24 May 1738), 104; his *Collection* (1799). 67; his *Free Grace* sermon (1740), 83, 250; his *Journal*, 92; his tune book *Sacred Melody*, 245; his Zanchius parody, 86

Wesley's Chapel (City Road, London), 78 (*see also* 'Foundery', the London).

Wesley, Susanna, 77

West country, 83
  Indies, 106

Westminster Abbey, 116, 209

Weymouth, Viscount, 31

Wexford, County, 84

Whig, 55

White, Cosby, 228

Whitefield, George (1714–70), 73, 83, 84, 85, 86, 87, 96, 101, 105, 107, 113; his 'Tabernacle' at Moorfields, 96, 107

Whitgift, John, Abp of Canterbury (1583–1604), 136

Whitsun, 74, 149, 175

Whitsunday, 162, 240

Wilberforce, Samuel, Bp of Oxford (1845–69), 160, 209, 256, 257

Wilberforce, William (1759–1833), 102, 115, 251, 252, 253

Wilde, Oscar, 128

Wilderness, 111, 150, 159

William III, King of Great Britain and Ireland (1689–1702), 28, 56, 142, 248–9

Will (of God), 202

Willows, 94

Wilson, Thomas, Bp of Sodor and Man (1697–1755), 141, 142, 146, 248, 249, 250; his *Catechism*, 143; his 'Ecclesiastical Constitutions', 142; his *Form for Receiving Penitents*, 142; his *Sacra Privata*, 143

Wiltshire, 32

Winchester, 23, 28, 127, 139

Wind, 102

Wine, 218

Winter, 118, 146

Wisdom, 38, 42, 53, 86, 176, 184, 194

Witness, 24, 25, 72, 141

Wits, 181, 207

Wittenberg, 5, 7, 9, 244

Woe, 215

Women, 68, 72, 92, 183
  ministry of, 183

Wonder, 66, 71

Word, of God, 8, 13, 15, 16, 30, 34, 42, 53, 72, 73, 85, 88, 91, 108, 122, 143, 152, 182, 211, 234, 240

Words, the 'comfortable', 67, 186

Wordsworth, Christopher, Bp of Lincoln (1869–85), 209, 227, 255

Wordsworth, William (1770–1850), 132, 146, 211, 212, 253

Working classes, 183

Works, good, 7, 12, 16, 86, 200

World, 54, 56, 61, 63, 73, 82, 133, 184, 195, 222, 235

Worms, Imperial Diet of (1521), 11, 12

Worship, Christian, xiii, xiv, xv, 5, 15, 17, 23, 25, 41 ,52, 53, 58, 59, 60, 62, 68, 74, 91, 105, 111, 112, 113, 114, 128, 152, 153, 162, 164, 165, 167, 174,

177, 194, 214, 223, 226, 230,
234, 243, 244, 245; daily
worship, 144; Hebrew worship,
175
Wounds, 59, 100
Wright, Thomas, 89
Writers, 181
Wyatt, William,143
Wykehamists, 24, 27, 31

YEAR, Church's, 131
Young, Peter, 140

ZANCHIUS, Jerôme, 86
Zeal, 42, 62, 73, 82, 161
Zeitungslieder, 15
Zion, 47